Sex Equality

EDITED BY

JANE ENGLISH

University of North Carolina

PRENTICE-HALL, INC., ENGLEWOOD CLIFFS, NEW JERSEY 07632

Library of Congress Cataloging in Publication Data

Main entry under title:

Sex equality.

Bibliography: p.
CONTENTS: The philosophical background: Plato.
The republic, book V. Aristotle. Politics, book I.
Locke, J. The second treatise of government.
Rousseau, J. J. Émile. Fichte, J. G. The science of
rights. Mill, J. S. The subjection of women. Engels, F.
The origin of the family, private property and the state.
Beauvoir, S. de. The second sex. [etc.]
    1. Feminism—Addresses, essays, lectures.
2. Equality—Addresses, essays, lectures. 3. Sex
role—Addresses, essays, lectures. I. English, Jane
(date)
HQ1154.S46   301.41   76-53000
ISBN 0-13-807594-8
ISBN 0-13-807586-7 pbk.

© 1977 by Prentice-Hall, Inc., Englewood Cliffs, N.J. 07632

10 9 8 7 6 5 4 3

Printed in the United States of America

PRENTICE-HALL INTERNATIONAL, INC., *London*
PRENTICE-HALL OF AUSTRALIA PTY. LIMITED, *Sydney*
PRENTICE-HALL OF CANADA, LTD., *Toronto*
PRENTICE-HALL OF INDIA PRIVATE LIMITED, *New Delhi*
PRENTICE-HALL OF JAPAN, INC., *Tokyo*
PRENTICE-HALL OF SOUTHEAST ASIA PTE. LTD., *Singapore*

CONTENTS

I
THE PHILOSOPHICAL BACKGROUND

II
CONTEMPORARY ARGUMENTS

III
THE POPULAR DEBATE

PREFACE

This collection is designed for use as a basic text in a philosophy of feminism course, as a second text in an introductory ethics course, or as "issues" reading in a general introduction to philosophy. Nearly all of the articles included are accessible to undergraduates with no previous philosophical training. No technical knowledge or terminology is presupposed. Thus the book will also be of interest to those members of the general public who are concerned about women's rights. On the other hand, answering the questions raised by the authors represented here remains a serious challenge for the most seasoned professional philosopher.

Many famous philosophers (such as Kant and Nietzsche) who have written about women have not been included because their writings do not contain reasoned defenses of their (usually misogynistic) views. The reader who wishes to practice distinguishing reason from rhetoric will find ample opportunity, especially in section III.

The inclusion of popular, nonphilosophical essays in a textbook is controversial. The articles in section III were chosen because they contain clear arguments intimately related to the views presented in the philosophical sections. They serve to relate the philosophers' sometimes abstract theories to practical concerns.

Several important aspects of feminism are not treated in this collection. Most notably, political theories about the nature of, origin of, and way to end women's oppression are sufficiently complex and numerous to deserve separate treatment. Another area of particular interest to women is human sexuality, including the issues of abortion, rape, contraception, premarital sex, and monogamy. These have also been omitted as not directly concerned with sex equality.

All the readings focus on one issue: are the sexes equal? Should they be? The nature of equality and the question of whether it is a good thing turn out to be difficult problems. They lead to controversies over equal opportunity, self-respect, reverse discrimination, sex roles, and the family. These issues are intertwined in such a way that it was impossible to group the articles into separate sections dealing with each issue. The introduction sets out the central issues, and the following list should help guide the reader to selections dealing with specific issues:

Equality: Williams, Jaggar, Plato, Lucas, Trebilcot, Ervin, DeWolf

Equal opportunity: Plato, Mill, O'Neill, Williams, Lucas, Trebilcot, Newton, Thalberg, Ginsburg, DeWolf

Preferential treatment: Newton, O'Neill, Thalberg

The family: Aristotle, Locke, Mill, Plato, Engels, Jaggar, Ervin, Bedell

Education: Plato, Rousseau, Mill, O'Neill, DeWolf, Fichte

Political equality: Fichte, Mill, Williams, Lucas, Newton, Ervin, Ginsburg

Natural sex differences: Aristotle, Rousseau, Jaggar, Lucas, Trebilcot, Pierce, Ervin, Goldberg, Weisstein, DeWolf

Self-respect: Hill, Bedell, Lakoff, de Beauvoir, Williams

Language: Levin, Lakoff, de Beauvoir

Sex roles: Trebilcot, Jaggar, Lucas, Plato, Aristotle, Rousseau, Mill, Pierce, Ervin, Goldberg, Weisstein, Lakoff

My heartfelt thanks go to the members of the Society for Women in Philosophy who have stimulated me to think and write about the philosophical aspects of sex equality. I am indebted to Mary Vetterling Braggin, whose idea it originally was to compile an anthology of philosophical issues about feminism. Fred Elliston brought Fichte's argument to my attention. Alison Jaggar, Lawrence Crocker, Janice Moulton, Sandra Harding, and Prentice-Hall's anonymous reviewers are among those whose many comments and ideas helped shape this collection.

INTRODUCTION

What is sex equality? Are the sexes equal? Should they be? The answers to these questions have often seemed to be obvious. Equality is one of the founding ideals of our society: "We hold these truths to be self evident: that all men [sic] are created equal. . . ." But even a brief inspection reveals that it is not at all clear which social arrangements are "equal," or even whether equality is a good thing.

In one sense, people simply are not equal. Some are taller, some are smarter, some can bear children, some can grow beards. If we treated people with complete equality, we would treat any two the same regardless of their distinctive characteristics. *Radical egalitarianism* is the extreme view:

E_1: Treat everyone alike, regardless of individual characteristics.

But this view has some unacceptable consequences: It tells us to assign the same grades to all students, regardless of their performance on exams; to pay the same wages to all workers, regardless of work or need; to give tonsillectomies to all, regardless of the state of their tonsils; to hire brain surgeons without regard to their skill; and so forth. If E_1 is what equality calls for, it is too strong a requirement. Equality would not be a good thing.

Rather, equality seems to call for treating people according to their characteristics:

E_2: Do not treat A differently from B unless there is some difference between A and B.

But E_2 turns out to be an empty ideal, for there exists some difference between *any* two individuals, A and B. Furthermore, E_2 would justify denying an education to A simply because A is black and B is white, or

1

a job to B simply because B is a woman and A is a man. Instead, we need to consider whether the characteristic in question is *relevant* to the difference in treatment, as skill is relevant to a job and sickness to a tonsillectomy. This suggests the principle:

> E_3: Do not treat A differently from B with respect to X unless there is a difference between A and B which is *relevant* to X.

This principle seems to be correct, but there remains the thorny problem of which characteristics are relevant to what.

Consider an apparently simple case such as giving people "equal" food. If this means that everyone is to receive the same diet as everyone else, it seems we do not want equality. A baby would have too much steak, while a 250-pound construction worker would go hungry. If we assigned food in proportion to weight instead, the thin would starve and the fat grow fatter. If people received food in amounts proportional to caloric output, those in sedentary occupations would no doubt complain that they were entitled to higher quality in their smaller quantity of food, arguing that equal monetary expenditures per individual would be "equal." In short, there is no one distribution method which we can call *the* equal distribution, even when we confine ourselves to relevant factors. Nor can we simply make it equal in *all* the "equal" ways. (This would be impossible, since we would have to give equal amounts per individual, per body weight, and per caloric output; but these conflict with each other, so the distribution cannot be equal in all these ways at once.)

Things become much more complex when we turn to equality of the sexes. To some matters, such as maternity leave, locker-room assignment, choosing a mate, or casting the part of Juliet, sex is obviously relevant. In other areas, sex is obviously irrelevant. When it comes to paying someone for putting a certain number of screws on a certain number of parts in an assembly line, for instance, the sex of the worker is irrelevant. Or if A digs ditches better than B, A is the more highly qualified ditch-digger, regardless of the sexes of A and B. Even in these areas of obvious irrelevance, women have often been denied equal treatment with men. Simple laws prohibiting discrimination and calling for equal pay for equal work follow from E_3 and are a relatively uncontroversial form of sex equality.

Often we find, however, that while sex itself is clearly irrelevant in some area, a characteristic highly correlated with sex *is* relevant. Men are typically taller, stronger, and heavier than women; these characteristics are relevant to being an effective professional football player, for example. Some claim that this is a sufficient reason to prohibit all women from becoming professional football players. This would follow not from E_3, however, but from the different principle:

E_4: You may treat A differently from B with respect to X if there is a difference between the *class* A belongs to and the *class* B belongs to, and that difference is relevant to X.

A problem with E_4 is that of specifying the classes or groups to be used. If we allow any classes to be used, then any individual A can be excluded by placing him or her in an arbitrary group whose average or typical member has a disqualifying feature which is relevant to X. If you wish to keep A out of college, for example, just consider the class containing all persons with IQ under 50 and A. Some people hold that sex is, but race is not, a permissible grouping to use in applying E_4.

When is it fair to treat individuals simply as members of groups? This is a difficult question not solvable by appeal to equality alone. Consider the current controversy over whether public high schools should be permitted to maintain sex-segregated teams. Unfortunately, no arrangement seems to be fair to everyone. If we maintain a team for each sex, and provide the equal funding, equal coaching, equal cheerleading, and equal facilities that have usually been absent in the past, the sexes are equal in the sense of E_4. But consider an individual girl who is fast, 6'3" tall, and a good ball-handler, who would make all-state if permitted to play basketball with the boys' team. Citing her sex to keep her on the girls' team would violate E_3 (but not E_4). If outstanding girls are permitted to play on the boys' team, however, the overall quality of and respect for the girls' team will decline. It might also seem unfair to smaller or less coordinated boys to prohibit them from playing on the girls' team on grounds of their sex alone. On the other hand, suppose we have just one team in each sport, open to members of both sexes. A problem is that some physical characteristics relevant to sports are highly correlated with sex, so that few or no girls may make the school's basketball, football, or track teams. (We should also note that in some areas girls are physiologically advantaged over boys, so that few or no boys may qualify in balance beam, synchronized swimming, or dance.) As in the equal food example, none of these arrangements can be claimed to be *the* equal one.

EQUAL OPPORTUNITY

Another shortcoming of E_3 is that it takes each individual's skills and other characteristics as a given. Yet if A has been raised with all the advantages of health, the best education money can buy, and encouragement to become a lawyer, while B suffered from malnutrition, little instruction, and less incentive, then we also think equality has been violated.

A society which follows E_3 is said to provide merely *formal equality*. To provide *equal opportunity* as well, we would have to add to E_3:

> E_5: A and B must be given the same opportunity and encouragement to acquire the skills relevant to performing X.

This principle does not require that A and B end up with the same probability of having the relevant skills or getting the job, however. After all, if X is the job of being a concert violinist and A is born tone-deaf while B has perfect pitch, this is a relevant difference which training and incentive alone cannot overcome.

Incentives, of course, include salary, fringe benefits, status, fame, and praise. This is an area in which women have often been denied equal opportunity in the past. For example, men working for the army received a dependency allowance for their wives which women in the same position did not receive for their husbands. There are more subtle incentives, however, that are often overlooked in discussions of equal opportunity. If parents encourage their daughter to be a nurse rather than a doctor when she bandages the puppy's tail, or if all the doctors depicted in her textbooks and television shows are male, then she has not been given the same incentive as a boy to pursue the goal of becoming a doctor. More subtly still, if a man gains status in his community for being a successful lawyer, while a woman's status is based on her housewifely accomplishments, her children's achievements, or her husband's success only, despite her own successes in law, then she too is being denied equal rewards and incentives to be a successful lawyer. The fact that many people today believe that a working woman's homemaking career is more important than her job and think of her salary as going only to buy "extras," shows that equal opportunity has not yet been attained.

Education is just one of many aspects of equal opportunity. But what constitutes equal education? Many people in the past argued that women ought to be educated differently from men because women's "nature" is different—and some of their arguments are not obviously mistaken. Depending on the facts, different educations may not be a denial of equal opportunity. Consider the following fictitious example: suppose it is discovered that boys perceive things in spatial terms, girls in linear or verbal ones. Furthermore, suppose that all spatial perceivers learn better if taught math first and reading later, and vice versa for the verbal learners. If this were true (which it probably is not), the principle of equal opportunity would actually call for different early educations for the two sexes. (We should *not* reason as follows, however: "Boys naturally fall behind in reading, so we must provide them with remedial help. Girls naturally fall behind in math, so they should be discouraged from studying it.") Here, then, is another case in which equality calls not for identical treatment of everyone, but for treating people differently depending upon their characteristics. Sex is often such a characteristic. Of course, determining just what are the characteristics of the two sexes will be a key to determining what treatment is fair or equal. But this calls for scientific investigation rather than philosophical speculation.

SELF-RESPECT

Individuals may also be deprived of equal skills and incentives by a lack of encouragement to have adequate self-respect. If you do not take your own views seriously, assume that your ideas are uninteresting, or believe that your happiness is less important than others', your lack of self-respect can lead to unequal opportunity. For example, an advertising executive who does not speak up at meetings because she assumes her ideas are inferior is less likely to be promoted. Indeed, she also harms the firm by depriving it of her creative input. A woman student who does all the housework so that her husband has time to study, reasoning that his education and happiness are more important than hers, deprives herself of an equal education.

Apart from such consequences, the absence of self-respect is wrong in itself. The very least equality requires is that each person be recognized as a person, that is, as having equal moral standing with others. This calls for taking oneself and one's interests to be important and for standing up for one's rights.

In most societies, whatever professions are dominated by woman are accorded less respect than those filled by men. Our very language encodes the subtle idea that women are atypical, not standard, "other," as in the notorious ambiguity of the word *man*. Even the tendency of women to phrase their statements as questions, and to add "isn't it?" or "don't you agree?" reinforces the impression that their ideas are more tentative, less forceful, and less likely to be true than those of men. These factors are both symptoms and causes of women's lower level of self-respect.

PREFERENTIAL TREATMENT

Given that women have not had equal access to powerful positions and prestigious careers in the past, what steps ought to be taken now to correct this situation? Some people advocate preferential treatment (or "reverse discrimination") as a temporary measure, to bring about equality. Preferential treatment consists of favoring women over equally or slightly more qualified men for a limited time wherever men have been unfairly favored over qualified women in the past. Opponents of preferential treatment object that equality itself requires us to treat people according to their relevant qualifications only; since the proponents of preferential treatment admit that sex is irrelevant to being hired or admitted, they violate E_3 itself in proposing that sex now be used as grounds for preferring women. And "two wrongs don't make a right," they claim.

Arguments in favor of preferential treatment can be grouped into two major types. One school of thought is that preferential treatment is required as a matter of *compensation* for past wrongs. Few people object that "two wrongs don't make a right" when a criminal is punished or society repays a victim of crime. In such circumstances it can be replied, of course, that preferential treatment is different because it is "group" compensation for past wrongs, somewhat in the spirit of E_4. In the typical case, a man, A, was unjustly favored over a qualified woman, B, years ago. But now it is not a question of compensating B by favoring her over A, but rather of favoring a younger woman, C, over an equally or slightly better qualified man, D. Under such forms of group compensation, D often complains that he should not be punished for an earlier favoritism of which not he but A was the beneficiary. It does seem that compensation can justify preferential treatment only if it is B, rather than D or the group of all women, who is being compensated.

A different approach is a *teleological* or goal-directed one: that preferential treatment is required not because of the past but because of the future. If we do not use preferential treatment, but simply start to observe E_3, it is argued, inequality will be perpetuated for several generations. Unless women executives and surgeons are present to fight discrimination in hiring and to break stereotypes now, inequality will continue too long. Either course of action admittedly leads to some injustice, but in the long run the use of temporary reverse discrimination would produce the smaller amount of injustice. Thus it is called for because it is the lesser of the two evils.

Preferential treatment may have adverse effects on self-respect, however, which must be added in to the calculation. If a fully qualified woman professor wonders whether she was hired merely because of her sex and begins to doubt her qualifications, her self-respect has been damaged. More serious from a teleological viewpoint is that she may be ineffective in ending discrimination and breaking stereotypes if her colleagues and students assume she is less qualified than the male professors. On the other hand, asking women to wait several generations for equality, rather than violating E_3 temporarily, may also infringe on self-respect.

BIOLOGICAL DIFFERENCES AND THE FAMILY

There are by definition biological differences between the sexes. To what extent do these justify differences in rights, duties, and opportunities? Writers from ancient times to the present have promulgated theories about what it is "natural" for women and men to do. Alleged disparities in mental abilities led to extreme claims about the inability of women to make decisions, manage property, and vote wisely. Hormonal differences may actually influence emotional characteristics and aggressiveness.

One serious problem with these approaches is that of determining scientifically which psychological differences between the sexes really do exist—as opposed to being merely assumed, expected, or socially induced. Until recently, scientific research has been scanty and biased. More important, it is not known whether the sexes would have different sorts of personalities if left to develop free from stereotypes. Would women be supportive, intuitive, emotional, self-sacrificing, and sympathetic; men courageous, rational, domineering, aggressive, and independent? If these "gender" traits are genetically determined, then they will develop even without the enforcement of sex stereotyping. And even if a difference does turn out to be natural, it does not follow that it ought to be tolerated, let alone intensified by social conditioning. Suppose it is natural to fear thunder or for the strong to dominate the weak. These would be "natural" human traits, but ones we should attempt to overcome with the use of reason and morality. The fact that something is natural does not imply that it is good.

No one disputes the existence of biological differences relating to reproduction, yet their implications for the relations between the sexes and the structure of the family are not clear. The physiological fact that most women can bear and nurse children and no men can has seemed to some to dictate that the "natural" or God-given arrangement is for the man to earn the living and the woman to raise the children and keep house. But this arrangement has not been the pattern throughout history or in all societies. Changing the family structure might result in some social disruption or inefficiency, but this does not dictate that the traditional family structure must not be disturbed. Rather, such costs would have to be weighed against the gains in equality and freedom that would result from making family arrangements a matter of personal choice.

There has also been considerable debate over whether the relationship between husband and wife is the "natural" rule of the superior over the inferior, or a mutual cooperation of independent and theoretically equal adults. A number of authors argue against equality for women on the grounds that it will lead to the destruction of the traditional family; meanwhile, others advocate the destruction of the traditional family for various reasons. A third, more moderate, group points out that equality in jobs and politics, even in housework and child care, need not spell the end of a loving, cooperative home environment for adults and children.

SEX ROLES

It is widely recognized today that most occupations and social roles are stereotyped by sex; for example, girls are encouraged to grow up to be stewardesses or nurses rather than pilots or doctors. Sometimes these customs are enforced by law—either explicitly, as when women were excluded from the armed forces, or indirectly, such as by setting a minimum weight of 165 pounds for state troopers.

Is there anything wrong with stereotyping jobs by sex? For one thing, it restricts individuals' freedom. For another, a woman who might lead a happy life as a pilot and a man who would find nursing rewarding are steered into professions they may not enjoy so much nor do so well. They lose happiness, and so do the rest of us in that we do not have the most talented people in society performing each job. Freedom, happiness, and efficiency have all been sacrificed.

An argument against this position asserts that the stereotyping of jobs serves both efficiency and happiness. For example, if only one woman in a hundred has the strength to be a successful construction worker, then discouraging all girls from that career is efficient. Although the abilities of the one in a hundred are lost, much effort is saved from not having to train or interview the other ninety-nine. And although the one in a hundred may be less happy as a result, much disappointment is saved on the part of some of the remaining ninety-nine who are doomed to failure in this occupation through no fault of their own. Even if efficiency has been served, however, freedom has not. It might be more efficient, too, if we had no choice as to the clothes we wear or the food we eat. But freedom often overrides considerations of efficiency. For example, democracy and freedom of speech would still be too valuable to give up, even if dictatorship and censorship were more efficient—as some people have asserted.

A more esoteric aspect of sex role stereotyping is that it limits and shapes the sorts of personalities individuals have, another clear limitation on freedom. Perhaps a more serious problem is that stereotyping actually discourages people from being the best possible individuals they can be. True, stereotyping encourages certain virtues: boys are taught to be brave, self-reliant problem-solvers; girls to be sympathetic, cooperative, and helpful. At the same time, however, in being discouraged from adopting the virtuous characteristics of the opposite sex, we are positively encouraged to be less than the most virtuous individuals we can be. Being self-reliant and rational are human virtues which girls are actively discouraged from having. Being sympathetic and supportive are also virtues, but boys are trained away from these "feminine" characteristics. In short, gender roles actually discourage the development of selected virtuous and beneficial traits. They also encourage some vices, such as aggressiveness and excessive dependency.

There is a third group of neutral characteristics, neither virtues nor vices, into which stereotypes enter, too. Men are supposed to be interested in cars and baseball scores, women in clothing and movie stars. While these are neither virtues nor vices, this situation does limit individual freedom for no beneficial reason. It also decreases the understanding, communication, and shared interests between the sexes—a serious loss affecting our daily lives, for example, in the case of the Sunday "football widow."

Finally, we come to the question whether equality calls for "unisex," for the end to all differences between the sexes except those immediately concerned with reproduction. Of course, the end of sex stereotyping does not mean that everyone would be alike. There would still be widely different professions, interests, personalities, and modes of dress. Indeed, with the removal of sex restrictions, we should expect to see more rather than less variety in society. Thus, the argument that people are happier with differences between the sexes will have to show why it is *sex* differences rather than simply *differences* which are beneficial.

It seems that it probably will not be possible, even if it were desirable, to eradicate all physical distinctions, including facial hair and voice pitch, which allow us readily to detect another's sex. If prejudice is to be undermined, must we either obliterate or at least be unaware of these differences? This is in part a psychological question whose answer is unknown. Surely the converse is true: if we were as unaware of a person's sex as we usually now are of his or her religion or left-handedness, it would be difficult to practice discrimination. (It is surprising that sex is such a central category in our thinking and makes such a difference to how we treat others that we feel uncomfortable when confronted with a stranger or even a baby of undetectable sex. This is partly because our pronoun system itself requires a knowledge of others' sex.) On the other hand, it will probably be possible to eradicate sex discrimination by methods less drastic than obliterating all sex differences. To the extent that equality is a good thing, what it calls for is justice rather than identical treatment. In this sense, the sexes could be "equal" without becoming indistinguishable.

I

The Philosophical Background

PLATO

The Republic

Plato's Republic *is a description of an ideal society, written as a conversation between Socrates and Glaucon, an Athenian friend of Socrates. Plato has described a special class, the Guardians, who are to be selected for their intelligence, bravery, and virtue; highly educated; and assigned the task of ruling the city-state. In Book V, Plato turns to the question of whether women should be Guardians too, and if so, whether they should have the same training and ruling power as the male Guardians.*

Plato assumes that women as a group are not only physically weaker than men but also inferior in most other areas. However, since some individual women are wise, brave, and strong, he concludes that they are eligible to be Guardians. Their characteristics are relevant to the job, and the "nature" of the sex as a whole is irrelevant, he reasons. We are to look to the abilities of the individual rather than to those of the group to which he or she belongs.

In the discussion which follows this selection, Plato prescribes the abolition of the traditional family for the Guardians (but not for the rest of the population). Their breeding is to be regulated on eugenic grounds, and possessiveness and favoritism are to be avoided by having no married couples and by concealing parentage. Plato also advocates complete social mobility, based on talent, between the Guardians and the lower classes.

Student of Socrates and teacher of Aristotle, Plato lived in Greece from 428 to 348 B.C. He is sometimes called the "first feminist," but this is an oversimplification. He did call for equal education and equal opportunity, but he believed women as a group to be inferior to men.

Further Reading

CHRISTINE PIERCE, "Equality: *Republic* V," *The Monist,* 57 (1973), 1–11.

ANNE DICKASON, "Anatomy and Destiny: The Role of Biology in Plato's View of Women," *The Philosophical Forum,* 5 (1973–74), 45–53; reprinted in Carol Gould and Marx Wartofsky, eds., *Women and Philosophy* (New York: G. P. Putnam's Sons, 1975).

CHRISTINE GARSIDE ALLEN, "Plato on Women," *Feminist Studies,* 2 (1975), 131–38.

JULIA ANNAS, "Plato's *Republic* and Feminism," *Philosophy,* 51 (1976), 307–21.

BOOK V

Socrates: We must go back, then, to a subject which ought, perhaps, to have been treated earlier in its proper place; though, after all, it may be suitable that the women should have their turn on the stage when the men have quite finished their performance, especially since you are so insistent. In my judgment, then, the question under what conditions people born and educated as we have described should possess wives and children, and how they should treat them, can be rightly settled only by keeping to the course on which we started them at the outset. We undertook to put these men in the position of watch-dogs guarding a flock. Suppose we follow up the analogy and imagine them bred and reared in the same sort of way. We can then see if that plan will suit our purpose.

Glaucon: How will that be?

In this way. Which do we think right for watch-dogs: should the females guard the flock and hunt with the males and take a share in all they do, or should they be kept within doors as fit for no more than bearing and feeding their puppies, while all the hard work of looking after the flock is left to the males?

They are expected to take their full share, except that we treat them as not quite so strong.

Can you employ any creature for the same work as another, if you do not give them both the same upbringing and education?

No.

Then, if we are to set women to the same tasks as men, we must teach them the same things. They must have the same two branches of training for mind and body and also be taught the art of war, and they must receive the same treatment.

That seems to follow.

Possibly, if these proposals were carried out, they might be ridiculed as involving a good many breaches of custom.

They might indeed.

From *The Republic of Plato* translated by F. M. Cornford 1941. Reprinted by permission of the Oxford University Press.

The most ridiculous—don't you think?—being the notion of women exercising naked along with the men in the wrestling-schools; some of them elderly women too, like the old men who still have a passion for exercise when they are wrinkled and not very agreeable to look at.

Yes, that would be thought laughable, according to our present notions.

Now we have started on this subject, we must not be frightened of the many witticisms that might be aimed at such a revolution, not only in the matter of bodily exercise but in the training of women's minds, and not least when it comes to their bearing arms and riding on horseback. Having begun upon these rules, we must not draw back from the harsher provisions. The wits may be asked to stop being witty and try to be serious; and we may remind them that it is not so long since the Greeks, like most foreign nations of the present day, thought it ridiculous and shameful for men to be seen naked. When gymnastic exercises were first introduced in Crete and later at Sparta, the humorists had their chance to make fun of them; but when experience had shown that nakedness is better uncovered than muffled up, the laughter died down and a practice which the reason approved ceased to look ridiculous to the eye. This shows how idle it is to think anything ludicrous but what is base. One who tries to raise a laugh at any spectacle save that of baseness and folly will also, in his serious moments, set before himself some other standard than goodness of what deserves to be held in honour.

Most assuredly.

The first thing to be settled, then, is whether these proposals are feasible; and it must be open to anyone, whether a humorist or serious-minded, to raise the question whether, in the case of mankind, the feminine nature is capable of taking part with the other sex in all occupations, or in none at all, or in some only; and in particular under which of these heads this business of military service falls. Well begun is half done, and would not this be the best way to begin?

Yes.

Shall we take the other side in this debate and argue against ourselves? We do not want the adversary's position to be taken by storm for lack of defenders.

I have no objection.

Let us state his case for him. "Socrates and Glaucon," he will say, "there is no need for others to dispute your position; you yourselves, at the very outset of founding your commonwealth, agreed that everyone should do the one work for which nature fits him." Yes, of course; I suppose we did. "And isn't there a very great difference in nature between man and woman?" Yes, surely. "Does not that natural difference imply a corresponding difference in the work to be given to each?" Yes. "But if so, surely you must be mistaken now and contradicting yourselves when you say that men and women, having such widely divergent natures, should do the same things?" What is your answer to that, my ingenious friend?

It is not easy to find one at the moment. I can only appeal to you to state the case on our own side, whatever it may be.

This, Glaucon, is one of many alarming objections which I foresaw some time ago. That is why I shrank from touching upon these laws concerning the possession of wives and the rearing of children.

It looks like anything but an easy problem.

True, I said; but whether a man tumbles into a swimming-pool or into mid-ocean, he has to swim all the same. So must we, and try if we can reach the shore, hoping for some Arion's dolphin or other miraculous deliverance to bring us safe to land.[1]

I suppose so.

Come then, let us see if we can find the way out. We did agree that different natures should have different occupations, and that the natures of man and woman are different; and yet we are now saying that these different natures are to have the same occupations. Is that the charge against us?

Exactly.

It is extraordinary, Glaucon, what an effect the practice of debating has upon people.

Why do you say that?

Because they often seem to fall unconsciously into mere disputes which they mistake for reasonable argument, through being unable to draw the distinctions proper to their subject; and so, instead of a philosophical exchange of ideas, they go off in chase of contradictions which are purely verbal.

I know that happens to many people; but does it apply to us at this moment?

Absolutely. At least I am afraid we are slipping unconsciously into a dispute about words. We have been strenuously insisting on the letter of our principle that different natures should not have the same occupations, as if we were scoring a point in a debate; but we have altogether neglected to consider what sort of sameness or difference we meant and in what respect these natures and occupations were to be defined as different or the same. Consequently, we might very well be asking one another whether there is not an opposition in nature between bald and long-haired men, and, when that was admitted, forbid one set to be shoemakers, if the other were following that trade.

---

[1] The musician Arion, to escape the treachery of Corinthian sailors, leapt into the sea and was carried ashore at Taenarum by a dolphin, Herod. i. 24.

That would be absurd.

Yes, but only because we never meant any and every sort of sameness or difference in nature, but the sort that was relevant to the occupations in question. We meant, for instance, that a man and a woman have the same nature if both have a talent for medicine; whereas two men have different natures if one is a born physician, the other a born carpenter.

Yes, of course.

If, then, we find that either the male sex or the female is specially qualified for any particular form of occupation, then that occupation, we shall say, ought to be assigned to one sex or the other. But if the only difference appears to be that the male begets and the female brings forth, we shall conclude that no difference between man and woman has yet been produced that is relevant to our purpose. We shall continue to think it proper for our Guardians and their wives to share in the same pursuits.

And quite rightly.

The next thing will be to ask our opponent to name any profession or occupation in civic life for the purposes of which woman's nature is different from man's.

That is a fair question.

He might reply, as you did just now, that it is not easy to find a satisfactory answer on the spur of the moment, but that there would be no difficulty after a little reflection.

Perhaps.

Suppose, then, we invite him to follow us and see if we can convince him that there is no occupation concerned with the management of social affairs that is peculiar to women. We will confront him with a question: When you speak of a man having a natural talent for something, do you mean that he finds it easy to learn, and after a little instruction can find out much more for himself; whereas a man who is not so gifted learns with difficulty and no amount of instruction and practice will make him even remember what he has been taught? Is the talented man one whose bodily powers are readily at the service of his mind, instead of being a hindrance? Are not these the marks by which you distinguish the presence of a natural gift for any pursuit?

Yes, precisely.

Now do you know of any human occupation in which the male sex is not superior to the female in all these respects? Need I waste time over exceptions like weaving and watching over saucepans and batches of cakes, though women are supposed to be good at such things and get laughed at when a man does them better?

It is true, he replied, in almost everything one sex is easily beaten by the other. No doubt many women are better at many things than many men; but taking the sexes as a whole, it is as you say.

To conclude, then, there is no occupation concerned with the management of social affairs which belongs either to woman or to man, as such. Natural gifts are to be found here and there in both creatures alike; and every occupation is open to both, so far as their natures are concerned, though woman is for all purposes the weaker.

Certainly.

Is that a reason for making over all occupations to men only?

Of course not.

No, because one woman may have a natural gift for medicine or for music, another may not.

Surely.

Is it not also true that a woman may, or may not, be warlike or athletic?

I think so.

And again, one may love knowledge, another hate it; one may be high-spirited, another spiritless?

True again.

It follows that one woman will be fitted by nature to be a Guardian, another will not; because these were the qualities for which we selected our men Guardians. So for the purpose of keeping watch over the commonwealth, woman has the same nature as man, save in so far as she is weaker.

So it appears.

It follows that women of this type must be selected to share the life and duties of Guardians with men of the same type, since they are competent and of a like nature, and the same natures must be allowed the same pursuits.

Yes.

We come round, then, to our former position, that there is nothing contrary to nature in giving our Guardians' wives the same training for mind and body. The practice we proposed to establish was not impossible or visionary, since it was in accordance with nature. Rather, the contrary practice which now prevails turns out to be unnatural.

So it appears.

Well, we set out to inquire whether the plan we proposed was feasible and also the best. That it is feasible is now agreed; we must next settle whether it is the best.

Obviously.

Now, for the purpose of producing a woman fit to be a Guardian, we shall not have one education for men and another for women, precisely because the nature to be taken in hand is the same.

True.

What is your opinion on the question of one man being better than another? Do you think there is no such difference?

Certainly I do not.

And in this commonwealth of ours which will prove the better men—the Guardians who have received the education we described, or the shoemakers who have been trained to make shoes?[2]

It is absurd to ask such a question.

Very well. So these Guardians will be the best of all the citizens?

By far.

And these women the best of all the women?

Yes.

Can anything be better for a commonwealth than to produce in it men and women of the best possible type?

No.

And that result will be brought about by such a system of mental and bodily training as we have described?

Surely.

We may conclude that the institution we proposed was not only practicable, but also the best for the commonwealth.

Yes.

The wives of our Guardians, then, must strip for exercise, since they will be clothed with virtue, and they must take their share in war and in the other social duties of guardianship. They are to have no other occupation; and in these duties the lighter part must fall to the women, because of the weakness of their sex. The man who laughs at naked women, exercising their bodies for the best of reasons, is like one that "gathers fruit unripe,"[3] for he does not know what it is that he is laughing at or what he is doing. There will never be a finer saying than the one which declares that whatever does good should be held in honour, and the only shame is in doing harm.

That is perfectly true.

[2]The elementary education of Chap. IX will be open to all citizens, but presumably carried further (to the age of 17 or 18) in the case of those who show special promise.

[3]An adapted quotation from Pindar (frag. 209, Schr.).

ARISTOTLE

The Politics

Aristotle (384–322 B.C.) concluded in his Nicomachean Ethics *(Book I, Chapter 7) that reason is the highest element in human nature. In Book I of* The Politics, *he considers three groups who, he claims, lack the full power of reason: slaves, women, and children. As a result, all three are judged to be inferior by their very "nature." But it is better for the inferior to be ruled by the superior—just as (inferior) emotions should be ruled by (superior) reason, and inferior animals by superior humans. From this basis, Aristotle develops his account of the three slightly different forms of rule in the household: master–slave, husband–wife, father–children. Although he discusses the case of slaves at more length, his conclusions apply directly to the status of women and children. He denies to women even the limited sort of equal opportunity which Plato would grant.*

This leads Aristotle to an interesting problem in Chapter XIII. A virtuous human being is rational, temperate, and so on. Can a woman or a slave be a virtuous human being? Aristotle's answer is no: a man's virtue is in commanding, a woman's in obeying, for example. And the man's virtue is the virtue of human beings as such, so a virtuous woman or slave is not a fully virtuous human being. Since women are inherently inferior and imperfect, the best virtue they can attain is relative to the perfect virtue of a free adult male.

Aristotle's comprehensive works, ranging from logic and ethics to physics and biology, formed the basis for research in these areas for many centuries. His general approach of deriving moral conclusions from assumptions about women's "nature" is prevalent even today.

Further Reading

ARISTOTLE, *The Politics*, Book II, Chapter 12.

JEAN BETHKE ELSHTAIN, "Moral Woman and Immoral Man: A Reconsideration of the Public/Private Split and Its Political Ramifications," *Politics and Society*, 4 (1974), 453–73.

BOOK I

Chapter I

Every state is a community of some kind, and every community is established with a view to some good; for mankind always act in order to obtain that which they think good. But, if all communities aim at some good, the state or political community, which is the highest of all, and which embraces all the rest, aims at good in a greater degree than any other, and at the highest good.

Some people think[1] that the qualifications of a statesman, king, householder, and master are the same, and that they differ, not in kind, but only in the number of their subjects. For example, the ruler over a few is called a master; over more, the manager of a household; over a still larger number, a statesman or king, as if there were no difference between a great household and a small state. The distinction which is made between the king and the statesman is as follows: When the government is personal, the ruler is a king; when, according to the rules of the political science, the citizens rule and are ruled in turn, then he is called a statesman.

But all this is a mistake; for governments differ in kind, as will be evident to any one who considers the matter according to the method[2] which has hitherto guided us. As in other departments of science, so in politics, the compound should always be resolved into the simple elements or least parts of the whole. We must therefore look at the elements of which the state is composed, in order that we may see in what the different kinds of rule differ from one another, and whether any scientific result can be attained about each one of them.

Chapter II

He who thus considers things in their first growth and origin, whether a state or anything else, will obtain the clearest view of them. In the first place there must be a union of those who cannot exist without each other; namely, of male and female, that the race may continue (and this is a union which is formed, not of deliberate purpose, but because, in common with other animals and with plants, mankind have a natural desire to leave

From Aristotle, *The Politics,* trans. Benjamin Jowett (Oxford: The Clarendon Press, 1885), lines 1252a1–1253b23, 1254a18–1255b15, 1259a37–1260b8.

[1]Cp. Plato, *Politicus,* 258e–259d.
[2]Cp. Book 1, ch. 8.

behind them an image of themselves), and of natural ruler and subject, that both may be preserved. For that which can foresee by the exercise of mind is by nature intended to be lord and master, and that which can with its body give effect to such foresight is a subject, and by nature a slave; hence master and slave have the same interest. Now nature has distinguished between the female and the slave. For [nature is not stingy], like the smith who fashions the Delphian knife for many uses; she makes each thing for a single use, and every instrument is best made when intended for one and not for many uses. But among barbarians no distinction is made between women and slaves, because there is no natural ruler among them: they are a community of slaves, male and female. Wherefore the poets say—

"It is meet that Hellenes should rule over barbarians";

as if they thought that the barbarian and the slave were by nature one.

Out of these two relationships between man and woman, master and slave, the first thing to arise is the family, and Hesiod is right when he says—

"First house and wife and an ox for the plough",

for the ox is the poor man's slave. The family is the association established by nature for the supply of men's everyday wants, and the members of it are called by Charondas "companions of the cupboard, " and by Epimenides the Cretan, "companions of the manger." But when several families are united, and the association aims at something more than the supply of daily needs, the first society to be formed is the village. And the most natural form of the village appears to be that of a colony from the family, composed of the children and grandchildren, who are said to be suckled "with the same milk." And this is the reason why Hellenic states were originally governed by kings; because the Hellenes were under royal rule before they came together, as the barbarians still are. Every family is ruled by the eldest, and therefore in the colonies of the family the kingly form of government prevailed because they were of the same blood. As Homer says:[3]

"Each one gives law to his children and to his wives."

For they lived dispersedly, as was the manner in ancient times. Wherefore men say that the Gods have a king, because they themselves either are or

---

[3]*Odyssey,* IX, 114, quoted by Plato, *Laws,* III, 680b, and by Aristotle in *Nicomachean Ethics,* X, 1180a28.

were in ancient times under the rule of a king. For they imagine, not only the forms of the Gods, but their ways of life to be like their own.

When several villages are united in a single complete community, large enough to be nearly or quite self-sufficing, the state comes into existence, originating in the bare needs of life, and continuing in existence for the sake of a good life. And therefore, if the earlier forms of society are natural, so is the state, for it is the end of them, and the nature of a thing is its end. For what each thing is when fully developed, we call its nature, whether we are speaking of a man, a horse, or a family. Besides, the final cause and end of a thing is the best, and to be self-sufficing is the end and the best.

Hence it is evident that the state is a creation of nature, and that man is by nature a political animal. And he who by nature and not by mere accident is without a state, is either a bad man or above humanity; he is like the

"Tribeless, lawless, hearthless one,"

whom Homer[4] denounces—the natural outcast is forthwith a lover of war; he may be compared to an isolated piece at draughts.

Now, that man is more of a political animal than bees or any other gregarious animals is evident. Nature, as we often say, makes nothing in vain,[5] and man is the only animal whom she has endowed with the gift of speech.[6] And whereas mere voice is but an indication of pleasure or pain, and is therefore found in other animals (for their nature attains to the perception of pleasure and pain and the intimation of them to one another, and no further), the power of speech is intended to set forth the expedient and inexpedient, and therefore likewise the just and the unjust. And it is a characteristic of man that he alone has any sense of good and evil, of just and unjust, and the like, and the association of living beings who have this sense makes a family and a state.

Further, the state is by nature clearly prior to the family and to the individual, since the whole is of necessity prior to the part; for example, if the whole body be destroyed, there will be no foot or hand, except in an equivocal sense, as we might speak of a stone hand; for when destroyed the hand will be no better than that. But things are defined by their working and power; and we ought not to say that they are the same when they no longer have their proper quality, but only that they have the same name. The proof that the state is a creation of nature and prior to the individual is that the individual, when isolated, is not self-sufficing; and

[4]*Iliad,* IX, 63.
[5]Cp. Book I, ch. 8.
[6]Cp. Book VII, ch. 14.

therefore he is like a part in relation to the whole. But he who is unable to live in society, or who has no need because he is sufficient for himself, must be either a beast or a god: he is no part of a state. A social instinct is implanted in all men by nature, and yet he who first founded the state was the greatest of benefactors. For man, when perfected, is the best of animals, but, when separated from law and justice, he is the worst of all; since armed injustice is the more dangerous, and he is equipped at birth with arms, meant to be used by intelligence and virtue, which he may use for the worst ends. Wherefore, if he have not virtue, he is the most unholy and the most savage of animals, and the most full of lust and gluttony. But justice is the bond of men in states, for the administration of justice, which is the determination of what is just,[7] is the principle of order in political society.

Chapter III

Seeing then that the state is made up of households, before speaking of the state we must speak of the management of the household. The parts of household management correspond to the persons who compose the household, and a complete household consists of slaves and freemen. Now we should begin by examining everything in its fewest possible elements; and the first and fewest possible parts of a family are master and slave, husband and wife, father and children. We have therefore to consider what each of these three relations is and ought to be:—I mean the relation of master and servant, the marriage relation (the conjunction of man and wife has no name of its own), and thirdly, the procreative relation (this also has no proper name). And there is another element of a household, the so-called art of getting wealth, which, according to some, is identical with household management, according to others, a principal part of it; the nature of this art will also have to be considered by us.

Let us first speak of master and slave, looking to the needs of practical life and also seeking to attain some better theory of their relation than exists at present. For some are of opinion that the rule of a master is a science, and that the management of a household, and the mastership of slaves, and the political and royal rule, as I was saying at the outset, are all the same. Others affirm that the rule of a master over slaves is contrary to nature, and that the distinction between slave and freeman exists by law only, and not by nature; and being an interference with nature is therefore unjust.

[7]Cp. *Nicomachean Ethics,* V, 1134a31.

. . .

Chapter V

But is there any one thus intended by nature to be a slave, and for whom such a condition is expedient and right, or rather is not all slavery a violation of nature?

There is no difficulty in answering this question, on grounds both of reason and of fact. For that some should rule and others be ruled is a thing not only necessary, but expedient; from the hour of their birth, some are marked out for subjection, others for rule.

And there are many kinds both of rulers and subjects (and that rule is the better which is exercised over better subjects—for example, to rule over men is better than to rule over wild beasts; for the work is better which is executed by better workmen, and where one man rules and another is ruled, they may be said to have a work); for in all things which form a composite whole and which are made up of parts, whether continuous or discrete, a distinction between the ruling and the subject element comes to light. Such a duality exists in living creatures, but not in them only; it originates in the constitution of the universe; even in things which have no life there is a ruling principle, as in a musical mode. But we are wandering from the subject. We will therefore restrict ourselves to the living creature, which, in the first place, consists of soul and body: and of these two, the one is by nature the ruler, and the other the subject. But then we must look for the intentions of nature in things which retain their nature, and not in things which are corrupted. And therefore we must study the man who is in the most perfect state both of body and soul, for in him we shall see the true relation of the two; although in bad or corrupted natures the body will often appear to rule over the soul, because they are in an evil and unnatural condition. At all events we may firstly observe in living creatures both a despotical and a constitutional rule; for the soul rules the body with a despotical rule, whereas the intellect rules the appetites with a constitutional and royal rule. And it is clear that the rule of the soul over the body, and of the mind and the rational element over the passionate, is natural and expedient; whereas the equality of the two or the rule of the inferior is always hurtful. The same holds good of animals in relation to men; for tame animals have a better nature than wild, and all tame animals are better off when they are ruled by man; for then they are preserved. Again, the male is by nature superior, and the female inferior; and the one rules, and the other is ruled; this principle, of necessity, extends to all mankind. Where then there is such a difference as that between soul and body, or between men and animals (as in the case of those whose business is to use their body, and who can do nothing better), the lower sort are by nature slaves, and it is better for them as for all inferiors that they should be under the rule of a master. For he who can be, and therefore is, another's and he who participates in rational principle enough to apprehend, but not to have, such a principle, is a slave by nature. Whereas the lower animals cannot even apprehend a principle; they obey their instincts. And indeed the use made of slaves and of tame animals is not very different; for both with their bodies minister to the needs of life. Nature would like to distinguish between the bodies of freemen and slaves, making the one strong for servile labour, the other upright, and although useless for such services, useful for political life in the arts both of war and peace. But the opposite often happens—that some have the souls and others have the bodies of freemen. And doubtless if men differed from one another in the mere forms of their bodies as much as the statues of the Gods do from all men, all would acknowledge that the inferior class should be slaves of the superior. And if this is true of the body, how much more just that a similar distinction should exist in the soul? but the beauty of the body is seen, whereas the beauty of the soul is not seen. It is clear, then, that some men are by nature free, and others slaves, and that for these latter slavery is both expedient and right.

Chapter VI

But that those who take the opposite view have in a certain way right on their side, may be easily seen. For the words slavery and slave are used in two senses. There is a slave or slavery by law as well as by nature. The law of which I speak is a sort of convention—the law by which whatever is taken in war is supposed to belong to the victors. But this right many jurists impeach, as they would an orator who brought forward an unconstitutional measure: they detest the notion that, because one man has the power of doing violence and is superior in brute strength, another shall be his slave and subject. Even among philosophers there is a difference of opinion. The origin of the dispute, and what makes the views invade each other's territory, is as follows: in some sense virtue, when furnished with means, has actually the greatest power of exercising force: and as superior power is only found where there is superior excellence of some kind, power seems to imply virtue, and the dispute to be simply one about justice (for it is due to one party identifying justice with goodwill,[8] while the other identifies it with the mere rule of the stronger). If these views

[8] I.e., mutual goodwill, which is held to be incompatible with the relation of master and slave.

are thus set out separately, the other views[9] have no force or plausibility against the view that the superior in virtue ought to rule, or be master. Others, clinging, as they think, simply to a principle of justice (for law and custom are a sort of justice), assume that slavery in accordance with the custom of war is justified by law, but at the same moment they deny this. For what if the cause of the war be unjust? And again, no one would ever say that he is a slave who is unworthy to be a slave. Were this the case, men of highest rank would be slaves and the children of slaves if they or their parents chance to have been taken captive and sold. Wherefore Hellenes do not like to call Hellenes slaves, but confine the term to barbarians. Yet, in using this language, they really mean the natural slave of whom we spoke at first;[10] for it must be admitted that some are slaves everywhere, others nowhere. The same principle applies to nobility. Hellenes regard themselves as noble everywhere, and not only in their own country, but they deem the barbarians noble only when at home, thereby implying that there are two sorts of nobility and freedom, the one absolute, the other relative. The Helen of Theodectes says:

> *"Who would presume to call me servant who am on both sides sprung from the stem of the Gods?"*

What does this mean but that they distinguish freedom and slavery, noble and humble birth, by the two principles of good and evil? They think that as men and animals beget men and animals, so from good men a good man springs. But this is what nature, though she may intend it, cannot always accomplish.

We see then that there is some foundation for this difference of opinion, and that all are not either slaves by nature or freemen by nature, and also that there is in some cases a marked distinction between the two classes, rendering it expedient and right for the one to be slaves and the others to be masters: the one practising obedience, the others exercising the authority and lordship which nature intended them to have. The abuse of this authority is injurious to both; for the interests of part and whole,[11] of body and soul, are the same, and the slave is a part of the master, a living but separated part of his bodily frame. Hence, where the relation of master and slave between them is natural they are friends and have a common interest, but where it rests merely on law and force the reverse is true.

[9]I.e., those stated in *Iliad* 5–12, that the stronger always has, and that he never has, a right to enslave the weaker. Aristotle finds that these views cannot maintain themselves against his intermediate view, that the superior in *virtue* should rule.

[10]Ch. 5.

[11]Cp. Book I, ch. 4.

...

Chapter XII

Of household management we have seen[12] that there are three parts—
one is the rule of a master over slaves, which has been discussed already,[13]
another of a father, and the third of a husband. A husband and father, we
saw, rules over wife and children, both free, but the rule differs, the rule
over his children being a royal, over his wife a constitutional rule. For
although there may be exceptions to the order of nature, the male is by
nature fitter for command than the female, just as the elder and full-grown
is superior to the younger and more immature. But in most constitutional
states the citizens rule and are ruled by turns, for the idea of a constitutional state implies that the natures of the citizens are equal, and do not
differ at all.[14] Nevertheless, when one rules and the other is ruled we
endeavour to create a difference of outward forms and names and titles of
respect, which may be illustrated by the saying of Amasis about his foot-
pan.[15] The relation of the male to the female is of this kind, but there the
inequality is permanent. The rule of a father over his children is royal, for
he rules by virtue both of love and of respect due to age, exercising a kind
of royal power. And therefore Homer has appropriately called Zeus "father
of Gods and men," because he is the king of them all. For a king is the
natural superior of his subjects, but he should be of the same kin or kind
with them, and such is the relation of elder and younger, of father and son.

Chapter XIII

Thus it is clear that household management attends more to men than
to the acquisition of inanimate things, and to human excellence more than
to the excellence of property which we call wealth, and to the virtue of
freemen more than to the virtue of slaves. A question may indeed be
raised, whether there is any excellence at all in a slave beyond and higher
than merely instrumental and ministerial qualities—whether he can have
the virtues of temperance, courage, justice, and the like; or whether slaves
possess only bodily and ministerial qualities. And, whichever way we
answer the question, a difficulty arises; for, if they have virtue, in what will
they differ from freemen? On the other hand, since they are men and share
in rational principle, it seems absurd to say that they have no virtue. A

[12]Book I, ch. 4.
[13]Book I, ch. 4–7.
[14]Cp. Book II, ch. 1; Book III, ch. 17.
[15]Herodotus, II, 172.

similar question may be raised about women and children, whether they too have virtues: ought a woman to be temperate and brave and just, and is a child to be called temperate, and intemperate, or not? So in general we may ask about the natural ruler, and the natural subject, whether they have the same or different virtues. For if a noble nature is equally required in both, why should one of them always rule, and the other always be ruled? Nor can we say that this is a question of degree, for the difference between ruler and subject is a difference of kind, which the difference of more and less never is. Yet how strange is the supposition that the one ought, and that the other ought not, to have virtue! For if the ruler is intemperate and unjust, how can he rule well? If the subject, how can he obey well? If he be licentious and cowardly, he will certainly not do his duty. It is evident, therefore, that both of them must have a share of virtue, but varying as natural subjects also vary among themselves. Here the very constitution of the soul has shown us the way; in it one part naturally rules, and the other is subject, and the virtue of the ruler we maintain to be different from that of the subject;—the one being the virtue of the rational, and the other of the irrational part. Now, it is obvious that the same principle applies generally, and therefore almost all things rule and are ruled according to nature. But the kind of rule differs;—the freeman rules over the slave after another manner from that in which the male rules over the female, or the man over the child; although the parts of the soul are present in all of them, they are present in different degrees. For the slave has no deliberative faculty at all; the woman has, but it is without authority, and the child has, but it is immature. So it must necessarily be supposed to be with the moral virtues also; all should partake of them, but only in such manner and degree as is required by each for the fulfilment of his duty. Hence the ruler ought to have moral virtue in perfection, for his function, taken absolutely, demands a master artificer, and rational principle is such an artificer; the subjects, on the other hand, require only that measure of virtue which is proper to each of them. Clearly, then, moral virtue belongs to all of them; but the temperance of a man and of a woman, or the courage and justice of a man and of a woman, are not, as Socrates maintained,[16] the same; the courage of a man is shown in commanding, of a woman in obeying. And this holds of all other virtues, as will be more clearly seen if we look at them in detail, for those who say generally that virtue consists in a good disposition of the soul, or in doing rightly, or the like, only deceive themselves. Far better than such definitions is their mode of speaking, who, like Gorgias,[17] enumerate the virtues. All classes must be deemed to have their special attributes; as the poet says of women,

[16]Plato, *Meno,* 72a–73c.
[17]*Meno,* 71e–72a.

"Silence is a woman's glory,"

but this is not equally the glory of man. The child is imperfect, and therefore obviously his virtue is not relative to himself alone, but to the perfect man and to his teacher, and in like manner the virtue of the slave is relative to a master. Now we determined[18] that a slave is useful for the wants of life, and therefore he will obviously require only so much virtue as will prevent him from failing in his duty through cowardice or lack of self-control. Some one will ask whether, if what we are saying is true, virtue will not be required also in the artisans, for they often fail in their work through the lack of self-control? But is there not a great difference in the two cases? For the slave shares in his master's life; the artisan is less closely connected with him, and only attains excellence in proportion as he becomes a slave. The meaner sort of mechanic has a special and separate slavery; and whereas the slave exists by nature, not so the shoemaker or other artisan. It is manifest, then, that the master ought to be the source of such excellence in the slave, and not a mere possessor of the art of mastership which trains the slave in his duties.[19] Wherefore they are mistaken who forbid us to converse with slaves and say that we should employ command only,[20] for slaves stand even more in need of admonition than children.

[18]Book I, ch. 5. Cf. Book I, ch. 12.
[19]Cp. Book I, ch. 7.
[20]Plato, *Laws*, VI, 777e.

JOHN LOCKE

The Second Treatise of Government

John Locke's Two Treatises of Government *were designed to justify the English Revolution of 1688, in which the Parliament replaced James II with William and Mary. To this end, Locke describes the first government or "civil society" as the result of an original agreement or contract rather than as the result of divine right. Before the formation of the first government, people lived in what he calls the "state of nature." Here people had some "natural rights" —not to be harmed in life, liberty, and possessions, and to punish anyone who does such harm, for example. The state of nature is rough and inconvenient, so people by mutual agreement formed civil society, giving up some of their natural rights to the state and acquiring some new rights along with the obligation to obey the government.*

The family is similarly formed before civil society by a mutual agreement between man and woman. So the sexes acquire equal rights and obligations, on Locke's account. Both have a duty to raise the resulting children, but their authority extends only so far as it promotes the children's welfare. The marriage may be dissolved by mutual consent after the children are grown.

Locke's account of the family thus embodies a significant advance over Aristotle. The wife is a rational and equal partner who can own property and participate in family decisions. However, when conflicts arise, says Locke, the final power rests with the husband because he is the "abler and stronger."

Locke's political theory has been extremely influential; for example, it stood behind the American Declaration of Independence. His extensive work in the philosophy of perception started the British Empiricist school of thought.

Further Reading

SANFORD A. LAKOFF, *Equality in Political Philosophy* (Cambridge, Mass.: Harvard University Press, 1964), pp. 92–101.

RICHARD WASSERSTROM, "Rights, Human Rights and Racial Discrimination," *Journal of Philosophy*, 61 (1964), 628–41; reprinted in *Moral Problems*, James Rachels, ed. (New York: Harper & Row, 1971), pp. 109–24.

ROBERT NOZICK, *Anarchy, State and Utopia* (New York: Basic Books, 1974), pp. 9–12, 131–33, 137–38, 174–78.

CHAPTER II

Of the State of Nature

4. To understand political power right and derive it from its original, we must consider what state all men are naturally in, and that is a state of perfect freedom to order their actions and dispose of their possessions and persons as they think fit, within the bounds of the law of nature, without asking leave or depending upon the will of any other man.

A state also of equality, wherein all the power and jurisdiction is reciprocal, no one having more than another; there being nothing more evident than that creatures of the same species and rank, promiscuously born to all the same advantages of nature and the use of the same faculties, should also be equal one amongst another without subordination or subjection; unless the lord and master of them all should, by any manifest declaration of his will, set one above another, and confer on him by an evident and clear appointment an undoubted right to dominion and sovereignty.

· · ·

6. But though this be a state of liberty, yet it is not a state of license; though man in that state have an uncontrollable liberty to dispose of his person or possessions, yet he has not liberty to destroy himself, or so much as any creature in his possession, but where some nobler use than its bare preservation calls for it. The state of nature has a law of nature to govern it, which obliges every one; and reason, which is that law, teaches all mankind who will but consult it that, being all equal and independent, no one ought to harm another in his life, health, liberty, or possessions. . . .

7. And that all men may be restrained from invading others' rights and from doing hurt to one another, and the law of nature be observed, which wills the peace and preservation of all mankind, the execution of the law of nature is, in that state, put into every man's hands, whereby everyone has a right to punish the transgressors of that law to such a degree as may hinder its violation; for the law of nature would, as all other laws that concern men in this world, be in vain if there were nobody that in that state of nature had a power to execute that law and thereby preserve the innocent and restrain offenders. And if anyone in the state of nature may

From *The Second Treatise of Government* (London, 1690).

punish another for any evil he has done, everyone may do so; for in that state of perfect equality, where naturally there is no superiority or jurisdiction of one over another, what any may do in prosecution of that law, everyone must needs have a right to do. . . .

12. . . . Each transgression may be punished to that degree and with so much severity as will suffice to make it an ill bargain to the offender, give him cause to repent, and terrify others from doing the like. Every offense that can be committed in the state of nature may in the state of nature be also punished equally, and as far forth as it may in a commonwealth; for though it would be beside my present purpose to enter here into the particulars of the law of nature, or its measures of punishment, yet it is certain there is such a law, and that, too, as intelligible and plain to a rational creature and a studier of that law as the positive laws of commonwealths, nay, possibly plainer, as much as reason is easier to be understood than the fancies and intricate contrivances of men, following contrary and hidden interests put into words; for so truly are a great part of the municipal laws of countries, which are only so far right as they are founded on the law of nature, by which they are to be regulated and interpreted.

13. To this strange doctrine—viz., that in the state of nature every one has the executive power of the law of nature—I doubt not but it will be objected that it is unreasonable for men to be judges in their own cases, that self-love will make men partial to themselves and their friends, and, on the other side, that ill-nature, passion, and revenge will carry them too far in punishing others, and hence nothing but confusion and disorder will follow; and that therefore God has certainly appointed government to restrain the partiality and violence of men. I easily grant that civil government is the proper remedy for the inconveniences of the state of nature, which must certainly be great where men may be judges in their own case; since it is easy to be imagined that he who was so unjust as to do his brother an injury will scarce be so just as to condemn himself for it; but I shall desire those who make this objection to remember that absolute monarchs are but men, and if government is to be the remedy of those evils which necessarily follow from men's being judges in their own cases, and the state of nature is therefore not to be endured, I desire to know what kind of government that is, and how much better it is than the state of nature, where one man commanding a multitude has the liberty to be judge in his own case, and may do to all his subjects whatever he pleases, without the least liberty to any one to question or control those who execute his pleasure, and in whatsoever he does, whether led by reason, mistake, or passion, must be submitted to? Much better it is in the state of nature, wherein men are not bound to submit to the unjust will of another; and if he that judges, judges amiss in his own or any other case, he is answerable for it to the rest of mankind.

. . .

15. To those that say there were never any men in the state of nature, I will not only oppose the authority of the judicious Hooker,[1] *Eccl. Pol.,* lib. i., sect. 10, where he says,

> The laws which have been hitherto mentioned (i.e., the laws of nature) do bind men absolutely, even as they are men, although they have never any settled fellowship, never any solemn agreement amongst themselves what to do, or not to do; but forasmuch as we are not by ourselves sufficient to furnish ourselves with competent store of things needful for such a life as our nature doth desire, a life fit for the dignity of man; therefore to supply those defects and imperfections which are in us, as living singly and solely by ourselves, we are naturally induced to seek communion and fellowship with others. This was the cause of men's uniting themselves at first in politic societies.

But I, moreover, affirm that all men are naturally in that state and remain so till by their own consents they make themselves members of some politic society; and I doubt not in the sequel of this discourse to make it very clear.

. . .

CHAPTER V

Of Property

25. Whether we consider natural reason, which tells us that men, being once born, have a right to their preservation, and consequently to meat and drink and such other things as nature affords for their subsistence; or revelation, which gives us an account of those grants God made of the world to Adam, and to Noah and his sons; it is very clear that God, as King David says (Psalm cxv. 16), "has given the earth to the children of men," given it to mankind in common. But this being supposed, it seems to some a very great difficulty how any one should ever come to have a property in anything. I will not content myself to answer that if it be difficult to make out property upon a supposition that God gave the world to Adam and his posterity in common, it is impossible that any man but one universal monarch should have any property upon a supposition that God gave the world to Adam and his heirs in succession, exclusive of all the rest of his posterity. But I shall endeavor to show how men might come to have a property in several parts of that which God gave to mankind in common, and that without any express compact of all the commoners.

[1]Richard Hooker, *The Laws of Ecclesiastical Polity.*

. . .

27. Though the earth and all inferior creatures be common to all men, yet every man has a property in his own person; this nobody has any right to but himself. The labor of his body and the work of his hands, we may say, are properly his. Whatsoever then he removes out of the state that nature has provided and left it in, he has mixed his labor with, and joined to it something that is his own, and thereby makes it his property. It being by him removed from the common state nature has placed it in, it has by this labor something annexed to it that excludes the common right of other men. For this labor being the unquestionable property of the laborer, no man but he can have a right to what that is once joined to, at least where there is enough and as good left in common for others.

. . .

31. It will perhaps be objected to this that "if gathering the acorns, or other fruits of the earth, etc., makes a right to them, then any one may engross as much as he will." To which I answer: not so. The same law of nature that does by this means give us property does also bound that property, too. "God has given us all things richly" (I Tim. vi. 17), is the voice of reason confirmed by inspiration. But how far has he given it us? To enjoy. As much as any one can make use of to any advantage of life before it spoils, so much he may by his labor fix a property in; whatever is beyond this is more than his share and belongs to others. . . .

CHAPTER VI

Of Paternal Power

52. It may perhaps be censured as an impertinent criticism, in a discourse of this nature, to find fault with words and names that have obtained in the world; and yet possibly it may not be amiss to offer new ones when the old are apt to lead men into mistakes, as this of "paternal power" probably has done, which seems so to place the power of parents over their children wholly in the father, as if the mother had no share in it; whereas, if we consult reason or revelation, we shall find she has an equal title. This may give one reason to ask whether this might not be more properly called "parental power," for whatever obligation nature and the right of genera- tion lays on children, it must certainly bind them equally to both concur- rent causes of it. And accordingly we see the positive law of God everywhere joins them together without distinction when it commands the obedience of children: "Honour thy father and thy mother" (Exod. xx. 12); "Whosoever curseth his father or his mother" (Lev. xx. 9); "Ye shall fear

every man his mother and his father" (Lev. xix. 5); "Children, obey your parents," etc. (Eph. vi. I), is the style of the Old and New Testament.

53. Had but this one thing been well considered, without looking any deeper into the matter, it might perhaps have kept men from running into those gross mistakes they have made about this power of parents, which, however it might without any great harshness bear the name of absolute dominion and regal authority, when under the title of "paternal power" it seemed appropriated to the father, would yet have sounded but oddly and in the very name shown the absurdity if this supposed absolute power over children had been called "parental," and thereby have discovered that it belonged to the mother, too; for it will but very ill serve the turn of those men who contend so much for the absolute power and authority of the fatherhood, as they call it, that the mother should have any share in it; and it would have but ill supported the monarchy they contend for, when by the very name it appeared that that fundamental authority from whence they would derive their government of a single person only was not placed in one but two persons jointly. But to let this of names pass.

54. Though I have said above (Chap. II) that all men by nature are equal, I cannot be supposed to understand all sorts of equality. Age or virtue may give men a just precedence; excellence of parts and merit may place others above the common level; birth may subject some, and alliance or benefits others, to pay an observance to those whom nature, gratitude, or other respects may have made it due; and yet all this consists with the equality which all men are in, in respect of jurisdiction or dominion one over another, which was the equality I there spoke of as proper to the business in hand, being that equal right that every man has to his natural freedom, without being subjected to the will or authority of any other man.

55. Children, I confess, are not born in this state of equality, though they are born to it. Their parents have a sort of rule and jurisdiction over them when they come into the world, and for some time after, but it is but a temporary one. The bonds of this subjection are like the swaddling clothes they are wrapped up in and supported by in the weakness of their infancy; age and reason, as they grow up, loosen them, till at length they drop quite off and leave a man at his own free disposal.

. . .

57. The law that was to govern Adam was the same that was to govern all his posterity—the law of reason. But his offspring having another way of entrance into the world, different from him, by a natural birth that produced them ignorant and without the use of reason, they were not presently under the law; for nobody can be under a law which is not promulgated to him; and this law being promulgated or made known by reason only, he that is not come to the use of his reason cannot be said to

be under this law; and Adam's children, being not presently as soon as born under this law of reason, were not presently free; for law, in its true notion, is not so much the limitation as the direction of a free and intelligent agent to his proper interest, and prescribes no further than is for the general good of those under that law. Could they be happier without it, the law, as a useless thing, would of itself vanish; and that ill deserves the name of confinement which hedges us in only from bogs and precipices. So that, however it may be mistaken, the end of law is not to abolish or restrain but to preserve and enlarge freedom; for in all the states of created beings capable of laws, where there is no law, there is no freedom. For liberty is to be free from restraint and violence from others, which cannot be where there is not law; but freedom is not, as we are told: a liberty for every man to do what he lists—for who could be free, when every other man's humor might domineer over him?—but a liberty to dispose and order as he lists his person, actions, possessions, and his whole property, within the allowance of those laws under which he is, and therein not to be subject to the arbitrary will of another, but freely follow his own.

58. The power, then, that parents have over their children arises from that duty which is incumbent on them—to take care of their offspring during the imperfect state of childhood. To inform the mind and govern the actions of their yet ignorant nonage till reason shall take its place and ease them of that trouble is what the children want and the parents are bound to; for God, having given man an understanding to direct his actions, has allowed him a freedom of will and liberty of acting as properly belonging thereunto, within the bounds of that law he is under. But while he is in an estate wherein he has not understanding of his own to direct his will, he is not to have any will of his own to follow; he that understands for him must will for him, too; he must prescribe to his will and regulate his actions; but when he comes to the estate that made his father a freeman, the son is a freeman, too.

. . .

CHAPTER VII

Of Political or Civil Society

77. God, having made man such a creature that in his own judgment it was not good for him to be alone, put him under strong obligations of necessity, convenience, and inclination to drive him into society, as well as fitted him with understanding and language to continue and enjoy it. The first society was between man and wife, which gave beginning to that between parents and children; to which, in time, that between master and

servant came to be added; and though all these might, and commonly did, meet together and make up but one family wherein the master or mistress of it had some sort of rule proper to a family—each of these, or all together, came short of political society, as we shall see if we consider the different ends, ties, and bounds of each of these.

78. Conjugal society is made by a voluntary compact between man and woman; and though it consist chiefly in such a communion and right in one another's bodies as is necessary to its chief end, procreation, yet it draws with it mutual support and assistance, and a communion of interests, too, as necessary not only to unite their care and affection, but also necessary to their common offspring, who have a right to be nourished and maintained by them till they are able to provide for themselves.

79. For the end of conjunction between male and female being not barely procreation but the continuation of the species, this conjunction betwixt male and female ought to last, even after procreation, so long as is necessary to the nourishment and support of the young ones who are to be sustained by those that got them till they are able to shift and provide for themselves. This rule, which the infinite wise Maker has set to the works of his hands, we find the inferior creatures steadily obey. In those viviparous animals which feed on grass, the conjunction between male and female lasts no longer than the very act of copulation, because the teat of the dam being sufficient to nourish the young till it be able to feed on grass, the male only begets, but concerns not himself for the female or young to whose sustenance he can contribute nothing. But in beasts of prey the conjunction lasts longer because, the dam not being able well to subsist herself and nourish her numerous offspring by her own prey alone, a more laborious as well as more dangerous way of living than by feeding on grass, the assistance of the male is necessary to the maintenance of their common family, which cannot subsist till they are able to prey for themselves but by the joint care of male and female. The same is to be observed in all birds —except some domestic ones, where plenty of food excuses the cock from feeding and taking care of the young brood—whose young needing food in the nest, the cock and hen continue mates till the young are able to use their wing and provide for themselves.

80. And herein, I think, lies the chief, if not the only, reason why the male and female in mankind are tied to a longer conjunction than other creatures, viz., because the female is capable of conceiving, and *de facto* is commonly with child again and brings forth, too, a new birth long before the former is out of a dependency for support on his parents' help and able to shift for himself and has all the assistance that is due to him from his parents; whereby the father, who is bound to take care for those he has begot, is under an obligation to continue in conjugal society with the same woman longer than other creatures whose young being able to subsist of

themselves before the time of procreation returns again, the conjugal bond dissolves of itself, and they are at liberty, till Hymen at his usual anniversary season summons them again to choose new mates. Wherein one cannot but admire the wisdom of the great Creator, who, having given to man foresight and an ability to lay up for the future as well as to supply the present necessity, has made it necessary that society of man and wife should be more lasting than of male and female amongst other creatures, that so their industry might be encouraged and their interest better united to make provision and lay up goods for their common issue, which uncertain mixture or easy and frequent solutions of conjugal society would mightily disturb.

81. But though these are ties upon mankind which make the conjugal bonds more firm and lasting in man than the other species of animals, yet it would give one reason to inquire why this compact, where procreation and education are secured and inheritance taken care for, may not be made determinable, either by consent, or at a certain time, or upon certain conditions, as well as any other voluntary compacts, there being no necessity in the nature of the thing nor to the ends of it that it should always be for life; I mean, to such as are under no restraint of any positive law which ordains all such contracts to be perpetual.

82. But the husband and wife, though they have but one common concern, yet having different understandings, will unavoidably sometimes have different wills, too; it therefore being necessary that the last determination—i.e., the rule—should be placed somewhere, it naturally falls to the man's share, as the abler and the stronger. But this, reaching but to the things of their common interest and property, leaves the wife in the full and free possession of what by contract is her peculiar right, and gives the husband no more power over her life than she has over his; the power of the husband being so far from that of an absolute monarch that the wife has in many cases a liberty to separate from him where natural right or their contract allows it, whether that contract be made by themselves in the state of nature, or by the customs or laws of the country they live in; and the children upon such separation fall to the father's or mother's lot, as such contract does determine.

83. For all the ends of marriage being to be obtained under politic government as well as in the state of nature, the civil magistrate does not abridge the right or power of either naturally necessary to those ends, viz., procreation and mutual support and assistance while they are together, but only decides any controversy that may arise between man and wife about them. If it were otherwise, and that absolute sovereignty and power of life and death naturally belonged to the husband and were necessary to the society between man and wife, there could be no matrimony in any of those countries where the husband is allowed no such absolute authority.

But the ends of matrimony requiring no such power in the husband, the condition of conjugal society put it not in him, it being not at all necessary to that state. Conjugal society could subsist and attain its ends without it; nay, community of goods and the power over them, mutual assistance and maintenance, and other things belonging to conjugal society, might be varied and regulated by that contract which unites man and wife in that society as far as may consist with procreation and the bringing up of children till they could shift for themselves, nothing being necessary to any society that is not necessary to the ends for which it is made.

. . .

86. Let us therefore consider a master of a family with all these subordinate relations of wife, children, servants, and slaves, united under the domestic rule of a family; which, what resemblance soever it may have in its order, offices, and number, too, with a little commonwealth, yet is very far from it, both in its constitution, power, and end; or, if it must be thought a monarchy, and the paterfamilias the absolute monarch in it, absolute monarchy will have but a very shattered and short power when it is plain, by what has been said before, that the master of the family has a very distinct and differently limited power both as to time and extent over those several persons that are in it; for excepting the slave—and the family is as much a family, and his power as paterfamilias as great, whether there be any slaves in his family or no—he has no legislative power of life and death over any of them, and none, too, but what a mistress of a family may have as well as he. And he certainly can have no absolute power over the whole family who has but a very limited one over every individual in it. But how a family or any other society of men differ from that which is properly political society, we shall best see by considering wherein political society itself consists.

. . .

89. Whenever, therefore, any number of men are so united into one society as to quit every one his executive power of the law of nature and to resign it to the public, there and there only is a political or civil society.

. . .

90. Hence it is evident that absolute monarchy, which by some men is counted the only government in the world, is indeed inconsistent with civil society, and so can be no form of civil government at all; for the end of civil society being to avoid and remedy these inconveniences of the state of nature which necessarily follow from every man being judge in his own case, by setting up a known authority to which everyone of that society may appeal upon any injury received or controversy that may arise, and

which everyone of the society ought to obey. Wherever any persons are who have not such an authority to appeal to for the decision of any difference between them, there those persons are still in the state of nature; and so is every absolute prince, in respect of those who are under his dominion.

JEAN JACQUES ROUSSEAU
Émile

Like John Locke, Jean Jacques Rousseau (1712–1778) based his social philosophy on the idea of a social contract. But for Rousseau, the natural *side of human beings is what is good; injustice, inequality, tyranny, and war are all the result of the "unnatural" introduction of property and the state. Only a state which effectively carries out the will of all can leave people as free as they would be naturally.*

Relative to his call for freedom and equality, Rousseau's position on women in an anachronism. Of all forms of society, only the family is "natural." Where he sees all other forms of rule or dominance as artificial and a distortion of human nature, Rousseau thinks the different roles of the sexes and the rule of the father in the family are natural—that is, good. Since the family arises prior to private property, and only property introduces the notion of justice, this domination cannot be unjust.

Émile (1762) is Rousseau's description of an ideal, "natural" education. Once he has described the education of his ideal man, Émile, he turns to the education of the ideal "helpmeet" for him, Sophy. In this selection it is clear that Rousseau believes many differences between the sexes, ranging from a double standard in chastity to an interest in needlework, are pre-social, natural, and should be reinforced by education.

Rousseau went beyond the political theory of Locke in using a social contract to justify the rule of all rather than merely the rights of an aristocratic parliament. This idea of Rousseau's was influential in the French Revolution.

Further Reading

MARY WOLLSTONECRAFT, *Thoughts on the Education of Daughters* (London: Joseph Johnson, 1786).

MARY WOLLSTONECRAFT, *Vindication of the Rights of Women,* chapter 5 (London: Joseph Johnson, 1792).

JEAN JACQUES ROUSSEAU, *A Discourse on the Origin of Inequality* (Amsterdam: M. M. Rey, 1755).

JEAN JACQUES ROUSSEAU, *The Social Contract,* Book I (Amsterdam: M. M. Rey, 1762).

SOPHY, OR WOMAN

Sophy should be as truly a woman as Émile is a man, *i.e.*, she must possess all those characters of her sex which are required to enable her to play her part in the physical and moral order. Let us inquire to begin with in what respects her sex differs from our own.

But for her sex, a woman is a man; she has the same organs, the same needs, the same faculties. The machine is the same in its construction; its parts, its working, and its appearance are similar. Regard it as you will the difference is only in degree.

Yet where sex is concerned man and woman are unlike; each is the complement of the other; the difficulty in comparing them lies in our inability to decide, in either case, what is a matter of sex, and what is not. General differences present themselves to the comparative anatomist and even to the superficial observer; they seem not to be a matter of sex; yet they are really sex differences, though the connection eludes our observation. How far such differences may extend we cannot tell; all we know for certain is that where man and woman are alike we have to do with the characteristics of the species; where they are unlike, we have to do with the characteristics of sex. Considered from these two standpoints, we find so many instances of likeness and unlikeness that it is perhaps one of the greatest of marvels how nature has contrived to make two beings so like and yet so different.

These resemblances and differences must have an influence on the moral nature; this inference is obvious, and it is confirmed by experience; it shows the vanity of the disputes as to the superiority or the equality of the sexes; as if each sex, pursuing the path marked out for it by nature, were not more perfect in that very divergence than if it more closely resembled the other. A perfect man and a perfect woman should no more be alike in mind than in face, and perfection admits of neither less nor more.

In the union of the sexes each alike contributes to the common end, but in different ways. From this diversity springs the first difference which may be observed between man and woman in their moral relations. The man should be strong and active; the woman should be weak and passive; the one must have both the power and the will; it is enough that the other should offer little resistance.

When this principle is admitted, it follows that woman is specially made for man's delight. If man in his turn ought to be pleasing in her eyes, the necessity is less urgent, his virtue is in his strength, he pleases because he is strong. I grant you this is not the law of love, but it is the law of nature, which is older than love itself.

From *Émile,* Chapter V, trans. Barbara Foxley (London: J. M. Dent & Sons, Ltd., 1911), pp. 321–33; first published in French (La Haye: J. Néaulme, 1762).

. . .

The mutual duties of the two sexes are not, and cannot be, equally binding on both. Women do wrong to complain of the inequality of man-made laws; this inequality is not of man's making, or at any rate it is not the result of mere prejudice, but of reason. She to whom nature has entrusted the care of the children must hold herself responsible for them to their father. No doubt every breach of faith is wrong, and every faithless husband, who robs his wife of the sole reward of the stern duties of her sex, is cruel and unjust; but the faithless wife is worse; she destroys the family and breaks the bonds of nature; when she gives her husband children who are not his own, she is false both to him and them, her crime is not infidelity but treason. To my mind, it is the source of dissension and of crime of every kind. Can any position be more wretched than that of the unhappy father who, when he clasps his child to his breast, is haunted by the suspicion that this is the child of another, the badge of his own dishonour, a thief who is robbing his own children of their inheritance? Under such circumstances the family is little more than a group of secret enemies, armed against each other by a guilty woman, who compels them to pretend to love one another.

Thus it is not enough that a wife should be faithful; her husband, along with his friends and neighbours, must believe in her fidelity; she must be modest, devoted, retiring; she should have the witness not only of a good conscience, but of a good reputation. In a word, if a father must love his children, he must be able to respect their mother. For these reasons it is not enough that the woman should be chaste, she must preserve her reputation and her good name. From these principles there arises not only a moral difference between the sexes, but also a fresh motive for duty and propriety, which prescribes to women in particular the most scrupulous attention to their conduct, their manners, their behaviour. Vague assertions as to the equality of the sexes and the similarity of their duties are only empty words; they are no answer to my argument.

. . .

I am quite aware that Plato, in the *Republic,* assigns the same gymnastics to women and men.[1] Having got rid of the family there is no place for women in his system of government, so he is forced to turn them into men. That great genius has worked out his plans in detail and has provided for every contingency; he has even provided against a difficulty which in all likelihood no one would ever have raised; but he has not succeeded in meeting the real difficulty. I am not speaking of the alleged community of wives which has often been laid to his charge; this assertion only shows

[1][See Plato, this volume, pp. 15 and 19.]

that his detractors have never read his works. I refer to that political promiscuity under which the same occupations are assigned to both sexes alike, a scheme which could only lead to intolerable evils; I refer to that subversion of all the tenderest of our natural feelings, which he sacrificed to an artificial sentiment which can only exist by their aid. Will the bonds of convention hold firm without some foundation in nature? Can devotion to the state exist apart from the love of those near and dear to us? Can patriotism thrive except in the soil of that miniature fatherland, the home? Is it not the good son, the good husband, the good father, who makes the good citizen?

When once it is proved that men and women are and ought to be unlike in constitution and in temperament, it follows that their education must be different. Nature teaches us that they should work together, but that each has its own share of the work; the end is the same, but the means are different, as are also the feelings which direct them. We have attempted to paint a natural man, let us try to paint a helpmeet for him.

. . .

The children's health depends in the first place on the mother's, and the early education of man is also in a woman's hands; his morals, his passions, his tastes, his pleasures, his happiness itself, depend on her. A woman's education must therefore be planned in relation to man. To be pleasing in his sight, to win his respect and love, to train him in childhood, to tend him in manhood, to counsel and console, to make his life pleasant and happy, these are the duties of woman for all time, and this is what she should be taught while she is young. The further we depart from this principle, the further we shall be from our goal, and all our precepts will fail to secure her happiness or our own.

. . .

Boys and girls have many games in common, and this is as it should be; do they not play together when they are grown up? They have also special tastes of their own. Boys want movement and noise, drums, tops, toy-carts; girls prefer things which appeal to the eye, and can be used for dressing-up—mirrors, jewellery, finery, and specially dolls. The doll is the girl's special plaything; this shows her instinctive bent towards her life's work. The art of pleasing finds it physical basis in personal adornment, and this physical side of the art is the only one which the child can cultivate.

. . .

We have here a very early and clearly-marked bent; you have only to follow it and train it. What the little girl most clearly desires is to dress her doll, to make its bows, its tippets, its sashes, and its tuckers; she is dependent on other people's kindness in all this, and it would be much pleasanter to be able to do it herself. Here is a motive for her earliest lessons, they are not tasks prescribed, but favours bestowed. Little girls always dislike learning to read and write, but they are always ready to learn to sew. They think they are grown up, and in imagination they are using their knowledge for their own adornment.

· · ·

If I object to little boys being made to learn to read, still more do I object to it for little girls until they are able to see the use of reading; we generally think more of our own ideas than theirs in our attempts to convince them of the utility of this art. After all, why should a little girl know how to read and write? Has she a house to manage? Most of them make a bad use of this fatal knowledge, and girls are so full of curiosity that few of them will fail to learn without compulsion. Possibly cyphering should come first; there is nothing so obviously useful, nothing which needs so much practice or gives so much opportunity for error as reckoning. If the little girl does not get the cherries for her lunch without an arithmetical exercise, she will soon learn to count.

· · ·

Show the sense of the tasks you set your little girls, but keep them busy. Idleness and insubordination are two very dangerous faults, and very hard to cure when once established. Girls should be attentive and industrious, but this is not enough by itself; they should early be accustomed to restraint. This misfortune, if such it be, is inherent in their sex, and they will never escape from it, unless to endure more cruel sufferings. All their life long, they will have to submit to the strictest and most enduring restraints, those of propriety. They must be trained to bear the yoke from the first, so that they may not feel it, to master their own caprices and to submit themselves to the will of others. If they were always eager to be at work, they should sometimes be compelled to do nothing. Their childish faults, unchecked and unheeded, may easily lead to dissipation, frivolity, and inconstancy. To guard against this, teach them above all things self-control. Under our senseless conditions, the life of a good woman is a perpetual struggle against self; it is only fair that woman should bear her share of the ills she has brought upon man.

· · ·

Just because they have, or ought to have, little freedom, they are apt to indulge themselves too fully with regard to such freedom as they have; they carry everything to extremes, and they devote themselves to their games with an enthusiasm even greater than that of boys. This is the second difficulty to which I referred. This enthusiasm must be kept in check, for it is the source of several vices commonly found among women, caprice and that extravagant admiration which leads a woman to regard a thing with rapture to-day and to be quite indifferent to it to-morrow. This fickleness of taste is as dangerous as exaggeration; and both spring from the same cause. Do not deprive them of mirth, laughter, noise, and romp-ing games, but do not let them tire of one game and go off to another; do not leave them for a moment without restraint. Train them to break off their games and return to their other occupations without a murmur. Habit is all that is needed, as you have nature on your side.

This habitual restraint produces a docility which woman requires all her life long, for she will always be in subjection to a man, or to man's judgment, and she will never be free to set her own opinion above his. What is most wanted in a woman is gentleness; formed to obey a creature so imperfect as man, a creature often vicious and always faulty, she should early learn to submit to injustice and to suffer the wrongs inflicted on her by her husband without complaint; she must be gentle for her own sake, not his.

J. G. FICHTE

The Science of Rights

Johann Gottlieb Fichte's moral philosophy is very closely related to Immanuel Kant's. The central principle is that a truly good person chooses to do the right thing simply because it is right, rather than because of its consequences. According to Fichte, one's conscience is the best guide to what is right.

In this selection from The Science of Rights *(1796), Fichte argues that married women should not vote, hold public office, write books, or have an equal education. But first he grants that women have reason and all the rights men do. However, because a woman's entire dignity rests on submitting herself to her husband, she should desire not to exercise these rights. The husband should hold the common property, vote for the whole family, and so forth. As for education, women have an advantage, he believes, in having to learn only the* results of *culture rather than being burdened with their theoretical foundations, which men learn in order to pass them on to the next generation.*

It is ironic that Fichte's other moral, political, and religious views were thought so radical that in 1799 he was forced to resign the professorship at the University of Jena.

Further Reading

ELIZABETH C. STANTON, SUSAN B. ANTHONY, and MATILDA J. GAGE, excerpts from *History of Woman Suffrage* (1881), in *The Feminist Papers,* Alice S. Rossi, ed. (New York: Columbia University Press, 1973), pp. 413–70.

JOHN STUART MILL, *Socialism, Being a Collection of His Writings on Socialism, Democracy, the Rights of Property in Land and the Enfranchisement of Women,* W. D. P. Bliss, ed. (New York: Humbold, 1891).

CARLOS WHITE, ed., *Ecce Femina: An Attempt to Solve the Women Question, Being an Examination of Arguments in Favor of Female Suffrage by John Stuart Mill and Others* (Boston: Ice & Shepard, 1870).

§3. CONCERNING THE LEGAL RELATION OF BOTH SEXES IN GENERAL TO EACH OTHER IN THE STATE.

I.

Has woman the same rights in the state which man has? This question may appear ridiculous to many. For if the only ground of all legal rights is reason and freedom, how can a distinction exist between two sexes which possess both the same reason and the same freedom?

Nevertheless, it seems that, so long as men have lived, this has been differently held, and the female sex seems not to have been placed on a par with the male sex in the exercise of its rights. Such a universal sentiment must have a ground, to discover which was never a more urgent problem than in our days.

If we grant that the female sex, so far as its rights are concerned, has really been thus treated, it by no means suffices to assign as ground a less degree of mental and physical power. For women would reply: "Firstly, you men do not give us the same degree of culture which you extend to your own sex; and secondly, that statement is not even true; for if you will make a list of the men who are the pride of their sex, we can make one of women, who will, justly estimated, be their peers in every thing; but finally, even if this inequality were as you state it to be, it would on no account involve such a decided inequality of rights, since there is also among men a great distinction of mental and bodily powers, which does not involve such an oppressive inequality of rights."

Hence, it will be necessary, above all things, to investigate whether women are really treated so badly and unjustly as some of them, and, still more, some uncalled-for advocates of their cause, assert.

II.

The question, whether the female sex has really a claim to all the rights of men and of citizens which belong to the male sex, could be raised only by persons who doubt whether women are complete human beings. We do not doubt it, as appears sufficiently from the above. But the question may certainly be asked, whether and in how far the female sex *can desire* to exercise all its rights? To facilitate the answering of this question, we shall consider the several conditions of women.

From *The Science of Rights,* trans. A. E. Kroeger (London: Trübner & Co., 1889), pp. 439–51.

III.

As a rule, woman is either a maid or married. If a maid, she is still under the care of her father, precisely as the unmarried young man. Herein both sexes are perfectly equal. Both become free by marriage, and in regard to their marriage both are equally free; or if there is to be a favor shown, it should be shown to the daughter. For she ought not even to be persuaded to marry, which may be permitted in the case of the son, as we have shown heretofore.

If she is *married,* her whole dignity depends upon her being completely subjected, and seeming to be so subjected, to her husband. Let it be well observed, what my whole theory expresses, but what it is perhaps necessary to repeat once more emphatically—woman is not subjected to her husband in such a manner as to give him a *right of compulsion* over her; she is subjected through her own continuous necessary wish—a wish which is the condition of her morality—to be so subjected. She has the *power* to withdraw her freedom, if she could have the *will* to do so; but that is the very point: she can not rationally will to be free. Her relation to her husband being publicly known, she must, moreover, will to appear to all whom she knows as utterly subjected to, and utterly lost in, the man of her choice.

Her husband is, therefore, the administrator of all her rights in consequence of her own necessary will; and she wishes those rights asserted and exercised only in so far as *he* wishes it. He is her natural representative in the state and in the whole society. This is her *public* relation to society. She can not even allow herself to think for a moment that she should exercise herself her rights in the state.

So far as her *private* and *internal* relation in the house is concerned, *the tenderness of the husband necessarily restores to her all and more than she has lost.* The husband will not relinquish her rights, because they are his own; and because, if he did so, he would dishonor himself and his wife before society. The wife has also rights in public affairs, for she is a citizen. I consider it the duty of the husband—in states which give to the citizen a vote on public matters—not to vote without having discussed the subject with his wife, and allowed her to modify his opinion through her own. His vote will then be the result of their common will. The father of a family, who represents not only his own but also the interests of his wife and children, ought indeed to have a greater influence and a more decisive vote in a commonwealth, than the citizen who represents only his own interests. The manner of arranging this is a problem for the science of politics.

Women, therefore, do really exercise the right of suffrage—not immediately, however, in their own person, because they can not wish to do so without lowering their dignity, but—through the influence which results from the nature of the marriage relation. This is, indeed, proved by the history of all great revolutions. They either emanated from, or at least were led and considerably modified by, women.

. . .

IV.

If the husband can not or refuses to vote, there is no reason why the wife should not appear in his place and cast their common vote, but always *as the vote of the husband.* (She could not cast it as her own without separating herself from her husband.) For the grounded extends no further than the ground; and the ground why the wife could not vote was, because the husband voted for both. If he does not, she can, therefore, vote.

This furnishes us the principle applicable to widows and divorced women, and to maids who are no longer under paternal authority and yet have never been married. All these classes of women are not subjected to a man; hence there is no reason why they should not themselves exercise all civil rights precisely as men do. In a republic they have the right to vote, to appear in court, and to defend their own cause. If from natural bashfulness and modesty they prefer to choose a guardian, they must be permitted to do so, but there is no legal ground why they should be forced to choose one.

V.

Every citizen in the state is to possess property and to administer it according to his will; hence, also, the woman who has no husband. This property need not be absolute property, money or valuables, but may also consist of civil rights or privileges. There is no reason why women should not have these. Woman can own land and carry on agriculture. Or she can carry on an art, or a profession, or some commercial business.

VI.

Women are ineligible to public offices for the following simple reasons: public officers are responsible to the state; and hence must be perfectly free, and dependent always only upon their own will; otherwise such a responsibility would be unjust and contradictory. Woman, however, is free and independent only so long as she has no husband. Hence the exclusive condition under which a woman might become eligible to office, would be the promise not to marry. But no rational woman can give such a promise, nor can the state rationally accept it. For woman is destined to love, and love comes to women of itself—does not depend upon her free will. But when she loves, it is her duty to marry, and the state must not form an obstacle to this duty. Now, if a woman, holding a public office, were to marry, two cases are possible. Firstly, she might not subject herself to her husband so far as her official duties were concerned. But this is utterly against female dignity; for she can not say then, that she has given herself up wholly to the husband. Moreover, where are the strict limits which separate official from private life? Or, secondly, she might subject herself utterly, as nature and morality require, to her husband, even so far as her official duties are concerned. But, in that case, she would cease to be the official, and he would become it. The office would become his by marriage, like the rest of his wife's property and rights. But this the state can not permit; for it must know the ability and the character of the person upon whom an office is conferred, and can not accept one chosen merely by love.

VII.

This fact, that women are not intended for public offices, has another consequence, which the advocates of woman's rights put forth as a new complaint against our political institutions. For, very naturally, they are not educated for duties they will never have to perform; are sent neither to colleges, nor to universities. Now they cry out, that men neglect their minds, and enviously and cunningly keep them in ignorance, and hold them removed from the sources of enlightening culture. We shall examine this charge carefully.

The learned man by profession studies not merely for himself; *as* student he studies, on the contrary, not at all for himself, but for others. If he wishes to become a preacher, or statesman, or doctor, he studies for the purpose of immediately applying what he has learned; hence he learns at the same time the form, or the manner of applying his science. Or if it is his intention to become a teacher of future students in schools or universities, it is also his intention to communicate again what he now learns, and to increase the stock of his knowledge by discoveries of his own, so that culture may not come to a stand-still. Hence he must know *how* to make these discoveries, and how to develop them out of the human soul. But this acquiring a knowledge of the *form* of science is precisely what they, women, can not make use of, since they are to become neither teachers, preachers, doctors, or lawyers.

For their own intellectual culture, men only require the *results* of culture; and these results women learn also in society: in each condition of society the results of the whole culture of that condition. That which they envy us is, therefore, the unessential, the formal, the mere hull. By their position and by our conversation they are saved the trouble of working through this hull, and can receive its contents directly. They could not, indeed, make use of the form at all. Women are not habituated, and can not be habituated, to look upon the form as means, because they could be accustomed to do so only by making use of the form. Hence they look upon it as an end in itself, as something noble and excellent in itself. This is the reason why really learned women—I do not speak of those who reason purely through their common sense, for these are very estimable—are usually pedantic.

To prevent my being misunderstood, let me explain this further. It can not be maintained that woman is inferior to man in regard to talents of mind; but it can certainly be maintained that the minds of man and woman have, by nature, a very different character. Man reduces all that is in and for him to clear conceptions, and discovers it only through reasoning— provided, of course, his knowledge is a true conviction, and not a mere historical knowledge. Woman, on the other hand, has a natural sentiment of what is good, true, and proper. Not as if this were given her through mere feeling, for that is impossible; but when it is externally given to her, she has the faculty of judging quickly through her feelings, and without clear insight into the grounds of such judgment, whether it be true and good, or not. It may be said, that man must first make himself rational; whereas, woman is already rational by nature. This is, indeed, clearly to be deduced from the fundamental distinction between woman and man. Her fundamental impulse originally unites with reason, because it would cancel reason unless it did so unite; it becomes a rational impulse. And this is the reason why woman's whole system of feeling is rational, and made to correspond to reason, as it were. Man, on the contrary, must first subordinate all his impulses to reason, through exertion and activity.

Woman, therefore, is especially practical, and not at all speculative in her womanly nature. She can not and shall not go beyond the limit of her feeling. (This explains the well-known phenomenon, why some women have been known to become distinguished in matters of memory, as languages, and even in mathematics, so far as they can be learned through memory; and some also in matters of invention, in the gentler forms of poetry, in novel-writing, and even in the writing of history. But no women are known to have been philosophers, or inventors of new theories in the mathematical science.)

JOHN STUART MILL

The Subjection of Women

John Stuart Mill's The Subjection of Women *(1869) stands out in history as the only essay by a famous moral philosopher devoted to this question, and the one most favorable to women since Plato. Mill persuasively presents a number of clear arguments against certain practices of his day. Upon marrying, for instance, a woman gave up her property, earnings, and many civil rights to her husband. Women were legally barred from many occupations, including public office. Mill points out, for example, that if women really are not qualified to hold certain jobs, it will not be necessary to make laws forbidding them from doing so. Like Plato, he says that the average characteristics of a sex are not sufficient reason to prohibit exceptional members from doing things the average cannot. In under-utilizing women's abilities, he says, society loses half the natural talent available to it. Not all these ideas were original with Mill, but he presents a cogent position.*

In applauding Mill's feminism, however, we should not overlook what we now realize to be serious errors. For instance, he claims it is only in the "lower classes" that boys and girls are raised differently. While arguing that husband and wife should both have a voice in family decisions, he says that the husband will have final say because he is the elder and earns the living. Nor should women hold jobs outside the home, lest child-rearing and household management suffer. When a woman marries, according to Mill, she chooses homemaking and renounces any outside career.

Mill (1806–1873) is best known as a proponent of Utilitarianism (the view that the right action is the one which produces the greatest happiness for the greatest number), a school of thought which had a significant impact on legislation in England in the nineteenth century.

Further Reading

HARRIET TAYLOR MILL, *The Enfranchisement of Women,* in *Essays on Sex Equality,* Alice Rossi, ed. (Chicago: University of Chicago Press, 1970), pp. 91–121.

SANFORD A. LAKOFF, *Equality in Political Philosophy* (Cambridge, Mass.: Harvard University Press, 1964), pp. 129–43.

L. P. BROCKETT, *Woman: Her Rights, Wrongs, Privileges and Responsibilities* (Brooklyn, N.Y., 1869); reprinted (Freeport, N.Y.: Books for Libraries Press, 1970).

JOHN STUART MILL, *On Liberty* (London: J.W. Parker & Son, 1859).

CHAPTER 1

The object of this Essay is to explain as clearly as I am able, the grounds of an opinion which I have held from the very earliest period when I had formed any opinions at all on social or political matters, and which, instead of being weakened or modified, has been constantly growing stronger by the progress of reflection and the experience of life: That the principle which regulates the existing social relations between the two sexes—the legal subordination of one sex to the other—is wrong in itself, and now one of the chief hindrances to human improvement; and that it ought to be replaced by a principle of perfect equality, admitting no power or privilege on the one side, nor disability on the other.

. . .

The generality of a practice is in some cases a strong presumption that it is, or at all events once was, conducive to laudable ends. This is the case, when the practice was first adopted, or afterwards kept up, as a means to such ends, and was grounded on experience of the mode in which they could be most effectually attained. If the authority of men over women, when first established, had been the result of a conscientious comparison between different modes of constituting the government of society; if, after trying various other modes of social organization—the government of women over men, equality between the two, and such mixed and divided modes of government as might be invented—it had been decided, on the testimony of experience, that the mode in which women are wholly under the rule of men, having no share at all in public concerns, and each in private being under the legal obligation of obedience to the man with whom she has associated her destiny, was the arrangement most conducive to the happiness and well being of both; its general adoption might then be fairly thought to be some evidence that, at the time when it was adopted, it was the best: though even then the considerations which rec-

From *The Subjection of Women* (London: Longmans, Green, Reader & Dyer, 1869).

ommended it may, like so many other primeval social facts of the greatest importance, have subsequently, in the course of ages, ceased to exist. But the state of the case is in every respect the reverse of this. In the first place, the opinion in favour of the present system, which entirely subordinates the weaker sex to the stronger, rests upon theory only; for there never has been trial made of any other: so that experience, in the sense in which it is vulgarly opposed to theory, cannot be pretended to have pronounced any verdict. And in the second place, the adoption of this system of inequality never was the result of deliberation, or forethought, or any social ideas, or any notion whatever of what conduced to the benefit of humanity or the good order of society. It arose simply from the fact that from the very earliest twilight of human society, every woman (owing to the value attached to her by men, combined with her inferiority in muscular strength) was found in a state of bondage to some man. Laws and systems of polity always begin by recognising the relations they find already existing between individuals. They convert what was a mere physical fact into a legal right, give it the sanction of society, and principally aim at the substitution of public and organized means of asserting and protecting these rights, instead of the irregular and lawless conflict of physical strength. Those who had already been compelled to obedience became in this manner legally bound to it. . . . But this dependence, as it exists at present, is not an original institution, taking a fresh start from considerations of justice and social expediency—it is the primitive state of slavery lasting on, through successive mitigations and modifications occasioned by the same causes which have softened the general manners, and brought all human relations more under the control of justice and the influence of humanity. It has not lost the taint of its brutal origin. No presumption in its favour, therefore, can be drawn from the fact of its existence. . . . The inequality of rights between men and women has no other source than the law of the strongest.

· · ·

But, it will be said, the rule of men over women differs from all these others in not being a rule of force: it is accepted voluntarily; women make no complaint, and are consenting parties to it. In the first place, a great number of women do not accept it. Ever since there have been women able to make their sentiments known by their writings (the only mode of publicity which society permits to them), an increasing number of them have recorded protests against their present social condition. . . .

All causes, social and natural, combine to make it unlikely that women should be collectively rebellious to the power of men. They are so far in a position different from all other subject classes, that their masters require something more from them than actual service. Men do not want solely the obedience of women, they want their sentiments. All men, except the most brutish, desire to have, in the woman most nearly connected with them, not a forced slave but a willing one, not a slave merely, but a favourite. They have therefore put everything in practice to enslave their minds. The masters of all other slaves rely, for maintaining obedience, on fear; either fear of themselves, or religious fears. The masters of women wanted more than simple obedience, and they turned the whole force of education to effect their purpose. All women are brought up from the very earliest years in the belief that their ideal of character is the very opposite to that of men; not self-will, and government by self-control, but submission, and yielding to the control of others. All the moralities tell them that it is the duty of women, and all the current sentimentalities that it is their nature, to live for others; to make complete abnegation of themselves, and to have no life but in their affections. And by their affections are meant the only ones they are allowed to have—those to the men with whom they are connected, or to the children who constitute an additional and indefeasible tie between them and a man. When we put together three things— first, the natural attraction between opposite sexes; secondly, the wife's entire dependence on the husband, every privilege or pleasure she has being either his gift, or depending entirely on his will; and lastly, that the principal object of human pursuit, consideration, and all objects of social ambition, can in general be sought or obtained by her only through him, it would be a miracle if the object of being attractive to men had not become the polar star of feminine education and formation of character. And, this great means of influence over the minds of women having been acquired, an instinct of selfishness made men avail themselves of it to the upmost as a means of holding women in subjection, by representing to them meekness, submissiveness, and resignation of all individual will into the hands of a man, as an essential part of sexual attractiveness. Can it be doubted that any of the other yokes which mankind have succeeded in breaking, would have subsisted till now if the same means had existed, and had been as sedulously used, to bow down their minds to it? . . .

Neither does it avail anything to say that the *nature* of the two sexes adapts them to their present functions and position, and renders these appropriate to them. Standing on the ground of common sense and the constitution of the human mind, I deny that any one knows, or can know, the nature of the two sexes, as long as they have only been seen in their present relation to one another. . . .

One thing we may be certain of—that what is contrary to women's nature to do, they never will be made to do by simply giving their nature free play. The anxiety of mankind to interfere in behalf of nature, for fear lest nature should not succeed in effecting its purpose, is an altogether unnecessary solicitude. . . .

CHAPTER 2

. . . Marriage being the destination appointed by society for women, the prospect they are brought up to, and the object which it is intended should be sought by all of them, except those who are too little attractive to be chosen by any man as his companion; one might have supposed that everything would have been done to make this condition as eligible to them as possible, that they might have no cause to regret being denied the option of any other. Society, however, both in this, and, at first, in all other cases, has preferred to attain its object by foul rather than fair means: but this is the only case in which it has substantially persisted in them even to the present day. Originally women were taken by force, or regularly sold by their father to the husband. . . .

[Today] the wife is the actual bond-servant of her husband: no less so, as far as legal obligation goes, than slaves commonly so called. She vows a life-long obedience to him at the altar, and is held to it all through her life by law. Casuists may say that the obligation of obedience stops short of participation in crime, but it certainly extends to everything else. She can do no act whatever but by his permission, at least tacit. She can acquire no property but for him; the instant it becomes hers, even if by inheritance, it becomes *ipso facto* his. In this respect the wife's position under the common law of England is worse than that of slaves in the laws of many countries. . . . The two are called "one person in law," for the purpose of inferring that whatever is hers is his, but the parallel inference is never drawn that whatever is his is hers; the maxim is not applied against the man, except to make him responsible to third parties for her acts, as a master is for the acts of his slaves or of his cattle. I am far from pretending that wives are in general no better treated than slaves; but no slave is a slave to the same lengths, and in so full a sense of the word, as a wife is. Hardly any slave, except one immediately attached to the master's person, is a slave at all hours and all minutes; in general he has, like a soldier, his fixed task, and when it is done, or when he is off duty, he disposes, within certain limits, of his own time, and has a family life into which the master rarely intrudes. "Uncle Tom" under his first master had his own life in his "cabin," almost as much as any man whose work takes him away from home, is able to have in his own family. But it cannot be so with the wife. Above all, a female slave has (in Christian countries) an admitted right, and is considered under a moral obligation, to refuse to her master the last familiarity. Not so the wife: however brutal a tyrant she may unfortunately be chained to—though she may know that he hates her, though it may be his daily pleasure to torture her, and though she may feel it impossible not to loathe him—he can claim from her and enforce the lowest degradation of a human being, that of being made the instrument of an animal function contrary to her inclinations. While she is held in this worst description of slavery as to her own person, what is her position in regard to the children in whom she and her master have a joint interest? They are by law *his* children. He alone has any legal rights over them. Not one act can she do towards or in relation to them, except by delegation from him. Even after he is dead she is not their legal guardian, unless he by will has made her so. He could even send them away from her, and deprive her of the means of seeing or corresponding with them, until this power was in some degree restricted by Serjeant Talfourd's Act. This is her legal state. And from this state she has no means of withdrawing herself. If she leaves her husband, she can take nothing with her, neither her children nor anything which is rightfully her own. If he chooses, he can compel her to return, by law, or by physical force; or he may content himself with seizing for his own use anything which she may earn, or which may be given to her by her relations. . . .

When we consider how vast is the number of men, in any great country, who are little higher than brutes, and that this never prevents them from being able, through the law of marriage, to obtain a victim, the breadth and depth of human misery caused in this shape alone by the abuse of the institution swells to something appalling. . . . I grant that the wife, if she cannot effectually resist, can at least retaliate; she, too, can make the man's life extremely uncomfortable, and by that power is able to carry many points which she ought, and many which she ought not, to prevail in. But this instrument of self-protection—which may be called the power of the scold, or the shrewish sanction—has the fatal defect, that it avails most against the least tyrannical superiors, and in favour of the least deserving dependents. It is the weapon of irritable and self-willed women; of those who would make the worst use of power if they themselves had it, and who generally turn this power to a bad use. . . .

But how, it will be asked, can any society exist without government? In a family, as in a state, some one person must be the ultimate ruler. Who shall decide when married people differ in opinion? Both cannot have their way, yet a decision one way or the other must be come to.

It is not true that in all voluntary association between two people, one of them must be absolute master: still less that the law must determine which of them it shall be. . . .

It is quite true that things which have to be decided every day, and cannot adjust themselves gradually, or wait for a compromise, ought to depend on one will: one person must have their sole control. But it does not follow that this should always be the same person. The natural arrangement is a division of powers between the two; each being absolute in the executive branch of their own department, and any change of system and principle requiring the consent of both. . . .

The real practical decision of affairs, to whichever may be given the legal authority, will greatly depend, as it even now does, upon comparative qualifications. The mere fact that he is usually the eldest, will in most cases give the preponderance to the man; at least until they both attain a time of life at which the difference in their years is of no importance. There will naturally also be a more potential voice on the side, whichever it is, that brings the means of support. . . .

After what has been said respecting the obligation of obedience, it is almost superfluous to say anything concerning the more special point included in the general one—a woman's right to her own property; for I need not hope that this treatise can make any impression upon those who need anything to convince them that a woman's inheritance or gains ought to be as much her own after marriage as before. The rule is simple: whatever would be the husband's or wife's if they were not married, should be under their exclusive control during marriage. . . .

When the support of the family depends, not on property, but on earnings, the common arrangement, by which the man earns the income and the wife superintends the domestic expenditure, seems to me in general the most suitable division of labour between the two persons. If, in addition to the physical suffering of bearing children, and the whole responsibility of their care and education in early years, the wife undertakes the careful and economical application of the husband's earnings to the general comfort of the family; she takes not only her fair share, but usually the larger share, of the bodily and mental exertion required by their joint existence. If she undertakes any additional portion, it seldom relieves her from this, but only prevents her from performing it properly. The care which she is herself disabled from taking of the children and the household, nobody else takes; those of the children who do not die, grow up as they best can, and the management of the household is likely to be so bad, as even in point of economy to be a great drawback from the value of the wife's earnings. In an otherwise just state of things, it is not, therefore, I think, a desirable custom, that the wife should contribute by her labour to the income of the family. In an unjust state of things, her doing so may be useful to her, by making her of more value in the eyes of the man who is legally her master; but, on the other hand, it enables him still farther to abuse his power, by forcing her to work, and leaving the support of the family to her exertions, while he spends most of his time in drinking and idleness. The *power* of earning is essential to the dignity of a woman, if she has not independent property. But if marriage were an equal contract, not implying the obligation of obedience; if the connexion were no longer enforced to the oppression of those to whom it is purely a mischief, but a separation, on just terms (I do not now speak of a divorce), could be obtained by any woman who was morally entitled to it; and if she would then find all honourable employments as freely open to her as to men; it would not be necessary for her protection, that during marriage she should make this particular use of her faculties. Like a man when he chooses a profession, so, when a woman marries, it may in general be understood that she makes choice of the management of a household, and the bringing up of a family, as the first call upon her exertions, during as many years of her life as may be required for the purpose; and that she renounces, not all other objects and occupations, but all which are not consistent with the requirements of this. The actual exercise, in a habitual or systematic manner, of outdoor occupations, or such as cannot be carried on at home, would by this principle be practically interdicted to the greater number of married women. But the utmost latitude ought to exist for the adaptation of general rules to individual suitabilities; and there ought to be nothing to prevent faculties exceptionally adapted to any other pursuit, from obeying their vocation notwithstanding marriage: due provision being made for supplying otherwise any falling-short which might become inevitable, in her full performance of the ordinary functions of mistress of a family. These things, if once opinion were rightly directed on the subject, might with perfect safety be left to be regulated by opinion, without any interference of law.

CHAPTER 3

On the other point which is involved in the just equality of women, their admissibility to all the functions and occupations hitherto retained as the monopoly of the stronger sex, I should anticipate no difficulty in convincing any one who has gone with me on the subject of the equality of women in the family. I believe that their disabilities elsewhere are only clung to in order to maintain their subordination in domestic life. . . . It is not sufficient to maintain that women on the average are less gifted than men on the average, with certain of the higher mental faculties, or that a smaller number of women than of men are fit for occupations and functions of the highest intellectual character. It is necessary to maintain that no women at all are fit for them, and that the most eminent women are inferior in mental faculties to the most mediocre of the men on whom those functions at present devolve. . . . Is there so great a superfluity of men fit for high duties, that society can afford to reject the service of any competent person? Are we so certain of always finding a man made to our hands for any duty or function of social importance which falls vacant, that we lose nothing by putting a ban upon one-half of mankind, and refusing beforehand to make their faculties available, however distinguished they may be? And even if we could do without them, would it be consistent with justice to refuse to them their fair share of honour and distinction, or to deny to them the equal moral right of all human beings to choose their occupation (short of injury to others) according to their own preferences, at their own risk? Nor is the injustice confined to them: it is shared by those who are in a position to benefit by their services. . . .

But (it is said) there is anatomical evidence of the superior mental capacity of men compared with women: they have a larger brain. I reply, that in the first place the fact itself is doubtful. It is by no means established that the brain of a woman is smaller than that of a man. . . . Next, I must observe that the precise relation which exists between the brain and the intellectual powers is not yet well understood, but is a subject of great dispute. . . . It would not be surprising—it is indeed an hypothesis which accords well with the differences actually observed between the mental operations of the two sexes—if men on the average should have the advantage in the size of the brain, and women in activity of cerebral circulation. The results which conjecture, founded on analogy, would lead us to expect from this difference of organization, would correspond to some of those which we most commonly see. In the first place, the mental operations of men might be expected to be slower. They would neither be so prompt as women in thinking, nor so quick to feel. Large bodies take more time to get into full action. On the other hand, when once got thoroughly into play, men's brain would bear more work. It would be more persistent in the line first taken; it would have more difficulty in changing from one mode of action to another, but, in the one thing it was doing, it could go on longer without loss of power or sense of fatigue. And do we not find that the things in which men most excel women are those which require most plodding and long hammering at a single thought, while women do best what must be done rapidly? A woman's brain is sooner fatigued, sooner exhausted; but given the degree of exhaustion, we should expect to find that it would recover itself sooner. I repeat that this speculation is entirely hypothetical. . . .

Let us take, then, the only marked case which observation affords, of apparent inferiority of women to men, if we except the merely physical one of bodily strength. No production in philosophy, science, or art, entitled to the first rank, has been the work of a woman. Is there any mode of accounting for this, without supposing that women are naturally incapable of producing them?

In the first place, we may fairly question whether experience has afforded sufficient grounds for an induction. It is scarcely three generations since women, saving very rare exceptions, have begun to try their capacity in philosophy, science, or art. It is only in the present generation that their attempts have been at all numerous; and they are even now extremely few, everywhere but in England and France. It is a relevant question, whether a mind possessing the requisites of first-rate eminence in speculation or creative art could have been expected, on the mere calculation of chances, to turn up during that lapse of time, among the women whose tastes and personal position admitted of their devoting themselves to these pursuits.

. . .

CHAPTER 4

There remains a question, not of less importance than those already discussed, and which will be asked the most importunately by those opponents whose conviction is somewhat shaken on the main point. What good are we to expect from the changes proposed in our customs and institutions? Would mankind be at all better off if women were free? If not, why disturb their minds, and attempt to make a social revolution in the name of an abstract right?

. . .

To which let me first answer, [there is] the advantage of having the most universal and pervading of all human relations regulated by justice instead of injustice. The vast amount of this gain to human nature, it is hardly possible, by any explanation or illustration, to place in a stronger light than it is placed by the bare statement, to any one who attaches a moral meaning to words. All the selfish propensities, the self-worship, the unjust self-preference, which exist among mankind, have their source and root in, and derive their principal nourishment from, the present constitution of the relation between men and women. Think what it is to a boy, to grow up to manhood in the belief that without any merit or any exertion of his own, though he may be the most frivolous and empty or the most ignorant and stolid of mankind, by the mere fact of being born a male he is by right the superior of all and every one of an entire half of the human race. . . . What must be the effect on his character, of this lesson? And men of the cultivated classes are often not aware how deeply it sinks into the immense majority of male minds. For, among right-feeling and well-bred people, the inequality is kept as much as possible out of sight; above all, out of sight of the children. As much obedience is required from boys to their mother as to their father: they are not permitted to domineer over their sisters, nor are they accustomed to see these postponed to them, but the contrary; the compensations of the chivalrous feeling being made prominent, while the servitude which requires them is kept in the background. . . .

The second benefit to be expected from giving to women the free use of their faculties, by leaving them the free choice of their employments, and opening to them the same field of occupation and the same prizes and encouragements as to other human beings, would be that of doubling the mass of mental faculties available for the higher service of humanity. . . . This great accession to the intellectual power of the species, and to the amount of intellect available for the good management of its affairs, would be obtained, partly, through the better and more complete intellectual education of women. . . .

The opinion of women would then possess a more beneficial, rather than a greater, influence upon the general mass of human belief and sentiment. I say a more beneficial, rather than a greater influence; for the influence of women over the general tone of opinion has always, or at least from the earliest known period, been very considerable. . . .

. . . The wife's influence tends, as far as it goes, to prevent the husband from falling below the common standard of approbation of the country. It tends quite as strongly to hinder him from rising above it. The wife is the auxiliary of the common public opinion. A man who is married to a woman his inferior in intelligence, finds her a perpetual dead weight, or, worse than a dead weight, a drag, upon every aspiration of his to be better than public opinion requires him to be. It is hardly possible for one who is in these bonds, to attain exalted virtue.

. . .

Though it may stimulate the amatory propensities of men, it does not conduce to married happiness, to exaggerate by differences of education whatever may be the native differences of the sexes. If the married pair are well-bred and well-behaved people, they tolerate each other's tastes; but is mutual toleration what people look forward to, when they enter into marriage? . . .

What marriage may be in the case of two persons of cultivated faculties, identical in opinions and purposes, between whom there exists that best kind of equality, similarity of powers and capacities with reciprocal superiority in them—so that each can enjoy the luxury of looking up to the other, and can have alternately the pleasure of leading and of being led in the path of development—I will not attempt to describe.[1] To those who can conceive it, there is no need; to those who cannot, it would appear the dream of an enthusiast. But I maintain, with the profoundest conviction, that this, and this only, is the ideal of marriage; and that all opinions, customs, and institutions which favour any other notion of it, or turn the

---

[1][This is a veiled reference to Mill's long romance and short marriage to Harriet Taylor Mill. See Alice Rossi's biographical introduction, "Sentiment and Intellect," in John Stuart Mill and Harriet Taylor Mill, *Essays on Sex Equality,* Alice S. Rossi, ed. (Chicago: University of Chicago Press, 1970).—Ed.]

conceptions and aspirations connected with it into any other direction, by whatever pretences they may be coloured, are relics of primitive barbarism. The moral regeneration of mankind will only really commence, when the most fundamental of the social relations is placed under the rule of equal justice, and when human beings learn to cultivate their strongest sympathy with an equal in rights and in cultivation.

FRIEDRICH ENGELS

The Origin of the Family,
Private Property and the State

Friedrich Engels (1820–1895) was a founder of Marxism, probably best known as co-author of The Communist Manifesto. The Origin of the Family, Private Property and the State *exhibits a combination of historical, anthropological, political, and philosophical approaches. Engels disagrees sharply with social contract theorists like Locke, finding most social institutions to be the result of oppressive economic domination, not of free and rational agreement.*

Monogamous marriage, for example, Engels analyzes as an institution that oppresses women as a class for the economic gains of men. The rise of private property led to the desire to pass accumulated wealth on to rightful heirs. Identifying heirs requires the faithfulness of the wife, but not of the husband. So the earlier, relatively equal arrangements of "group marriage" and "pairing marriage" gave way, he says, to the double standard of monogamy for women and continued promiscuity for men. Thus, monogamy naturally led to prostitution, which according to Engels demoralizes men even more than it does the women who are forced to become prostitutes. Hence the dual oppression of women—as prostitutes and as wives bound into unequal marriages arranged by parents for financial reasons—is essentially linked to the private ownership of capital.

For women to be liberated, Engels reasons, it will be necessary to end this private ownership. But Engels does not call for the end of the nuclear family. Quite the reverse: he hopes to free love from such monetary motives in order to make "true" monogamy possible for men as well as for women.

Further Reading

KATHLEEN GOUGH, "An Anthropologist Looks at Engels," in *Woman in a Man-Made World,* Nona Glazer-Malbin and Helen Youngelson Waehrer, eds. (Chicago: Rand McNally, 1972), pp. 107–18.

ALISON JAGGAR, "Political Philosophies of Women's Liberation," in *Feminism and Philosophy*, M. Braggin, F. Elliston, and J. English, eds. (Totowa, N.J.: Littlefield, Adams, 1977).

ELI ZARETSKY, "Capitalism, the Family and Personal Life," *Socialist Revolution*, 3 (1973), no. 1–2, pp. 69–126; no. 3, pp. 19–70.

. . . [Monogamy] was not in any way the fruit of individual sex-love, with which it had nothing whatever to do; marriages remained as before marriages of convenience. It was the first form of the family to be based, not on natural, but on economic conditions—on the victory of private property over primitive, natural communal property. The Greeks themselves put the matter quite frankly: the sole exclusive aims of monogamous marriage were to make the man supreme in the family, and to propagate, as the future heirs to his wealth, children indisputably his own. Otherwise, marriage was a burden, a duty which had to be performed, whether one liked it or not, to gods, state, and one's ancestors. In Athens the law exacted from the man not only marriage but also the performance of a minimum of so-called conjugal duties.

Thus when monogamous marriage first makes its appearance in history, it is not as the reconciliation of man and woman, still less as the highest form of such a reconciliation. Quite the contrary. Monogamous marriage comes on the scene as the subjugation of the one sex by the other; it announces a struggle between the sexes unknown throughout the whole previous prehistoric period. In an old unpublished manuscript, written by Marx and myself in 1846, I find the words: "The first division of labor is that between man and woman for the propagation of children." And today I can add: The first class opposition that appears in history coincides with the development of the antagonism between man and woman in monogamous marriage, and the first class oppression coincides with that of the female sex by the male. Monogamous marriage was a great historical step forward; nevertheless, together with slavery and private wealth, it opens the period that has lasted until today in which every step forward is also relatively a step backward, in which prosperity and development for some is won through the misery and frustration of others. It is the cellular form of civilized society, in which the nature of the oppositions and contradictions fully active in that society can be already studied.

From *The Origin of the Family, Private Property and the State*, translated by Alec West (New York: International Publishers Co., 1942), pp. 128–29; 134–39. Reprinted by permission of International Publishers Co.

. . .

Nowadays there are two ways of concluding a bourgeois marriage. In Catholic countries the parents, as before, procure a suitable wife for their young bourgeois son, and the consequence is, of course, the fullest development of the contradiction inherent in monogamy: the husband abandons himself to hetaerism and the wife to adultery. Probably the only reason why the Catholic Church abolished divorce was because it had convinced itself that there is no more a cure for adultery than there is for death. In Protestant countries, on the other hand, the rule is that the son of a bourgeois family is allowed to choose a wife from his own class with more or less freedom; hence there may be a certain element of love in the marriage, as, indeed, in accordance with Protestant hypocrisy, is always assumed, for decency's sake. Here the husband's hetaerism is a more sleepy kind of business, and adultery by the wife is less the rule. But since, in every kind of marriage, people remain what they were before, and since the bourgeois of Protestant countries are mostly philistines, all that this Protestant monogamy achieves, taking the average of the best cases, is a conjugal partnership of leaden boredom, known as "domestic bliss." . . .

In both cases, however, the marriage is conditioned by the class position of the parties and is to that extent always a marriage of convenience. In both cases this marriage of convenience turns often enough into crassest prostitution—sometimes of both partners, but far more commonly of the woman, who only differs from the ordinary courtesan in that she does not let out her body on piece-work as a wage-worker, but sells it once and for all into slavery. . . .

Our jurists, of course, find that progress in legislation is leaving women with no further ground of complaint. Modern civilized systems of law increasingly acknowledge, first, that for a marriage to be legal, it must be a contract freely entered into by both partners, and, secondly, that also in the married state both partners must stand on a common footing of equal rights and duties. If both these demands are consistently carried out, say the jurists, women have all they can ask.

This typically legalist method of argument is exactly the same as that which the radical republican bourgeois uses to put the proletarian in his place. The labor contract is to be freely entered into by both partners. But it is considered to have been freely entered into as soon as the law makes both parties equal on *paper*. The power conferred on the one party by the difference of class position, the pressure thereby brought to bear on the other party—the real economic position of both—that is not the law's business. . . .

As regards the legal equality of husband and wife in marriage, the position is no better. The legal inequality of the two partners, bequeathed to us from earlier social conditions, is not the cause but the effect of the economic oppression of the woman. In the old communistic household, which comprised many couples and their children, the task entrusted to the women of managing the household was as much a public and socially necessary industry as the procuring of food by the men. With the patriarchal family, and still more with the single monogamous family, a change came. Household management lost its public character. It no longer concerned society. It became a *private service;* the wife became the head servant, excluded from all participation in social production. Not until the coming of modern large-scale industry was the road to social production opened to her again—and then only to the proletarian wife. But it was opened in such a manner that, if she carries out her duties in the private service of her family, she remains excluded from public production and unable to earn; and if she wants to take part in public production and earn independently, she cannot carry out family duties. And the wife's position in the factory is the position of women in all branches of business, right up to medicine and the law. The modern individual family is founded on the open or concealed domestic slavery of the wife, and modern society is a mass composed of these individual families as its molecules.

In the great majority of cases today, at least in the possessing classes, the husband is obliged to earn a living and support his family, and that in itself gives him a position of supremacy, without any need for special legal titles and privileges. Within the family he is the bourgeois and the wife represents the proletariat. In the industrial world, the specific character of the economic oppression burdening the proletariat is visible in all its sharpness only when all special legal privileges of the capitalist class have been abolished and complete legal equality of both classes established. The democratic republic does not do away with the opposition of the two classes; on the contrary, it provides the clear field on which the fight can be fought out. And in the same way, the peculiar character of the supremacy of the husband over the wife in the modern family, the necessity of creating real social equality between them, and the way to do it, will only be seen in the clear light of day when both possess legally complete equality of rights. Then it will be plain that the first condition for the liberation of the wife is to bring the whole female sex back into public industry, and that this in turn demands the abolition of the monogamous family as the economic unit of society.

We thus have three principal forms of marriage which correspond broadly to the three principal stages of human development. For the period of savagery, group marriage; for barbarism, pairing marriage; for civilization, monogamy, supplemented by adultery and prostitution. Between pairing marriage and monogamy intervenes a period in the upper stage of barbarism when men have female slaves at their command and polygamy is practiced.

As our whole presentation has shown, the progress which manifests itself in these successive forms is connected with the peculiarity that women, but not men, are increasingly deprived of the sexual freedom of group marriage. In fact, for men group marriage actually still exists even to this day. What for the woman is a crime, entailing grave legal and social consequences, is considered honorable in a man or, at the worse, a slight moral blemish which he cheerfully bears. But the more the hetaerism of the past is changed in our time by capitalist commodity production and brought into conformity with it, the more, that is to say, it is transformed into undisguised prostitution, the more demoralizing are its effects. And it demoralizes men far more than women. Among women, prostitution degrades only the unfortunate ones who become its victims, and even these by no means to the extent commonly believed. But it degrades the character of the whole male world. A long engagement, particularly, is in nine cases out of ten a regular preparatory school for conjugal infidelity.

We are now approaching a social revolution in which the economic foundations of monogamy as they have existed hitherto will disappear just as surely as those of its complement—prostitution. Monogamy arose from the concentration of considerable wealth in the hands of a single individual —a man—and from the need to bequeath this wealth to the children of that man and of no other. For this purpose, the monogamy of the woman was required, not that of the man, so this monogamy of the woman did not in any way interfere with open or concealed polygamy on the part of the man. But by transforming by far the greater portion, at any rate, of permanent, heritable wealth—the means of production—into social property, the coming social revolution will reduce to a minimum all this anxiety about bequeathing and inheriting. Having arisen from economic causes, will monogamy then disappear when these causes disappear?

One might answer, not without reason: far from disappearing, it will, on the contrary, be realized completely. For with the transformation of the means of production into social property there will disappear also wage-labor, the proletariat, and therefore the necessity for a certain—statistically calculable—number of women to surrender themselves for money. Prostitution disappears; monogamy, instead of collapsing, at last becomes a reality—also for men.

SIMONE DE BEAUVOIR

The Second Sex

The idea discussed by Hegel, that every self needs to set up an opposite, an "other," to define itself against, finds a central place in existentialist views such as that of Simone de Beauvoir. Many societies have recognized groupings of characteristics like yin *and* yang, *such as sky, light, reason, male, dry, good versus earth, dark, irrational, female, moist, evil. When men define themselves by projecting these undesirable characteristics onto women, who are cast in the role of "other," women's sense of self suffers.*

A similar analysis is found in Freudian psychology, according to which the little boy is forced to develop a sense of self and independence because he must define himself as different from his mother. The little girl, who does not have this task but sees herself as similar to her mother, does not develop as strong a sense of self. Later she, too, sees boys as standard and normal, and herself as "other," a defective boy at best.

Appearing in 1949, The Second Sex *fell between two major waves of feminism. Today it seems a surprising combination of modern insight into the deep-seated causes of women's lower status, and older armchair anthropology which fails to challenge fundamental masculine values or call for political action.*

Further Reading

G. W. F. HEGEL, *The Phenomenology of Mind,* trans. J. B. Baillie (New York: Macmillan, 1910), pp. 175–88, 440–58.

CAROLINE WHITBECK, "Theories of Sex Difference," *The Philosophical Forum,* 5 (1973–74), 54–80; reprinted in *Women and Philosophy,* Carol C. Gould and Mary W. Wartofsky, eds. (New York: G. P. Putnam's Sons, 1976).

JULIET MITCHELL, *Psychoanalysis and Feminism* (New York: Pantheon Books, 1974).

... What is a woman?

To state the question is, to me, to suggest, at once, a preliminary answer. The fact that I ask it is in itself significant. A man would never get the notion of writing a book on the peculiar situation of the human male.[1] But if I wish to define myself, I must first of all say: "I am a woman"; on this truth must be based all further discussion. A man never begins by presenting himself as an individual of a certain sex; it goes without saying that he is a man. The terms *masculine* and *feminine* are used symmetrically only as a matter of form, as on legal papers. In actuality the relation of the two sexes is not quite like that of two electrical poles, for man represents both the positive and the neutral, as is indicated by the common use of *man* to designate human beings in general; whereas woman represents only the negative, defined by limiting criteria, without reciprocity. In the midst of an abstract discussion it is vexing to hear a man say: "You think thus and so because you are a woman"; but I know that my only defense is to reply: "I think thus and so because it is true," thereby removing my subjective self from the argument. It would be out of the question to reply: "And you think the contrary because you are a man," for it is understood that the fact of being a man is no peculiarity. A man is in the right in being a man; it is the woman who is in the wrong. It amounts to this: just as for the ancients there was an absolute vertical with reference to which the oblique was defined, so there is an absolute human type, the masculine. Woman has ovaries, a uterus; these peculiarities imprison her in her subjectivity, circumscribe her within the limits of her own nature. It is often said that she thinks with her glands. Man superbly ignores the fact that his anatomy also includes glands, such as the testicles, and that they secrete hormones. He thinks of his body as a direct and normal connection with the world, which he believes he apprehends objectively, whereas he regards the body of woman as a hindrance, a prison, weighed down by everything peculiar to it. "The female is a female by virtue of a certain *lack* of qualities," said Aristotle; "we should regard the female nature as afflicted with a natural defectiveness." And St. Thomas for his part pronounced woman to be an "imperfect man," an "incidental" being. This is symbolized in Genesis where Eve is depicted as made from what Bossuet called "a supernumerary bone" of Adam.

Thus humanity is male and man defines woman not in herself but as relative to him; she is not regarded as an autonomous being. Michelet

From *The Second Sex*, by Simone de Beauvoir, translated by H. M. Parshley. Copyright 1952 by Alfred A. Knopf, Inc. Reprinted by permission of Alfred A. Knopf, Inc.

[1]The Kinsey Report [Alfred C. Kinsey and others: *Sexual Behavior in the Human Male* (W. B. Saunders Co., 1948)] is no exception, for it is limited to describing the sexual characteristics of American men, which is quite a different matter.

writes: "Woman, the relative being. . . ." And Benda is most positive in his *Rapport d'Uriel:* "The body of man makes sense in itself quite apart from that of woman, whereas the latter seems wanting in significance by itself. . . . Man can think of himself without woman. She cannot think of herself without man." And she is simply what man decrees; thus she is called "the sex," by which is meant that she appears essentially to the male as a sexual being. For him she is sex—absolute sex, no less. She is defined and differentiated with reference to man and not he with reference to her; she is the incidental, the inessential as opposed to the essential. He is the Subject, he is the Absolute—she is the Other.[2]

The category of the *Other* is as primordial as consciousness itself. In the most primitive societies, in the most ancient mythologies, one finds the expression of a duality—that of the Self and the Other. This duality was not originally attached to the division of the sexes; it was not dependent upon any empirical facts. It is revealed in such works as that of Granet on Chinese thought and those of Dumézil on the East Indies and Rome. The feminine element was at first no more involved in such pairs as Varuna-Mitra, Uranus-Zeus, Sun-Moon, and Day-Night than it was in the contrasts between Good and Evil, lucky and unlucky auspices, right and left, God and Lucifer. Otherness is a fundamental category of human thought.

Thus it is that no group ever sets itself up as the One without at once setting up the Other over against itself. If three travelers chance to occupy the same compartments, that is enough to make vaguely hostile "others" out of all the rest of the passengers on the train. In small-town eyes all persons not belonging to the village are "strangers" and suspect; to the native of a country all who inhabit other countries are "foreigners"; Jews are "different" for the anti-Semite, Negroes are "inferior" for American racists, aborigines are "natives" for colonists, proletarians are the "lower class" for the privileged.

Lévi-Strauss, at the end of a profound work on the various forms of primitive societies, reaches the following conclusion: "Passage from the

[2]E. Lévinas expresses this idea most explicitly in his essay, *Temps et L'Autre.* "Is there no case in which otherness, alterity [altérité] unquestionably marks the nature of a being, as its essence, an instance of otherness not consisting purely and simply in the opposition of two species of the same genus? I think that the feminine represents the contrary in its absolute sense, this contrariness being in no wise affected by any relation between it and its correlative and thus remaining absolutely other. Sex is not a certain specific difference . . . no more is the sexual difference a mere contradiction. . . . Nor does this difference lie in the duality of two complementary terms, for two complementary terms imply a pre-existing whole. . . . Otherness reaches its full flowering in the feminine, a term of the same rank as consciousness but of opposite meaning."

I suppose that Lévinas does not forget that woman, too, is aware of her own consciousness, or ego. But it is striking that he deliberately takes a man's point of view, disregarding the reciprocity of subject and object. When he writes that woman is mystery, he implies that she is mystery for man. Thus his description, which is intended to be objective, is in fact an assertion of masculine privilege.

state of Nature to the state of Culture is marked by man's ability to view biological relations as a series of contrasts; duality, alternation, opposition, and symmetry, whether under definite or vague forms, constitute not so much phenomena to be explained as fundamental and immediately given data of social reality."[3] These phenomena would be incomprehensible if in fact human society were simply a *Mitsein* or fellowship based on solidarity and friendliness. Things become clear, on the contrary, if, following Hegel, we find in consciousness itself a fundamental hostility toward every other consciousness; the subject can be posed only in being opposed—he sets himself up as the essential, as opposed to the other, the inessential, the object.

But the other consciousness, the other ego, sets up a reciprocal claim. The native traveling abroad is shocked to find himself in turn regarded as a "stranger" by the natives of neighboring countries. As a matter of fact, wars, festivals, trading, treaties, and contests among tribes, nations, and classes tend to deprive the concept *Other* of its absolute sense and to make manifest its relativity; willy-nilly, individuals and groups are forced to realize the reciprocity of their relations. How is it, then, that this reciprocity has not been recognized between the sexes, that one of the contrasting terms is set up as the sole essential, denying any relativity in regard to its correlative and defining the latter as pure otherness? Why is it that women do not dispute male sovereignty? No subject will readily volunteer to become the object, the inessential; it is not the Other who, in defining himself as the Other, establishes the One. The Other is posed as such by the One in defining himself as the One. But if the Other is not to regain the status of being the One, he must be submissive enough to accept this alien point of view. Whence comes this submission in the case of woman?

There are, to be sure, other cases in which a certain category has been able to dominate another completely for a time. Very often this privilege depends upon inequality of numbers—the majority imposes its rule upon the minority or persecutes it. But women are not a minority, like the American Negroes or the Jews; there are as many women as men on earth. Again, the two groups concerned have often been originally independent; they may have been formerly unaware of each other's existence, or perhaps they recognized each other's autonomy. But a historical event has resulted in the subjugation of the weaker by the stronger. The scattering of the Jews, the introduction of slavery into America, the conquests of imperialism are examples in point. In these cases the oppressed retained at least the memory of former days; they possessed in common a past, a tradition, sometimes a religion or a culture.

[3]See C. Lévi-Strauss: *Les Structures élementaires de la parenté.* My thanks are due to C. Lévi-Strauss for his kindness in furnishing me with the proofs of his work.

The parallel drawn by Bebel between women and the proletariat is valid in that neither ever formed a minority or a separate collective unit of mankind. And instead of a single historical event it is in both cases a historical development that explains their status as a class and accounts for the membership of *particular individuals* in that class. But proletarians have not always existed, whereas there have always been women. They are women in virtue of their anatomy and physiology. Throughout history they have always been subordinated to men,[4] and hence their dependency is not the result of a historical event or a social change—it was not something that *occurred*. The reason why otherness in this case seems to be an absolute is in part that it lacks the contingent or incidental nature of historical facts. A condition brought about at a certain time can be abolished at some other time, as the Negroes of Haiti and others have proved; but it might seem that a natural condition is beyond the possibility of change. In truth, however, the nature of things is no more immutably given, once for all, than is historical reality. If woman seems to be the inessential which never becomes the essential, it is because she herself fails to bring about this change. Proletarians say "We"; Negroes also. Regarding themselves as subjects, they transform the bourgeois, the whites, into "others." But women do not say "We," except at some congress of feminists or similar formal demonstration; men say "women," and women use the same word in referring to themselves. They do not authentically assume a subjective attitude. The proletarians have accomplished the revolution in Russia, the Negroes in Haiti, the Indo-Chinese are battling for it in Indo-China; but the women's effort has never been anything more than a symbolic agitation. They have gained only what men have been willing to grant; they have taken nothing, they have only received.

The reason for this is that women lack concrete means for organizing themselves into a unit which can stand face to face with the correlative unit. They have no past, no history, no religion of their own; and they have no such solidarity of work and interest as that of the proletariat. They are not even promiscuously herded together in the way that creates community feeling among the American Negroes, the ghetto Jews, the workers of Saint-Denis, or the factory hands of Renault. They live dispersed among the males, attached through residence, housework, economic condition, and social standing to certain men—fathers or husbands—more firmly than they are to other women. If they belong to the bourgeoisie, they feel solidarity with men of that class, not with proletarian women; if they are white, their allegiance is to white men, not to Negro women. The proletariat can propose to massacre the ruling class, and a sufficiently fanatical Jew or Negro might dream of getting sole possession of the atomic bomb and

---

[4]With rare exceptions, perhaps, like certain matriarchal rulers, queens, and the like—*Tr.*

making humanity wholly Jewish or black; but woman cannot even dream of exterminating the males. The bond that unites her to her oppressors is not comparable to any other. The division of the sexes is a biological fact, not an event in human history. Male and female stand opposed within a primordial *Mitsein,* and woman has not broken it. The couple is a fundamental unity with its two halves riveted together, and the cleavage of society along the line of sex is impossible. Here is to be found the basic trait of woman: she is the Other in a totality of which the two components are necessary to one another.

II

Contemporary Arguments

BERNARD WILLIAMS
The Idea of Equality

Bernard Williams distinguishes three different interpretations of the ideal of equality. First, calling people "equal" might merely remind us of our common humanity. This is not as empty as the statement that all humans are human, because it reminds us that women as well as men, blacks as well as whites, have interests and affections, value self-respect, and feel pain. Typically, a reminder of common humanity may help rectify unequal treatment due to the use of irrelevant characteristics; we can put ourselves in the other's shoes and see that the characteristic is irrelevant.

A second sort of equality is based on Kant's moral view that all those with a capacity for moral thought deserve to be accorded equal worth. All those with this capacity have the same rights and duties. Treating others as ends, never merely as means to our own ends, is called for by the respect for moral persons central to Kant's philosophy. This is stronger than the reminder of our common humanity.

The third and strongest ideal is that of equal opportunity. This does not require giving equal jobs to all, or even equal probabilities of attaining equal jobs. Rather, any two people born with equal native abilities and developing these with equal effort ought to have equal chances for the same attainment. Here it is important and difficult to distinguish the individual and his or her abilities at any stage from the circumstances that have influenced the development of those abilities.

Further Reading

GREGORY VLASTOS, "Human Worth, Merit and Equality," in *Moral Concepts*, Joel Feinberg, ed. (London: Oxford University Press, 1970), pp. 141–52.

J. R. LUCAS, "Against Equality," *Philosophy*, 40 (1965), 296–307; reprinted in *Justice and Equality*, Hugo Bedau, ed. (Englewood Cliffs, N.J.: Prentice-Hall, 1971), pp. 138–51.

HUGO BEDAU, "Egalitarianism and the Idea of Equality," in *Justice and Equality*, Hugo Bedau, ed. (Englewood Cliffs, N.J.: Prentice-Hall, 1971), pp. 168–80.

The idea of equality is used in political discussion both in statements of fact, or what purport to be statements of fact—that men *are* equal—and in statements of political principles or aims—that men *should be* equal, as at present they are not. The two can be, and often are, combined: the aim is then described as that of securing a state of affairs in which men are treated as the equal beings which they in fact already are, but are not already treated as being. In both these uses, the idea of equality notoriously encounters the same difficulty: that on one kind of interpretation the statements in which it figures are much too strong, and on another kind much too weak, and it is hard to find a satisfactory interpretation that lies between the two.[1]

To take first the supposed statement of fact: it has only too often been pointed out that to say that all men are equal in all those characteristics in respect of which it makes sense to say that men are equal or unequal, is a patent falsehood; and even if some more restricted selection is made of these characteristics, the statement does not look much better. Faced with this obvious objection, the defender of the claim that all men are equal is likely to offer a weaker interpretation. It is not, he may say, in their skill, intelligence, strength or virtue that men are equal, but merely in their being men: it is their common humanity that constitutes their equality. On this interpretation, we should not seek for some special characteristics in respect of which men are equal, but merely remind ourselves that they are all men. Now to this it might be objected that being men is not a respect in which men can strictly speaking be said to be *equal;* but, leaving that aside, there is the more immediate objection that if all that the statement does is to remind us that men are men, it does not do very much, and in particular does less than its proponents in political argument have wanted it to do. What looked like a paradox has turned into a platitude.

I shall suggest in a moment that even in this weak form the statement is not so vacuous as this objection makes it seem; but it must be admitted that when the statement of equality ceases to claim more than is warranted, it rather rapidly reaches the point where it claims less than is interesting. A similar discomfiture tends to overcome the practical maxim of equality. It cannot be the aim of this maxim that all men should be treated alike in all circumstances, or even that they should be treated alike as much as possible. Granted that, however, there is no obvious stopping point before the interpretation which makes the maxim claim only that men should be treated alike in similar circumstances; and since "circum-

From *Problems of the Self* by Bernard Williams, © 1973 Cambridge University Press. Reprinted by permission.

[1]For an illuminating discussion of this and related questions, see R. Wollheim and I. Berlin, "Equality," *Proceedings of the Aristotelian Society,* LVI (1955–6), p. 281 seq.

stances" here must clearly include reference to what a man is, as well as to his purely external situation, this comes very much to saying that for every difference in the way men are treated, some general reason or principle of differentiation must be given. This may well be an important principle; some indeed have seen in it, or in something very like it, an essential element of morality itself.[2] But it can hardly be enough to constitute the principle that was advanced in the name of *equality*. It would be in accordance with this principle, for example, to treat black men differently from others just because they were black, or poor men differently just because they were poor, and this cannot accord with anyone's idea of equality.

In what follows I shall try to advance a number of considerations that can help to save the political notion of equality from these extremes of absurdity and of triviality. These considerations are in fact often employed in political argument, but are usually bundled together into an unanalysed notion of equality in a manner confusing to the advocates, and encouraging to the enemies, of that ideal. These considerations will not enable us to define a distinct third interpretation of the statements which use the notion of equality; it is rather that they enable us, starting with the weak interpretations, to build up something that in practice can have something of the solidity aspired to by the strong interpretations. In this discussion, it will not be necessary all the time to treat separately the supposedly factual application of the notion of equality, and its application in the maxim of action. Though it is sometimes important to distinguish them, and there are clear grounds for doing so, similar considerations often apply to both. The two go significantly together: on the one hand, the point of the supposedly factual assertion is to back up social ideals and programmes of political action; on the other hand—a rather less obvious point, perhaps—those political proposals have their force because they are regarded not as gratuitously egalitarian, aiming at equal treatment for reasons, for instance, of simplicity or tidiness, but as affirming an equality which is believed in some sense already to exist, and to be obscured or neglected by actual social arrangements.

1. COMMON HUMANITY

The factual statement of men's equality was seen, when pressed, to retreat in the direction of merely asserting the equality of men as men; and this was thought to be trivial. It is certainly insufficient, but not, after all, trivial. That all men are human is, if a tautology, a useful one, serving as a reminder that those who belong anatomically to the species *homo sapiens,* and can speak a language, use tools, live in societies, can interbreed despite

[2]For instance, R. M. Hare: see his *Language of Morals* (Oxford: The Clarendon Press, 1952).

racial differences, etc., are also alike in certain other respects more likely to be forgotten. These respects are notably the capacity to feel pain, both from immediate physical causes and from various situations represented in perception and in thought; and the capacity to feel affection for others, and the consequences of this, connected with the frustration of this affection, loss of its objects, etc. The assertion that men are alike in the possession of these characteristics is, while indisputable and (it may be) even necessarily true, not trivial. For it is certain that there are political and social arrangements that systematically neglect these characteristics in the case of some groups of men, while being fully aware of them in the case of others; that is to say, they treat certain men as though they did not possess these characteristics, and neglect moral claims that arise from these characteristics and which would be admitted to arise from them.

Here it may be objected that the mere fact that ruling groups in certain societies treat other groups in this way does not mean that they neglect or overlook the characteristics in question. For, it may be suggested, they may well recognize the presence of these characteristics in the worse-treated group, but claim that in the case of that group, the characteristics do not give rise to any moral claim; the group being distinguished from other members of society in virtue of some further characteristic (for instance, by being black), this may be cited as the ground of treating them differently, whether they feel pain, affection, etc., or not.

This objection rests on the assumption, common to much moral philosophy that makes a sharp distinction between fact and value, that the question whether a certain consideration is *relevant* to a moral issue is an evaluative question: to state that a consideration is relevant or irrelevant to a certain moral question is, on this view, itself to commit oneself to a certain kind of moral principle or outlook. Thus, in the case under discussion, to say (as one would naturally say) that the fact that a man is black is, by itself, quite irrelevant to the issue of how he should be treated in respect of welfare, etc., would, on this view, be to commit oneself to a certain sort of moral principle. This view, taken generally, seems to me quite certainly false. The principle that men should be differentially treated in respect of welfare merely on grounds of their colour is not a special sort of moral principle, but (if anything) a purely arbitrary assertion of will, like that of some Caligulan ruler who decided to execute everyone whose name contained three "R"s.

This point is in fact conceded by those who practice such things as colour discrimination. Few can be found who will explain their practice merely by saying, "But they're black: and it is my moral principle to treat black men differently from others." If any reasons are given at all, they will be reasons that seek to correlate the fact of blackness with certain other considerations which are at least candidates for relevance to the question of how a man should be treated: such as insensitivity, brute stupidity, ineducable irresponsibility, etc. Now these reasons are very often rationalizations, and the correlations claimed are either not really believed, or quite irrationally believed, by those who claim them. But this is a different point; the argument concerns what counts as a moral reason, and the rationalizer broadly agrees with others about what counts as such—the trouble with him is that his reasons are dictated by his policies, and not conversely. The Nazis' "anthropologists" who tried to construct theories of Aryanism were paying, in very poor coin, the homage of irrationality to reason.

The question of relevance in moral reasons will arise again, in a different connexion, in this paper. For the moment its importance is that it gives a force to saying that those who neglect the moral claims of certain men that arise from their human capacity to feel pain, etc., are *overlooking* or *disregarding* those capacities; and are not just operating with a special moral principle, conceding the capacities to these men, but denying the moral claim. Very often, indeed, they have just persuaded themselves that the men in question have those capacities in a lesser degree. Here it is certainly to the point to assert the apparent platitude that these men are also human.

I have discussed this point in connexion with very obvious human characteristics of feeling pain and desiring affection. There are, however, other and less easily definable characteristics universal to humanity, which may all the more be neglected in political and social arrangements. For instance, there seems to be a characteristic which might be called "a desire for self-respect"; this phrase is perhaps not too happy, in suggesting a particular culturally-limited, bourgeois value, but I mean by it a certain human desire to be identified with what one is doing, to be able to realize purposes of one's own, and not to be the instrument of another's will unless one has willingly accepted such a role. This is a very inadequate and in some ways rather empty specification of a human desire; to a better specification, both philosophical reflection and the evidences of psychology and anthropology would be relevant. Such investigations enable us to understand more deeply, in respect of the desire I have gestured towards and of similar characteristics, what it is to be human; and of what it is to be human, the apparently trivial statement of men's equality as men can serve as a reminder.

2. MORAL CAPACITIES

So far we have considered respects in which men can be counted as all alike, which respects are, in a sense, negative: they concern the capacity to suffer, and certain needs that men have, and these involve men in moral relations as the recipients of certain kinds of treatment. It has certainly been a part, however, of the thought of those who asserted that men were equal, that there were more positive respects in which men were alike: that they were equal in certain things that they could do or achieve, as well as in things that they needed and could suffer. In respect of a whole range of abilities, from weight lifting to the calculus, the assertion is, as was noted at the beginning, not plausible, and has not often been supposed to be. It has been held, however, that there are certain other abilities, both less open to empirical test and more essential in moral connexions, for which it is true that men are equal. These are certain sorts of moral ability or capacity, the capacity for virtue or achievement of the highest kind of moral worth.

The difficulty with this notion is that of identifying any purely moral capacities. Some human capacities are more relevant to the achievement of a virtuous life than others: intelligence, a capacity for sympathetic understanding, and a measure of resoluteness would generally be agreed to be so. But these capacities can all be displayed in non-moral connexions as well, and in such connexions would naturally be thought to differ from man to man like other natural capacities. That this is the fact of the matter has been accepted by many thinkers, notably, for instance, by Aristotle. But against this acceptance, there is a powerful strain of thought that centres on a feeling of ultimate and outrageous absurdity in the idea that the achievement of the highest kind of moral worth should depend on natural capacities, unequally and fortuitously distributed as they are; and this feeling is backed up by the observation that these natural capacities are not themselves the bearers of the moral worth, since those that have them are as gifted for vice as for virtue.

This strain of thought has found many types of religious expression; but in philosophy it is to be found in its purest form in Kant. Kant's view not only carries to the limit the notion that moral worth cannot depend on contingencies, but also emphasizes, in its picture of the Kingdom of Ends, the idea of *respect* which is owed to each man as a rational moral agent— and, since men are equally such agents, is owed equally to all, unlike admiration and similar attitudes, which are commanded unequally by men in proportion to their unequal possession of different kinds of natural excellence. These ideas are intimately connected in Kant, and it is not possible to understand his moral theory unless as much weight is given to what he says about the Kingdom of Ends as is always given to what he says about duty.

. . . It seems empty to say that all men are equal as moral agents, when the question, for instance, of men's responsibility for their actions is one to which empirical considerations are clearly relevant, and one which moreover receives answers in terms of different degrees of responsibility and different degrees of rational control over action. To hold a man responsible for his actions is presumably the central case of treating him as a moral agent, and if men are not treated as equally responsible, there is not much left to their equality as moral agents.

If, without its transcendental basis, there is not much left to men's equality as moral agents, is there anything left to the notion of the *respect* owed to all men? This notion of "respect" is both complex and unclear, and I think it needs, and would repay, a good deal of investigation. Some content can, however, be attached to it; even if it is some way away from the ideas of moral agency. There certainly is a distinction, for instance, between regarding a man's life, actions or character from an aesthetic or technical point of view, and regarding them from a point of view which is concerned primarily with what it is *for him* to live that life and do those actions in that character. Thus from the technological point of view, a man who has spent his life in trying to make a certain machine which could not possibly work is merely a failed inventor, and in compiling a catalogue of those whose efforts have contributed to the sum of technical achievement, one must "write him off": the fact that he devoted himself to this useless task with constant effort and so on, is merely irrelevant. But from a human point of view, it is clearly not irrelevant: we are concerned with him, not merely as "a failed inventor," but as a man who wanted to be a successful inventor. Again, in professional relations and the world of work, a man operates, and his activities come up for criticism, under a variety of professional or technical titles, such as "miner" or "agricultural labourer" or "junior executive." The technical or professional attitude is that which regards the man solely under that title, the human approach that which regards him as *a man who has* that title (among others), willingly, unwillingly, through lack of alternatives, with pride, etc.

That men should be regarded from the human point of view, and not merely under these sorts of titles, is part of the content that might be attached to Kant's celebrated injunction "treat each man as an end in himself, and never as a means only." But I do not think that this is all that should be seen in this injunction, or all that is concerned in the notion of "respect." What is involved in the examples just given could be explained by saying that each man is owed an effort at identification: that he should not be regarded as the surface to which a certain label can be applied, but one should try to see the world (including the label) from his point of view. This injunction will be based on, though not of course fully explained by, the notion that men are conscious beings who necessarily have intentions and purposes and see what they are doing in a certain light. But there seem to be further injunctions connected with the Kantian maxim, and with the notion of "respect," that go beyond these considerations. There are forms of exploiting men or degrading them which would be thought to be excluded by these notions, but which cannot be excluded merely by considering how the exploited or degraded men see the situation. For it is precisely a mark of extreme exploitation or degradation that those who suffer it do *not* see themselves differently from the way they are seen by the exploiters; either they do not see themselves as anything at all, or they acquiesce passively in the role for which they have been cast. Here we evidently need something more than the precept that one should respect and try to understand another man's consciousness of his own activities; it is also that one may not suppress or destroy that consciousness.

...

3. EQUALITY IN UNEQUAL CIRCUMSTANCES

The notion of equality is invoked not only in connexions where men· are claimed in some sense all to be equal, but in connexions where they are agreed to be unequal, and the question arises of the distribution of, or access to, certain goods to which their inequalities are relevant. It may be objected that the notion of equality is in fact misapplied in these connexions, and that the appropriate ideas are those of fairness or justice, in the sense of what Aristotle called "distributive justice," where (as Aristotle argued) there is no question of regarding or treating everyone as equal, but solely a question of distributing certain goods in proportion to men's recognized inequalities.

I think it is reasonable to say against this objection that there is some foothold for the notion of equality even in these cases. It is useful here to make a rough distinction between two different types of inequality, inequality of *need* and inequality of *merit*, with a corresponding distinction between goods—on the one hand, goods demanded by the need, and on the other, goods that can be earned by the merit. In the case of needs, such as the need for medical treatment in case of illness, it can be presumed for practical purposes that the persons who have the need actually desire the goods in question, and so the question can indeed be regarded as one of distribution in a simple sense, the satisfaction of an existing desire. In the case of merit, such as for instance the possession of abilities to profit from a university education, there is not the same presumption that everyone who has the merit has the desire for the goods in question, though it may, of course, be the case. Moreover, the good of a university education may be legitimately, even if hopelessly, desired by those who do not possess the merit; while medical treatment or unemployment benefits are either not desired, or not legitimately desired, by those who are not ill or unemployed, that is do not have the appropriate need. Hence the distribution of goods in accordance with merit has a competitive aspect lacking in the case of distribution according to need. For these reasons, it is appropriate to speak, in the case of merit, not only of the distribution of the good, but of the distribution of the opportunity of achieving the good. But this, unlike the good itself, can be said to be distributed equally to everybody, and so one does encounter a notion of *general* equality, much vaunted in our society today, the notion of equality of opportunity.

Before considering this notion further, it is worth noticing certain resemblances and differences between the cases of need and of merit. In both cases, we encounter the matter (mentioned before in this paper) of the relevance of reasons. Leaving aside preventive medicine, the proper ground of distribution of medical care is ill health: this is a necessary truth. Now in very many societies, while ill health may work as a necessary condition of receiving treatment, it does not work as a sufficient condition, since such treatment costs money, and not all who are ill have the money; hence the possession of sufficient money becomes in fact an additional necessary condition of actually receiving treatment. Yet more extravagantly, money may work as a sufficient condition by itself, without any medical need, in which case the reasons that actually operate for the receipt of this good are just totally irrelevant to its nature; however, since only a few hypochondriacs desire treatment when they do not need it, this is, in this case, a marginal phenomenon.

When we have the situation in which, for instance, wealth is a further necessary condition of the receipt of medical treatment, we can once more apply the notions of equality and inequality: not now in connexion with the inequality between the well and the ill, but in connexion with the inequality between the rich ill and the poor ill, since we have straightforwardly the situation of those whose needs are the same not receiving the same treatment, though the needs are the ground of the treatment. This is an irrational state of affairs.

It may be objected that I have neglected an important distinction here. For, it may be said, I have treated the ill health and the possession of money as though they were regarded on the same level, as "reasons for receiving medical treatment," and this is a muddle. The ill health is, at most, a ground of the *right* to receive medical treatment; whereas the money is, in certain circumstances, the causally necessary condition of securing the right, which is a different thing. There is something in the distinction that this objection suggests: there is a distinction between a man's rights, the reasons why he should be treated in a certain way, and his power to secure those rights, the reasons why he can in fact get what he deserves. But this objection does not make it inappropriate to call the situation of inequality an "irrational" situation: it just makes it clearer what is meant by so calling it. What is meant is that it is a situation in which reasons are insufficiently *operative;* it is a situation insufficiently controlled by reasons—and hence by reason itself. The same point arises with another form of equality and equal rights, equality before the law. It may be said that in a certain society, men have equal rights to a fair trial, to seek redress from the law for wrongs committed against them, etc. But if a fair trial or redress from the law can be secured in that society only by moneyed and educated persons, to insist that everyone *has* this right, though only these particular persons can *secure* it, rings hollow to the point of cynicism: we are concerned not with the abstract existence of rights, but with the extent to which those rights govern what actually happens.

Thus when we combine the notions of the *relevance* of reasons, and the *operativeness* of reasons, we have a genuine moral weapon, which can be applied in cases of what is appropriately called unequal treatment, even where one is not concerned with the equality of people as a whole. This represents a strengthening of the very weak principle mentioned at the beginning of this paper, that for every difference in the way men are treated, a reason should be given: when one requires further that the reasons should be relevant, and that they should be socially operative, this really says something.

Similar considerations will apply to cases of merit. There is, however, an important difference between the cases of need and merit, in respect of the relevance of reasons. It is a matter of logic that particular sorts of needs constitute a reason for receiving particular sorts of good. It is, however, in general a much more disputable question whether certain sorts of merit constitute a reason for receiving certain sorts of good. For instance, let it be agreed, for the sake of argument, that the private schools provide a superior type of education, which it is a good thing to receive. It is then objected that access to this type of education is unequally distributed, because of its cost: among children of equal promise or intelligence, only those from wealthy homes will receive it, and, indeed, children of little promise or intelligence will receive it, if from wealthy homes; and this, the objection continues, is irrational.

. . .

Now the notion of equality of opportunity might be said to be the notion that a limited good shall in fact be allocated on grounds which do not *a priori* exclude any section of those that desire it. But this formulation is not really very clear. For suppose grammar school education (a good perhaps contingently, and certainly fortuitously, limited) is allocated on grounds of ability as tested at the age of eleven; this would normally be advanced as an example of equality of opportunity, as opposed to a system of allocation on grounds of parents' wealth. But does not the criterion of ability exclude *a priori* a certain section of people, namely those that are not able—just as the other excludes *a priori* those who are not wealthy? Here it will obviously be said that this was not what was meant by *a priori* exclusion: the present argument just equates this with exclusion of anybody, that is, with the mere existence of some condition that has to be satisfied. What then is *a priori* exclusion? It must mean exclusion on grounds *other* than those appropriate or rational for the good in question. But this still will not do as it stands. For it would follow from this that so long as those allocating grammar school education on grounds of wealth thought that such grounds were appropriate or rational (as they might in one of the ways discussed above in connexion with private schools), they could sincerely describe their system as one of equality of opportunity—which is absurd.

Hence it seems that the notion of equality of opportunity is more complex than it first appeared. It requires not merely that there should be no exclusion from access on grounds other than those appropriate or rational for the good in question, but that the grounds considered appropriate for the good should themselves be such that people from all sections of society have an equal chance of satisfying them. What now is a "section of society"? Clearly we cannot include under this term sections of the populace identified just by the characteristics which figure in the grounds for allocating the good—since, once more, any grounds at all must exclude some section of the populace. But what about sections identified by characteristics which are *correlated* with the grounds of exclusion? There are important difficulties here: to illustrate this, it may help first to take an imaginary example.

Suppose that in a certain society great prestige is attached to membership of a warrior class, the duties of which require great physical strength. This class has in the past been recruited from certain wealthy families only; but egalitarian reformers achieve a change in the rules, by which warriors are recruited from all sections of the society, on the results of a suitable competition. The effect of this, however, is that the wealthy families still provide virtually all the warriors, because the rest of the populace is so undernourished by reason of poverty that their physical strength is inferior to that of the wealthy and well nourished. The reformers protest that equality of opportunity has not really been achieved; the wealthy reply that in fact it has, and that the poor now have the opportunity of becoming warriors—it is just bad luck that their characteristics are such that they do not pass the test. "We are not," they might say, "excluding anyone *for* being poor; we exclude people for being weak, and it is unfortunate that those who are poor are also weak."

This answer would seem to most people feeble, and even cynical. This is for reasons similar to those discussed before in connexion with equality before the law; that the supposed equality of opportunity is quite empty —indeed, one may say that it does not really exist—unless it is made more effective than this. For one knows that it could be made more effective; one knows that there is a causal connexion between being poor and being undernourished, and between being undernourished and being physically weak. One supposes further that something could be done—subject to whatever economic conditions obtain in the imagined society—to alter the distribution of wealth. All this being so, the appeal by the wealthy to the "bad luck" of the poor must appear as disingenuous.

It seems then that a system of allocation will fall short of equality of opportunity if the allocation of the good in question in fact works out unequally or disproportionately between different sections of society, if the unsuccessful sections are under a disadvantage which could be removed by further reform or social action. This was very clear in the imaginary example that was given, because the causal connexions involved are simple and well known. In actual fact, however, the situations of this type that arise are more complicated, and it is easier to overlook the causal connexions involved. This is particularly so in the case of educational selection, where such slippery concepts as "intellectual ability" are involved. It is a known fact that the system of selection for grammar schools by the "11+" examination favours children in direct proportion to their social class, the children of professional homes having proportionately greater success than those from working class homes. We have every reason to suppose that these results are the product, in good part, of environmental factors; and we further know that imaginative social reform, both of the primary educational system and of living conditions, would favourably affect those environmental factors. In these circumstances, this system of educational selection falls short of equality of opportunity.[3]

This line of thought points to a connexion between the idea of equality of opportunity, and the idea of equality of persons, which is stronger than might at first be suspected. We have seen that one is not really offering equality of opportunity to Smith and Jones if one contents oneself with applying the same criteria to Smith and Jones at, say, the age of eleven; what one is doing there is to apply the same criteria to Smith as affected by favourable conditions and to Jones as affected by unfavourable but curable conditions. Here there is a necessary pressure to equal up the conditions: to give *Smith* and *Jones* equality of opportunity involves regarding their conditions, where curable, as themselves part of what is done to Smith and Jones, and not part of Smith and Jones themselves. Their identity, for these purposes, does not include their curable environment, which is itself unequal and a contributor of inequality. This abstraction of persons in themselves from unequal environments is a way, if not of

[3]See on this C. A. R. Crosland, "Public Schools and English Education," *Encounter,* July 1961.

regarding them as equal, at least of moving recognizably in that direction; and is itself involved in equality of opportunity.

One might speculate about how far this movement of thought might go. The most conservative user of the notion of equality of opportunity is, if sincere, prepared to abstract the individual from some effects of his environment. We have seen that there is good reason to press this further, and to allow that the individuals whose opportunities are to be equal should be abstracted from more features of social and family background. Where should this stop? Should it even stop at the boundaries of heredity? Suppose it were discovered that when all curable environmental disadvantages had been dealt with, there was a residual genetic difference in brain constitution, for instance, which was correlated with differences in desired types of ability; but that the brain constitution could in fact be changed by an operation.[4] Suppose further that the wealthier classes could afford such an operation for their children, so that they always came out top of the educational system; would we then think that poorer children did not have equality of opportunity, because they had no opportunity to get rid of their genetic disadvantages?

. . .

This conflict within the ideals of equality arises even without resort to the fantasy world. It exists to-day in the feeling that a thorough-going emphasis on equality of opportunity must destroy a certain sense of common humanity which is itself an ideal of equality.[5] The ideals that are felt to be in conflict with equality of opportunity are not necessarily other ideals of equality—there may be an independent appeal to the values of community life, or to the moral worth of a more integrated and less competitive society. Nevertheless, the idea of equality itself is often invoked in this connexion, and not, I think, inappropriately.

If the idea of equality ranges as widely as I have suggested, this type of conflict is bound to arise with it. It is an idea which, on the one hand, is invoked in connexion with the distribution of certain goods, some at least of which are bound to confer on their possessors some preferred status or prestige. On the other hand, the idea of equality of respect is one which urges us to give less consideration to those structures in which people enjoy status or prestige, and to consider people independently of those goods, on the distribution of which equality of opportunity precisely focuses our, and their, attention. There is perhaps nothing formally incom-

[4] A yet more radical situation—but one more likely to come about—would be that in which an individual's characteristics could be *pre-arranged* by interference with the genetic material. The dizzying consequences of this I shall not try to explore.

[5] See, for example, Michael Young, *The Rise of the Meritocracy* (London: Thames and Hudson, 1958).

patible in these two applications of the idea of equality: one might hope for a society in which there existed both a fair, rational and appropriate distribution of these goods, and no contempt, condescension or lack of human communication between persons who were more and less successful recipients of the distribution. Yet in actual fact, there are deep psychological and social obstacles to the realization of this hope; as things are, the competitiveness and considerations of prestige that surround the first application of equality certainly militate against the second. How far this situation is inevitable, and how far in an economically developed and dynamic society, in which certain skills and talents are necessarily at a premium, the obstacles to a wider realization of equality might be overcome, I do not think that we know: these are in good part questions of psychology and sociology, to which we do not have the answers.

When one is faced with the spectacle of the various elements of the idea of equality pulling in these different directions, there is a strong temptation, if one does not abandon the idea altogether, to abandon some of its elements: to claim, for instance, that equality of opportunity is the only ideal that is at all practicable, and equality of respect a vague and perhaps nostalgic illusion; or, alternatively, that equality of respect is genuine equality, and equality of opportunity an inegalitarian betrayal of the ideal —all the more so if it were thoroughly pursued, as now it is not. To succumb to either of these simplifying formulae would, I think, be a mistake. Certainly, a highly rational and efficient application of the ideas of equal opportunity, unmitigated by the other considerations, could lead to a quite inhuman society (if it worked—which, granted a well-known desire of parents to secure a position for their children at least as good as their own, is unlikely). On the other hand, an ideal of equality of respect that made no contact with such things as the economic needs of society for certain skills, and human desire for some sorts of prestige, would be condemned to a futile Utopianism, and to having no rational effect on the distribution of goods, position and power that would inevitably proceed. If, moreover, as I have suggested, it is not really known how far, by new forms of social structure and of education, these conflicting claims might be reconciled, it is all the more obvious that we should not throw one set of claims out of the window; but should rather seek, in each situation, the best way of eating and having as much cake as possible. It is an uncomfortable situation, but the discomfort is just that of genuine political thought. It is no greater with equality than it is with liberty, or any other noble and substantial political ideal.

ALISON JAGGAR

On Sexual Equality

What is meant by the demand for sexual equality? Alison Jaggar considers a variety of positions falling under this description. Does equality require that the sexes be indistinguishable? Not necessarily, although such indistinguishability would surely make discrimination difficult. The appeal of the distinctive dress and behavior of the sexes is often cited, but this "entertainment value" is readily outweighed by considerations of freedom.

Equality does call for changes in the role structure of society. A society would be impossible without some roles, but they need not be assigned by sex. Androgyny is the view that the good or desirable human characteristics should not be differentially encouraged by sex, but that all good traits should be encouraged in all individuals; that is, the same ideals would be set for both sexes.

Does equality mean giving men and women the same rights (as the Equal Rights Amendment asks), or different rights depending on the different needs of the sexes? Jaggar argues that it is best not to postulate special female rights, such as abortion and maternity leave, but to see these as part of the general medical, reproductive, and child-rearing rights of all people, rather than as special liabilities of women.

Finally, we confront the integrationist ideal versus the demand for separate but equal groups. Jaggar examines the view that women's special psychology and culture should be separately preserved. Some of these traits and customs are undesirable, she argues, remnants of a slave mentality. Others, such as empathetic understanding and child-rearing skills, should be shared by men. Her ideal society would be sexually integrated with no distinctions specifically sex-based, except those directly related to reproduction.

Further Reading

W. E. COOPER, "What Is Sexual Equality and Why Does Tey Want It?" *Ethics*, 85 (1975), 256–57.

W. T. BLACKSTONE, "Freedom and Women," *Ethics*, 85 (1975), 243–48.

Oh Ma, what is a feminist?
A feminist, my daughter,
Is any woman now who cares
To organize her own affairs
As men don't think she oughter.

I. SEXUAL EQUALITY: INTEGRATION OR SEPARATION?

A more conventional, though not more apt, definition of a feminist is
one who believes that justice requires equality between women and men.
Not that equality is a sufficient condition of human or of women's liberation, but it is at least a necessary one. For this reason, and since the concept
of equality is already notoriously elusive, it seems worthwhile to spend a
little time reflecting on what it would mean for the sexes to be equal.

Equality, in the sense with which social philosophers are concerned, is
a social ideal. Therefore, sexual equality does not mean that individuals of
different sexes should be physically indistinguishable from each other (as
misogynists sometimes pretend is the goal of women's liberation). It means
rather that those of one sex, in virtue of their sex, should not be in a
socially advantageous position vis-à-vis those of the other sex. A society
in which this condition obtained would be a nonsexist society. Although
all feminists, by definition, agree that sexism should be eliminated, disagreement arises among us over how this should be done and how our
common goal of sexual equality should be achieved.

The traditional feminist answer to this question has been that a sexually
egalitarian society is one in which virtually no public recognition is given
to the fact that there is a physiological sex difference between persons.
This is not to say that the different reproductive functions of each sex
should be unacknowledged in such a society nor that there should be no
physicians specializing in female and male complaints, etc. But it is to say
that, except in this sort of context, the question whether someone is female
or male should have no significance.

It is easy to see why both traditional feminism and much of the contemporary women's liberation movement take this view of sexual equality.
Since the distinction between the sexes is embedded in our most basic
institutions (employment, marriage, the draft, even our language),[1] and

Reprinted with omissions from *Ethics*, 84 (1974), 275–92, by permission of Alison Jaggar
and the University of Chicago Press. ©1974 by The University of Chicago. All rights reserved.

[1]The sexism implicit in our language is documented by Robert Baker in " 'Pricks' and
'Chicks': A Plea for 'Persons,' " in *Philosophy and Sex*, R. Baker and F. Elliston, eds. (Buffalo,
New York: Prometheus Books, 1975). It is also shown by Kate Miller and Casey Swift in an
article called "De-Sexing the English Language," *Ms.* (Spring 1972).

since the societal disadvantages of being female are well known, it is natural to suppose that the one is the cause of the other and hence that equality requires the de-institutionalization of sexual differences. For this reason, feminists have always fought hard against the notion that an individual's sex should be an acceptable test for ter[2] fitness to do such things as fill a certain job, borrow money, etc. Much of their effort has been expended in trying to provide legal guarantees to protect women from differential treatment in so-called public life. Recently, and in accord with the contemporary rejection of the old public/private dichotomy on which classical liberalism laid so much stress, some radical feminists have extended the principle that equality requires the minimization of sexual differences even into what used to be called private life. Thus, Shulamith Firestone believes that a sexually egalitarian society requires that an individual may freely express ter "natural" "polymorphous perversity" by sexual encounters with other people of any age and of either sex,[3] and Ti-Grace Atkinson advocates the total abolition of what she calls "the institution of sexual intercourse."[4]

In order to understand more clearly what is meant by this call for the de-institutionalization of sexual differences, let me pause for a moment to consider what it is for an activity to be institutionalized. Some of the radical feminists' proposals may be confusing if they are thought to suggest that every cooperative activity constitutes a social institution. One unfortunate consequence of taking this suggestion seriously would be to undermine the distinction between individual and institutional prejudice, a distinction which is very useful in the analysis of discriminatory behavior.[5] At least for present purposes, then, I shall take a social institution to be a relatively stable way of organizing a significant social activity. To institutionalize activity streamlines social intercourse by defining socially recognized roles and thus enables prediction of what those participating in the practice are likely to do. It also, and perhaps more importantly, provides a standard of correctness by reference to which the propriety of certain kinds of behavior may be judged. It is clear from this definition why even such an apparently individual matter as sexual intercourse, to the extent that it is governed by community norms and even regulated by law,

[2]In this paper I adopt the suggestions of Miller and Swift for a new form of the generic singular pronoun. Instead of using "he," "him," and "his," I employ their suggested common-gender form, derived from the plural, namely, "tey," "tem," and "ter(s)."

[3]Shulamith Firestone, *The Dialectic of Sex: The Case for Feminist Revolution* (New York: Bantam Books, 1971).

[4]Ti-Grace Atkinson, "The Institution of Sexual Intercourse" and "Radical Feminism," in *Notes from the Second Year,* ed. S. Firestone (New York, 1970).

[5]As far as I know, this distinction was first made with respect to racial prejudice by Stokely Carmichael and Charles V. Hamilton in their book *Black Power: The Politics of Liberation in America* (New York: Vintage Books, 1967).

should be acknowledged as a social institution. This definition also makes it clear that some forms of activity may be institutionalized in one society and not in another; it depends on the extent of social regulation and control.

Institutional sexism is a social disadvantage which attaches to individuals of one sex or the other as the result of a certain way of institutionalizing activity. In this, it differs from individual sexism which occurs when a certain individual or group of individuals express hatred or contempt for an individual or group of (usually) the other sex by an act of hostility which may or may not be violent but which is not part of a socially stabilized pattern of discrimination. As social philosophers, we must obviously be concerned primarily with the former type of discrimination, for our first task is to articulate a social ideal.

Let us now return to what I see as my central question, namely, does equality between the sexes require that there should be no institutional recognition of sexual differences, that is, no institutions which differentiate systematically between women and men? I have already remarked that the mainstream of feminist thought has held almost continuously that the answer to this question is yes. In the mainstream tradition, the nonsexist society is one which is totally integrated sexually, one in which sexual differences have ceased to be a matter of public concern. That this should be the ultimate goal of the women's liberation movement follows logically from one very natural interpretation of such familiar slogans as "Women want to be treated as human beings" or "as persons" or "as individuals." On this interpretation, to treat someone as a person is to ignore ter sex.[6]

Recently, however, the traditional feminist goal of sexual integration has been challenged—and challenged by those who, on the criterion of their belief in sexual equality, are undeniably feminists. Just as there is a faction within the black liberation movement which rejects the ideals of "color blindness" and racial integration in favor of black pride and racial separatism, so there are now some feminists who argue that a person's sex is an inescapable and important fact about tem which ought to be socially recognized rather than ignored.

The issue between these two groups of feminists is not entirely clear. In some cases, it seems to be merely a matter of tactics or strategy: what is the best way of improving the position of women in this society? But the disagreement is also a philosophical one, philosophical in two senses. On the one hand, it involves certain more or less familiar conceptual problems: what constitutes justice or equality? what constitutes a person? even, what constitutes a sexual difference? And, on the other hand, it

---

[6]This is suggested, for example, by the subtitle of Baker's paper (n. 1 above).

involves a normative disagreement over the kind of society for which we should aim.

In this paper, I shall explore the philosophical differences between these two groups of feminists and try to establish that sexual separation, or the institutionalization of sexual differences, is neither necessary nor desirable. I shall begin by attempting to refute various philosophical arguments to the conclusion that it is impossible, logically and practically, to ignore a person's sex. I shall then deal with other arguments which purport to present good reasons for the institutionalization of sexual differences. Thus, I shall move from the more clearly conceptual to the more explicitly normative claims. My overriding aim will be to defend the traditional feminist conception of sexual equality as the de-institutionalization of sexual differences.

· · ·

III. THE DISTINCTION BETWEEN THE SEXES

The traditional feminist claim that sexual equality is to be achieved by ignoring sexual differences obviously presupposes a certain view of what a sexual difference is. As a matter of historical fact (though not conceptual necessity), sexual integrationists have regarded an individual's sex as being an entirely physiological characteristic.[7] It is assumed that the physiological differences are not accompanied by any significant differences between the sexes in such apparently nonphysical functions as sensitivity, reasoning, moral deliberation, etc. This makes it plausible to claim that sexual differences can be ignored in most social contexts except those directly concerned with reproduction.

The picture might change, however, if this view about what constitutes a sexual difference were shown to be inadequate, if it could be argued successfully that the concept of sex should include not only a difference in reproductive organs but also certain nonphysical differences. Empirical research in this area is still inconclusive, to say the least, but if a philosophical argument could demonstrate that sexual differences necessarily stretch beyond the physical, this should force us to rethink the claim that such differences are socially irrelevant. And if sexual differences were shown to be much more far-reaching than we had hitherto supposed, we might come to believe that it was practically if not logically impossible to ignore a person's sex.

[7] Although the difference in reproductive capacity is what makes the physiological differences between the sexes important to us, the physiological distinction is normally taken as the primary criterion for determining the sex of an individual, and one who is unable to reproduce is not thereby described as sexless. Therefore, I call the distinction physiological rather than functional.

There are, of course, a number of arguments by misogynists purporting to show that women are intellectually and morally inferior to men. But I shall take these as already refuted by other writers and turn instead to the one author I have been able to discover who deals with the question in a manner which is both philosophical and feminist. This is Professor Christine Garside, who first takes up the issue in a paper entitled "Women and Persons":[8]

> ... women will always be different from men as the result of self-determination, because we differ in physical structure, we differ in our present social experience, we differ in our inherited past and so on.
>   I suspect that it was in some part the fear of loss of polarity between the sexes which led to the traditional denial of self-determination for women. This fear, however, is groundless for a true polarity will emerge when women and men press forward in active self-determination.[9]

The concluding paragraph of her paper runs thus:

> Finally, I would like to reiterate my belief that there is no need to fear loss of polarity when women do achieve liberation on the level of self-determination. . . . There is no way that women can ever become identical to men. Nor is there any reason why they should desire to do so. The heritage and experience of women is as rich as the heritage and experience as [of?] men; and once women recognize their right to self-determination and release their creative energies into the world this will be obvious.[10]

Now, in its narrowest interpretation, the claim that women can never be identical to men is simply tautologous, trivially true, just like the claim that people with big feet can never be identical to people with small ones. But of course Garside is saying more than this, and her most recent paper, "True Sex-Polarity,"[11] gives a fuller exposition of her views. In this account, she utilizes Scriven's notion of "normical" properties, properties which do not belong analytically to an object but whose presence is not purely accidental or, as she says, "arbitrary." "A normical property is one which is needed in a thorough explanation of the thing which has the property."[12] An object may lack any one of its normical properties, but it could not lack them all and still be an object of that type.

[8]Christine Garside's "Women and Persons" was the winning entry in "The Problem of Women" prize essay competition. It is published in *Mother Was Not a Person*, ed. Margret Andersen (Montreal: Content, 1972). My criticism of Garside's argument should in no way be taken, of course, as reflecting a lack of admiration for her work.

[9]Ibid., p. 196.

[10]Ibid., p. 202.

[11]Parts of this paper were read in response to mine at the Western Division meetings of the American Philosophical Association in April 1973. It is as yet unpublished, but copies can probably be obtained by writing to the author at Sir George Williams University in Montreal.

[12]Christine Garside, "True Sex-Polarity," p. 10 of the typescript.

Garside claims that there is only one property which belongs analytically to women, namely, that of being a person, but she believes that this one property is supplemented by a number of normical properties. "What it is to be a woman includes having a particular kind of body, having a recent history of being brought up in a patriarchal society, having an inherited history of female archetypes, having present experiences which occur because one is female, and having a future which calls for a revolution from being oppressed. There are other things as well, but these are most central."[13]

In elaborating this definition, Garside gives a rich and evocative account of what it is to be female. The alternative account, which I wish to espouse, is much starker. For me, to be a woman is no more and no less than to be a female human being. All and only female human beings are women. To be female and to be human are the necessary and sufficient conditions for being a woman.

. . .

Neither Garside nor I dispute the empirical facts regarding women's history, socialization, etc. But we do differ, apparently, in the significance that we attach to those facts. Garside seems to believe that they are of great importance, that they result in distinct and permanent differences between male and female nature, if that is an acceptable gloss for her term "sex-polarity." I'm less sure about this. I simply don't know how important these factors are. I suppose the importance of at least some of them might be investigated empirically—although I don't know how one could investigate empirically her claim that "it feels different to be a woman than to be a man."[14] At the moment, given the oppressive conditions of the present and the past, those factors may be very important. But one may hope that, as conditions improve, as women experience less discrimination, for example, those factors may weigh less heavily. So not only is it not conceptually true, it may not even be empirically true that, in a more than trivial philosophical sense, there will always be a sexual polarity.

Garside's presumption that there are certain necessary features of personal experience seems to be philosophically sound. I would accept that it is indeed a conceptual truth that persons must have physical experiences, social experiences, and some kind of cultural heritage. But what does not seem to be conceptually true is that these features have an inescapably sexual character. I am not, of course, asserting, *a priori*, that the differences between women and men have been shown conclusively to be limited to

---

[13]Ibid., pp. 10–11.

[14]For a discussion of some of the problems of investigating empirically whether there are innate psychological differences between the sexes, see my "On Female Nature," forthcoming in *The Problem of Women,* incorporating prize essays on "The Problem of ♀," a competition sponsored by SUNY at Fredonia.

the purely reproductive and that, therefore, complete sexual integration is possible in all social contexts except those directly involving reproduction. What I am claiming, however, is that we have as yet no good reason, either *a priori* or empirical, for denying the possibility of sexual integration. So, since I believe that integration is a desirable ideal, I claim that we should work on the assumption that it is possible. Only if empirical research or new philosophical arguments demonstrate other differences between the sexes shall we need to question again the possibility of this ideal.

IV. THE RIGHTS OF WOMEN

Even in the absence of reason to believe in a sexual polarity which transcends the physiological distinction, it might be argued that the simple physiological differences between women and men were alone sufficient to justify the institutionalization of sexual differences. The facts that women are, in general, smaller and (in some ways) weaker than men, that we give birth to children, and so on, may be thought to constitute in themselves inequalities which require social remedy. In the past, such arguments have been used by male supremacists as justification for forcing on women a kind of "protection" which guarantees to us an inferior social position, but the biological facts may also be used by feminists as grounds for arguing that women should receive special treatment in order to offset our biological inequality. Such a feminist is Shulamith Firestone, who believes that the goal of social equality between the sexes requires a technological advance which will allow for the extrauterine reproduction of children, thus freeing women from what Firestone calls "the fundamental inequality of the bearing and raising of children."[15]

This claim apparently takes for granted the conclusion of my argument in the last section that one's sex should be essentially determined by the shape of ter reproductive organs. Its novelty seems to lie in its view of equality. For it presupposes that equality is not merely equality of opportunity, that is, not merely the absence of social impediments based on sex to any individual's attaining whatever position in society tey chooses to aim for. Instead, equality is viewed in a more positive sense, as a certain level of physical and economic security which society ought to provide for each of its members. In order that each individual should reach this level, it may be necessary to grant special social rights to certain disadvantaged

[15] *The Dialectic of Sex* (n. 3 above).

groups, and it is claimed that women constitute a group which requires such rights in order to achieve social equality with men.

In order to qualify as a genuine female right, any proposal must be envisioned as a permanent feature of a nonsexist society. It cannot be viewed simply as a temporary measure, like alimony or the preferential hiring of women, which are usually advocated as necessary only to correct an unequal situation but which should be discontinued as soon as the imbalance is remedied. To be a genuine "female right," the alleged right must be seen as belonging permanently to all women simply in virtue of our sex and not, for example, in virtue of our social status or in virtue simply of our being human. When the sexual distinction is seen primarily as a difference in reproductive organs, it follows that the kind of special rights which women are said to need in a sexually egalitarian society should be connected with our reproductive function. They include the right to protection from assault and rape, the right to abortion, the right to maternity leave, and the right to guaranteed care and/or financial support for our children.

In my opinion, the trouble with this position lies not in its vision of social equality as a positive condition but, rather, in its view of the sexual distinction. Despite its apparent acceptance of the view that sex is merely physiological, I think that those who claim the need for special female rights are surreptitiously extending the sexual distinction to cover more than a physiological difference. For example, it may well be true that society in general should take on the responsibility of providing and caring for children, but this proposal should not be presented as a *female* right. To do so is to make the obviously false assumption that the sexual difference consists not only in women's capacity to give birth to children but also in our having an obligation to raise them. Even on the dubious presumption that the welfare of children is the total responsibility of whoever produced them, it is clear that this measure would provide relief to *both* parents of the children, the father as well as the mother. But perhaps a preferable way of seeing this proposal is not as a right of parents at all but rather as a right of children.

Similarly, to suggest that the right to freedom from assault and rape is a specifically female right is to presuppose that women alone are desirable sexual objects or that women alone are incapable of defending themselves. Such suggested female rights are far better viewed as applications of general human rights, so that adequate protection may be afforded to any individual, male or female, who needs it. Thus, the right to maternity leave should be covered by the statement that those who are temporarily incapable of contributing to material production should not be expected to do so. The stress on the special nature of maternity leave does indeed emphasize that pregnancy and childbirth are not sicknesses, but it also suggests that women need special privileges which men don't require. This suggestion is misleading. We do not, after all, elevate "prostate leave" into a special right of men.

The proposed female right to abortion is more complicated. It is certainly something which does not apply to men, but it is often defended either as a way of allowing women to enjoy the general human right of "control over one's own body" or, perhaps more plausibly, as a way of allowing women the general human right of sexual freedom.[16] The former right, however, is extremely ill-determined and controversial; how much control over ter own body should a typhoid carrier have, for example? And the latter right, of sexual freedom, may well be thought to be limited by a consideration of the rights of the fetus. If this is so, however, then a feminist could argue that, in the absence of foolproof contraceptive methods, the right to sexual freedom should be limited for men as well as for women. The complexity of this special case makes it impossible to discuss adequately here, but it certainly does not seem to me to present a clear case of a special female right which ought to be guaranteed by a sexually egalitarian society.

In general, I would argue that, so long as we view the difference between the sexes as a simple physiological difference—and we have no conclusive grounds for doing more—then there is no reason to draw up a special bill of rights for women in order to ensure our equality. The rights of women can be protected quite adequately in a society which recognizes basic human rights.

V. THE PRESERVATION OF FEMALE "CULTURE"

Another challenge to the belief that sexual equality requires complete sexual integration is rooted in the rejection of the classical liberal model of a society as composed of a multitude of isolated individuals, each intent on pursuing ter own private advantage to the best of ter ability. It is now frequently argued that this model is inadequate to account for the complexities of modern society and that it should be superseded by a different picture of society as composed of a series of groups organized on a variety of different bases. It is this latter model which underlies the arguments of some feminists who argue for a kind of sexual separation. These feminists claim that women, like it or not, form a series of special-interest groups and that in order to gain social equality we ought to seek power for our

[16]The latter suggestion was made by Carolyn Korsmeyer of the State University of New York at Buffalo.

groups as a whole in order to rival the power of the groups presently formed by men. Such feminists often deny that integration on an individual level is a realistic goal. This pluralist model of equality contrasts sharply with that view which sees equality in terms of assimilation and integration by individuals. It is generally associated with the type of conservatism and reaction which is perhaps most clearly typified by the South African system of apartheid, so it is interesting to see that the motto of "separate but equal" can also be adopted by genuine feminists.[17]

The pluralistic model of equality is supported by arguments which are sometimes strikingly similar to those used by the factions of the U.S. black liberation movement which advocate racial separatism. One such argument is that women have a distinctive culture which would be lost if complete sexual integration were to occur. It is also contended that individual women will not be recognized by men as genuine equals in any sphere so long as we belong to an inferior "caste." For this reason, it is claimed, the assimilation of individuals is impossible until the prestige of women as a group has been raised through the establishment of strong female institutions capable of challenging the power of the present male-dominated institutions. The institutions most generally regarded as crucial to feminism are education, health, and the media, but there are some advocates of separate female financial institutions and even a female military force. Persuaded by such arguments, a number of women even deny that a genuine heterosexual love relationship is possible in the present conditions of male/female inequality and they therefore recommend exclusively lesbian sexual arrangements. Finally, it is claimed that women need to have strong supportive female groups behind them before they can "get it together" as individuals sufficiently to face integration with men. For this reason, too, therefore, sexual separation is seen as a more appropriate goal for the women's liberation movement than complete sexual integration on an individual level.

The trouble with most of these arguments is that they rest on empirical premises about the psychology of oppressed groups whose truth is, to say the least, controversial. But in any case, they do not directly attack the notion of individual sexual integration as an ideal; they claim merely that sexual separation is a necessary step on the way to this ultimate goal. The only argument which challenges the *ultimate* desirability of complete sexual integration is the one which advocates the preservation of a distinctive female "culture" and sees separation as the only way of achieving this.

[17] I am using here my original definition of a feminist, namely, someone who believes in sexual equality.

For the sake of evaluating this argument, let us assume that there does indeed exist a worldwide split between female and male "culture."[18] "Male culture" consists of the art, philosophy, and science which are identified with national culture and from which, it is claimed, women have been excluded almost totally. "Female culture," on the other hand, is less visible and less closely tied to national boundaries. In the past, it has included many invaluable contributions to civilization, such as folk medicine, the preparation and preservation of food, spinning, weaving, pottery, and so on. Nowadays, however, it has been reduced to a number of relatively simple domestic skills, mainly involving such tasks as cooking, cleaning, and child care, in a few unprestigious skills such as typing which are used in work outside the home, and in the subtle skills which women use to make themselves attractive to men. "Female culture" is said to embody values which are contrary, antipathetic, to those embodied in the institutions of "male culture," such as the government, army, religion, and economy. In particular, it is claimed that "female culture" demands and fosters such values as empathy, intuition, love, responsibility, endurance, practicality, and humanization.

It is certainly true that the above-mentioned characteristics are highly valued in few, if any, national or "male" cultures. Instead, these cultures often emphasize such qualities as discipline, self-control, efficiency, etc. But there are other aspects of "female culture," especially in its debased modern aspect, which are perhaps less admirable. They include lack of initiative, dependence, timidity, narcissism, cunning, manipulativeness, etc. Nor can the existence of these features be written off entirely as propagandist examples of sexual stereotyping. On the contrary, they are the necessary concomitants of the culture of an economically dependent group; they typify a slave culture. And this being so, it seems obvious that they represent aspects of "female culture" which liberated women will not want to preserve.

It is doubtful, indeed, whether those aspects even could be preserved in a society where women were organizing their own institutions in competition with those of men. The necessity of competition would entail that women would have to adopt the "male" values of discipline, efficiency, etc., simply in order to face the male challenge. This is, of course, the same problem that faces utopian socialist or anarchist groups who wish to institute values different from those which prevail at present but who have to

[18]It has become fashionable to use the term "culture" very loosely to describe the special practices of a certain group within a larger society. A more accurate term might be "subculture," but in this discussion I shall follow the usage of the writers whose views I am discussing. Much of the characterization of male and female "culture" which follows is taken from the *Fourth World Manifesto,* by Barbara Burris, reprinted in *Notes from the Third Year* (Women's Liberation), edited by Anne Koedt and Shulamith Firestone (New York, 1971), pp. 102–19.

survive in a world where their values are at a practical disadvantage, at least with respect to quantity of production.

Whatever may be the solution to this dilemma in other spheres, it seems clear that the problem as it arises for women cannot be solved by sexual separation. Not only is it extremely unlikely that female institutions could ever challenge successfully the dominant male ones, but they would be corrupted if they did so. They would have to abandon those values we have designated as characteristically female ones, and thus women would be forced to become imitations of men.

What we now call female culture could not survive if it were placed in competition with, instead of in subordination to, the male culture. Nor, I would argue, should we want it to. We should recognize that our culture is to a large extent the culture of an oppressed group, and while we may not wish to let it be forgotten entirely, at the same time we should distinguish those elements which we want to keep alive. Obviously we do not really want to perpetuate the supposedly feminine skills of hair curling or straightening, makeup, and the "arts" of seduction. What we must do instead is to create a new androgynous culture which incorporates the best elements of both the present male and the present female cultures, which values both personal relationships and efficiency, both emotion and rationality.

This result cannot be achieved through sexual separation. Our ideal of sexual equality must go beyond the achievement of a balance of economic and political power for contending female and male groups. Ultimately, I believe that we must seek total integration on a personal level, so that an individual's sex is viewed as a fact which is irrelevant to ter place in society.

VI. SEXUAL DIFFERENTIATION AS INTRINSICALLY VALUABLE

I want to consider one more argument against sexual integration. The proponents of this argument may well accept the simple physiological view of the sexual distinction, but they still propose, on what seem to be semiaesthetic grounds, that it is desirable to preserve a social distinction between the sexes. Freud seems to be taking this position when he suggests that, if women leave "the calm uncompetitive activity of home" and join "the struggle for existence exactly as men," we should mourn "the passing away of the most delightful thing the world can offer us—our ideal of womanhood."[19]

[19]This well-known passage from one of Freud's letters to his fiancée is quoted in *Masculine/Feminine: Readings in Sexual Mythology and the Liberation of Women,* ed. Betty Roszak and Theodore Roszak (New York: Harper & Row, 1969).

I call arguments on these lines *vive la différence* arguments. They recur with predictable regularity whenever women's liberation is being discussed. They claim that the basic physiological differences between the sexes should be the grounds of social differentiation because in this way we can add a spice of pleasurable variety to life. They argue that sexual equality in the sense that one sex should not have more social advantages than the other does not entail that the sexes should have identical social roles. They ask, rhetorically, "Wouldn't it be unfortunate if we were all alike?" These arguments are persuasive because of their suggestion that those who do not recognize the pleasures of institutionalizing sexual differences are gloomy puritans. They suggest that their proponents are advocating not sexual inequality but merely a kind of healthy hedonism.

Simone de Beauvoir's response to Freud's argument is to point out what both women and men invariably lose as well as what we gain when a sexual role system is established. She agrees "that he would be a barbarian indeed who failed to appreciate exquisite flowers, rare lace, the crystal-clear voice of the eunuch, and feminine charm."[20] But then she asks, "Does a fugitive miracle—and one so rare—justify us in perpetuating a situation that is baneful for both sexes? One can appreciate the beauty of flowers, the charm of women, and appreciate them at their true value; if these treasures cost blood or misery, they must be sacrificed."[21]

De Beauvoir's point is well taken. The forcing of women into a socially shaped mold of femininity may indeed have its compensations, but, as contemporary women's liberation literature never tires of reminding us, those advantages have been more than offset in practice by their corresponding disadvantages. Such disadvantages include not only female frustration, the wasting of female potential and talent, loss of female initiative, and so on, but also a corresponding denial of self-realization to men. Insofar as sexual discrimination exists in contexts other than the reproductive, and hence is based on a difference which is irrelevant in those contexts, it is bound to limit arbitrarily the options of both women and men.

There is, however, a more far-reaching argument against sexual separation. This is hinted at by some radical feminists, such as Ti-Grace Atkinson, when they claim that the sexual role system should be abolished not just because the goal of "separate but equal" seems to be unrealizable in fact but because it is one aspect of a role system which ideally should be abolished in its entirety. I take such talk about the desirability of a "role system" to be a way of talking about the desirability of institutionalizing human activity. This claim is sometimes thought to be involved in the political theory of anarchism, and since many of the radical feminist writ-

---

[20]Simone de Beauvoir, *The Second Sex* (New York: Bantam Books, 1961), p. 686.
[21]Ibid., p. 687.

ings, especially those of Firestone and Atkinson, pay homage to some fundamental anarchist ideals, I shall draw on the anarchist tradition in an attempt to reconstruct the kind of considerations which may well have influenced Atkinson in rejecting a role system.[22]

One general objection to a role system is that it might tempt us to define a person by ter relation to a social institution. Thus, a person comes to be seen simply as a tinker, a tailor, a soldier, or a sailor. Not only is such stereotyping an obvious disfigurement of an individual's humanity, but it seems to conflict with the anarchist ideal of a person able to do many different kinds of work in a society where specialization of human function has been minimized if not eliminated.

The institutionalization of human activity might also be thought inimical to the anarchist ideal of social freedom. To the extent that social institutions embody norms of behavior and impose sanctions, even if only as mild as social disapproval, on individuals who depart from those norms, the freedom of the individual might be thought to be compromised. Indeed, it is a conceptual truth that, in order to be playing a role at all, the behavior of the player must be circumscribed by the requirements of that role.

Finally, the existence of a role system might appear to be incompatible with the moral autonomy of the individual.[23] If the obligations of a person's role are taken as defining the whole of ter moral obligations, then it becomes impossible for that individual to rise above the conventional morality of professional ethics. Insofar as one conforms to ter role, one may be forced to do what is morally wrong or be unable to do what is morally right. A soldier may have to kill and a salaried employee may be unable to avoid contributing to the war effort. In order to act morally, therefore, it seems to be necessary to transcend one's role, to examine critically the obligations which define it. Thus, a morally autonomous person must, despite the functionalist theory of contemporary sociologists, be more than the sum of ter roles.

These arguments are very persuasive, and in my original draft of this paper I accepted them. However, I now believe that they can be answered, that human freedom and equality do not require the de-institutionalization of all human activity.[24] I doubt, in fact, whether the very concept of a society without some kind of "role system" is coherent. It seems to me now that a society necessarily includes social institutions which define

[22]For some of the following ideas I am indebted to my former colleague, Peter M. Schuller of Miami University, Ohio, who explains them in an unpublished paper entitled "Antinomic Elements in Higher Education."

[23]This seems to be an implication of Robert Paul Wolff's thesis in his *In Defense of Anarchism* (New York: Harper & Row, 1970).

[24]I was forced to this realization by argument with Marlene Fried.

social roles, in fact, that it is precisely the norms embodied in those institutions which provide the criteria for the identification of that society.

Not only are norms logically necessary to a society; by ensuring a certain degree of social predictability, they are also practically necessary. However, in order that social institutions should not be oppressive, certain conditions must be fulfilled. The norms which we endorse should be determined rationally by all concerned. Such norms should help rather than hinder justice and personal self-determination; to use a couple of obvious examples, such things as exploitation and rape should not be permissible. And the norms which define a social role should not be viewed as absolutely binding on the one who is performing that role: roles should be seen, rather, as imposing *prima facie* duties which may, in certain circumstances, be overridden. In this case, to adopt a role will not per se limit one's moral autonomy.[25] Finally, a person should not be assigned any role involuntarily; instead, tey should be able to choose from a variety of roles.

These requirements necessitate the abolition of a role system based on sex. Sex roles are not determined by those concerned. They are irrational whenever they regulate our behavior in contexts other than the reproductive, for in doing so they unwarrantably presuppose that the difference between the sexes is more than a simple physiological distinction. Sex roles are restrictive and oppressive, in fact if not in principle. And, necessarily, they are ascribed by others rather than assumed voluntarily. Hence, while I cannot agree that personal liberation and equality require the total de-institutionalization of all human activity, I do believe that women's and men's liberation and sexual equality require that the distinction between the sexes should ultimately be de-institutionalized. I am not, of course, advocating that a genuine feminist should refuse to recognize physiological sexual differences. To do this would suggest that feminism involves a reversion to the kind of Victorian hypocrisy which preferred to call a woman's legs her "limbs." But I do claim that a sexually egalitarian society must be integrated in the sense that sexual differences should not be institutionally recognized.

VII. CONCLUSION

This account of sexual equality is obviously not purely analytic, nor is it intended to be. It is designed to persuade. And if it is accepted, various practical conclusions follow from it. If sexual equality requires integration, then a feminist should seek to modify our language by the use of neuter proper names and the elimination of gender in order to undermine the

[25]For a fuller discussion of this claim, see my "The Just State as a Round Square," *Dialogue* 11, no. 4 (December 1972): 580–83.

sexist consciousness which presently permeates it.[26] Tey must, of course, continue the long and tedious struggle against institutionalized sexual discrimination. And when people complain that you can't tell the boys from the girls nowadays, the feminist response must be to point out that it should make no difference. As Florynce Kennedy demanded, "Why do they want to know anyway? So that they can discriminate?"

[26]These measures are among those suggested by Baker (n. 1 above).

J. R. LUCAS

"Because You Are a Woman"

While granting that we should not treat two individuals differently without citing a relevant difference between them, J. R. Lucas argues that sex itself is a relevant difference. He concludes that it is permissible to deny a gifted woman an equal education or an opportunity to have a military career simply "because she is a woman."

Lucas's many reasons for his position fall into several groups. First he cites genetic differences (X- and Y-chromosomes), pointing out that many traits, such as baldness, are sex-linked. Feminists advocate "dualism," he claims—the view that there are physical but no mental or intellectual differences between the sexes. Here Lucas holds that even if a statistical difference in some skill shows up between the sexes, this is not a sufficient reason to exclude exceptional individuals from the usually less-skilled sex.

Using a social utility argument, however, he finds a justification for the opposite conclusion. Perhaps Miss Amazon would make a fine soldier and not disrupt the army at all, but if other women would, then she, too, can be excluded. Her loss of freedom and happiness is outweighed by the greater social good gained by excluding the others, he reasons. It is "easier" to exclude all women than to screen them.

Third, Lucas distinguishes sex as more "integral" to some social roles than to others. For example, one's sex is more integral to being a mother, a priest, or a nurse than to being a pilot or a secretary. Hence it is reasonable, he concludes, to prefer individuals from the appropriate sex for such roles.

Finally he claims that equality would lead to the depersonalization of women, because ignoring a woman's "essential femininity" would lead to viewing her simply as an inferior by male standards.

Further Reading

Sara Ann Ketchum and Christine Pierce, "Implicit Racism," Analysis, 36 (1976), 91–95.

SUSAN HAACK, "On the Moral Relevance of Sex," *Philosophy*, 49 (1974), 90–95.

TRUDY GOVIER, "Woman's Place," *Philosophy*, 49 (1974), 305–9.

Plato was the first feminist. In the *Republic* he puts forward the view that women are just the same as men, only not quite so good. It is a view which has often been expressed in recent years, and generates strong passions. Some of these have deep biological origins, which a philosopher can only hope to recognize and not to assuage. But much of the heat engendered is due to unnecessary friction between views which are certainly compatible and probably correct. And here a philosopher can help. If we can divide the issues neatly, at the joints, then we need not quarrel with one another for saying something, probably true, because what is being maintained is misconstrued and taken to mean something else, probably false.

The feminist debate turns on the application of certain concepts of justice, equality and humanity. Should the fact—"the mere fact"—of a person's being a woman disqualify her from being a member of the Stock Exchange, the Bench of Bishops or the House of Lords, or from obtaining a mortgage, owning property, having a vote or going to heaven? Is it not, say the feminists, just as irrational and inequitable as disqualifying a man on the grounds of the colour of his hair? Is it not, counter the anti-feminists, just as rational as drawing a distinction between men on the one hand and children, animals, lunatics, Martians and computers on the other? Whereupon we come to enunciate the formal platitude that women are the same as men in some respects, different from them in others, just as men are the same in some respects as children, animals, lunatics, Martians and computers, and different in others. And then we have to embark on more substantial questions of the respects in which men and women are the same, and those in which they are different; and of whether any such differences could be relevant to the activity or institution in question, or could be comparable to the differences, generally acknowledged to exist, between *homo sapiens* and the rest of creation. Even if women are different from men, a feminist might argue, why should this be enough to debar them from the floor of the Stock Exchange, when, apparently, there is no objection to the presence of computers?

We are faced with two questions. We need to know first what exactly are the ways in which women differ from men, and this in turn raises issues

" 'Because You Are a Woman,' " by J. R. Lucas, from *Philosophy*, Vol. 48 (1973). © 1973 by the Royal Institute of Philosophy. Reprinted by permission of Cambridge University Press.

of the methods whereby such questions may be answered. Only when these methodological issues have been discussed can we turn to the more substantial ones of morals and politics concerned with whether it can ever be right to treat a woman differently from a man on account of her sex, or whether that is a factor which must always be regarded as in itself irrelevant.

I

The facts of femininity are much in dispute. The development of genetic theory is some help, but not a decisive one. We know that men differ from women in having one Y-chromosome and only one X-chromosome whereas women have two X-chromosomes. Apart from the X- and Y-chromosomes, exactly the same sort of chromosomes turn up in men and women indifferently. The genetic make-up of each human being is constituted by his chromosomes, which occur in pairs, one of each pair coming from the father, the other from the mother. Men and women share the same gene pool. So far as chromosomes, other than the X- and Y-ones, are concerned, men and women of the same breeding community are far more alike than members of different species, or even men of different races. This constitutes a powerful argument against the doctrine, attributed by some to the Mahometans, that women have no souls; contrary to the view of many young males, they are not just birds; or, in more modern parlance, it gives empirical support to arguments based on the principle of Universal Humanity.[1] Women are worthy of respect, for the same reasons as men are. If it is wrong to hurt a man, to harm him, humiliate him or frustrate him, then it is wrong to hurt, harm, humiliate or frustrate a woman; for she is of the same stock as he, and they share the same inheritance and have almost all their chromosome-types in common.

Early genetic theory assumed a one–one correlation between pairs of hereditary genetic factors and their manifested effects in the individual. Whether I had brown eyes or blue eyes depended on whether I had the pair of factors BB, Bb or bB, in all of which cases I should have brown eyes, or whether I had bb, in which case I should have blue eyes. No other genetic factor was supposed to be relevant to the colour of my eyes, nor was the possession of a B or a b gene relevant to anything else about me. If this theory represented the whole truth, the feminist case would be simple. Sex is irrelevant to everything except sex. The fact of a man's being male or a woman's being female would be a "mere fact" with no bearing on anything except sexual intercourse and the procreation of children. It

[1][See Williams, this volume, p. 81.]

would be rational to hold that only a male could be guilty of rape, and it might be permissible to have marriage laws which countenanced only heterosexual unions, and to look for proofs of paternity as well as of maternity. Perhaps we might go a very little further, and on the same grounds as we admit that negroes are not really eligible for the part of Iago, admit that males could not really expect to be employed as models for female fashions, and *vice versa*. Beyond these few and essentially unimportant exceptions, it would be as wrong for the law to discriminate between the sexes as it would be if it were to prefer blondes.

Simple genetic theory is, however, too simple. It needs to be complicated in two ways. First, although chromosomes occur in pairs, each single one being inherited more or less independently of every other one, each chromosome contains not just one, but many, many genetic factors, and these are not all independently inherited, and some, indeed, like the one responsible for haemophilia, are sex-linked. There are, so far as we know, relatively few effects—and those mostly bad—which are caused by factors contained in the Y-chromosome, and there is a slight *a priori* argument against many features being thus transmitted (because the Y-chromosome is much smaller than the others, and so, presumably, carries less genetic information): but there could well be more complicated effects due to a relatively rare recessive gene not being marked in the male as it probably would have been in the female. Mathematical talent might be like haemophilia or colour-blindness: it is consonant with what we know of genetic theory that only one in a thousand inherit the genetic factor, which if it is inherited by a boy then becomes manifest, but which if it is inherited by a girl, still in 999 cases out of a thousand is marked by a dominant unmathematicality. The second complication is more fundamental than the first. Genetic factors not only are not inherited independently of the others, but do not operate independently of the others. What is important is not simply whether I have BB, Bb, or bb, but whether I have one of these pairs in conjunction with some set of other pairs of factors. In particular, whether a person is male or female may affect whether or not some other hereditary factor manifests itself or not. Only men go bald. There are many physical features and physiological processes which are affected by whether a person is male or female. So far as our bodies are concerned, the fact of a person's being a man or a woman is not "a mere fact" but a fundamental one. Although there are many similarities between men and women, the differences are pervasive, systematic and of great biological significance. Almost the first question a hospital needs to ask is "M or F?"

Many feminists are dualists, and while conceding certain bodily differences between men and women, deny that there is any inheritance of intellectual ability or traits of character at all. Genetic theory, as far as it goes, is against them. There is reasonable evidence for the inheritance of skills and patterns of behaviour in other animals, and in particular of those patterns of behaviour we should normally ascribe to the maternal instinct.

. . .

[A] methodological issue is raised by those who acknowledge that there have been and are differences in the intellectual achievements and the typical behaviour of women as compared with men, but attribute all of them exclusively to the social pressures brought to bear upon women which have prevented them from exercising their talents to the full or giving rein to their natural inclinations. When the advocate of male supremacy marshals his masses of major poets against a solitary Sappho, the feminist explains that women have been so confined by domestic pressures and so inhibited by convention that those few with real poetic talent have never had opportunity to bring it to flower. Poets might be poor, but at least they could listen to the Muse undistracted by baby's cries: whereas potential poetesses, unless their lot were cast in Lesbos, were married off and made to think of clothes and nappies[2] to the exclusion of all higher thoughts.

It is difficult to find hard evidence either for or against this thesis. In this it is like many rival explanations or interpretations in history or literature. What moves us to adopt one rather than another is that it seems to us more explanatory or more illuminating than the alternative; and what seems to us more explanatory or illuminating depends largely on our own experience and understanding—and our own prejudices. But although we are very liable to be swayed by prejudice, it does not follow that we inevitably are, and although we are often guided by subjective considerations in deciding between various hypotheses, it does not follow that there is nothing, really, to choose between them. We can envisage evidence, even if we cannot obtain it, which would decide between the two alternatives. The feminist claim would be established if totally unisex societies sprang up and flourished; or if there were as many societies in which the roles of men and women were reversed as there were traditional ones. Indeed, the existence of any successful and stable society in which the roles of the sexes are reversed is evidence in favour of the claim. Evidence against is more difficult to come by. Few people deny that social pressures have a very considerable bearing on our behaviour and capacities. Some people argue from the analogy with other animals, whose behaviour is indubitably determined genetically and differs according to their sex; or argue, as I have done, by extrapolation from purely physical features. Both arguments are respectable, neither conclusive. Man is an animal, but very unlike other animals, particularly in respect of the extreme plasticity of

[2][Diapers.]

human behaviour, nearly all of which is learned. Very few of our responses
are purely instinctive; and it is unsafe to claim confidently that maternal
feelings must be. What would constitute evidence against the feminist
claim would be some intellectual ability or character trait which seemed
to be both relatively independent of social circumstance and distributed
unevenly between the sexes. Mathematical talent might be a case in point.
It seems to be much more randomly distributed in the population than
other forms of intellectual ability. If Ramanujan could triumph over his
circumstances, then surely numerate sisters to Sappho should abound. But
this is far from being a conclusive argument.

There are no conclusive arguments about feminine abilities and attitudes. But the discoveries of the scientists, so far as they go, lend some
support to traditional views. It could well be the case that intellectual and
psychological characteristics are, like physical ones, influenced by genetic
factors. If this is so, the way in which a particular pair of genes in an
individual genotype will be manifested in the phenotype will depend on
the other genes in the genotype, and may depend greatly on whether there
are two X chromosomes or one X and one Y. It could be that the masculine
mind is typically more vigorous and combative, and the feminine mind
typically more intuitive and responsive, with correspondingly different
ranges of interests and inclinations. It would make evolutionary sense if
it were, and would fit in with what else we know about the nature of man:
but it is still possible to maintain the contrary view; and even if there are
in fact differences between men and women, it does not follow that their
treatment should be different too.

II

If it could be established that there were no innate intellectual or emotional differences between men and women, the feminists' case would be
pretty well made; but it does not follow that to admit that there are
differences carries with it an adequate justification for every sort of discrimination, and it is useful to consider what sort of bearing various types
of difference might have. Suppose, for example, that mathematical ability
were distributed unevenly and according to the same pattern as haemophilia, so that only one in n males have it and only one in n^2 females. This
would be a highly relevant factor in framing our educational policy. It
would justify the provision of far more opportunities for boys to study
higher mathematics than for girls. But it would not justify the total exclusion of girls. Most girls prefer nursing to numeracy, but those few who
would rather solve differential equations ought not to be prevented from
doing so on the grounds that they are female. Two principles underlie this

judgment. First that the connexion between sex and mathematical ability is purely contingent; and secondly that we are in a position in which considerations of the individual's interests and deserts are paramount. Even if there are very few female mathematicians, there is no reason why any particular woman should not be a mathematician. And if any particular woman is, then her being a woman is irrelevant to her actual performance in mathematics. Her being a woman created a presumption, a purely contingent although usually reliable presumption, that she was no good at mathematics. It is like presumptive evidence in a court of law, which could be rebutted, and in this case was, and having been rebutted is of no more relevance in this individual situation, which is all we are concerned with.

Female mathematicians are rare. Few disciplines are so pure as mathematics. In most human activities—even in most academic pursuits—the whole personality is much more involved, and the irrelevance of a person's sex far more dubious. Differences between the sexes are likely to come into play most in ordinary human relations where one person tells another what to do, or persuades, or cajoles or encourages or warns or threatens or acquiesces. In so far as most positions in society are concerned with social relations, it cannot be argued that the differences between the sexes are, of necessity, irrelevant. Although it might be the case that working men would as readily take orders from a fore-woman as a foreman, or that customers would be as pleased to find a handsome boy receptionist as a pretty girl, there is no reason to suppose that it must be so. . . . To deny people the fruits of their examination success or to deprive them of their liberty on any grounds irrelevant to their own desert is wrong: but it is not so evidently wrong to frustrate Miss Amazon's hopes of a military career in the Grenadier Guards on the grounds not that she would make a bad soldier but that she would be a disturbing influence in the mess room. Laws and institutions are characteristically two-faced. They set norms for the behaviour of different parties, and need to take into consideration the interests and claims of more than one person. They also need to apply generally, and cannot be tailor-made to each particular situation: they define roles rather than fit actual personalities, and roles need to fit the typical rather than the special case. Even if Miss Amazon is sure not to attract sidelong glances from the licentious soldiery, her sisters may not be; and it may be easier to operate an absolute bar than leave it to the recruiting officer to decide whether a particular woman is sufficiently unattractive to be safe. This type of case turns up in many other laws and public regulations. We lay down rigid speed limits because they are easier to apply. There are many towns in which to drive at thirty m.p.h. would be dangerous, and many suburbs in which to drive at forty-five m.p.h. would sometimes be safe. Some boys of ten are better informed about public affairs than other voters of thirty. But the advantage of having a fixed speed limit or a fixed voting age outweighs its admitted unfairness.

We can now see what sort of facts would bring what sort of principles to bear upon our individual decisions and the general structure of our laws and institutions. We need to know not only whether there are differences, but whether these differences are integrally or only contingently connected with a person's sex, and whether they apply in all cases or only as a rule. The more integrally and the more invariably a difference is connected with a person's sex, the more we are entitled to insist that the mere fact of being male or female can constitute a conclusive reason against being allowed to do something. The less integral a difference is, the more the arguments from Formal Equality (or Universalizability) and from Justice will come into play, requiring us to base our decisions only on the features relevant to the case in hand. The less invariable a difference is, the more the arguments from Humanity and again from Justice will come into play, requiring us to pay respect to the interests and inclinations of each individual person, and to weigh her actual interests, as against those of the community at large, on the basis of her actual situation and actual and reasonable desires.

However much I, a male, want to be a mother, a wife or a girlfriend, I am disqualified from those roles on account of my sex, and I cannot reasonably complain. Not only can I not complain if individuals refuse to regard me as suitable in those roles, but I have to acknowledge that it is reasonable for society generally to do so, and for the state to legislate accordingly. The state is justified in not countenancing homosexual "marriages," because of our general understanding of what marriage really is, and the importance we attach to family life. For exactly the same reasons, women are debarred from being regarded in a fatherly or husbandly light; and hence also in those parts of the Christian Church that regard priests as being essentially fathers in God from being clergymen or bishops. How far roles should be regarded as being integrally dependent on sex is a matter of dispute. In very intimate and personal relationships it is evident that the whole personality is involved, and that since a man—or at least many, non-Platonic men—responds to a woman in a different way from that in which he responds to a man or a woman to a woman, it is natural that these roles should be essentially dependent on sex. But as the roles become more limited, so the dependence becomes less. I could hardly complain if I was not given the part of Desdemona or a job as an *au pair*[3] boy on account of my sex: but if I had very feminine features and had grown my hair long and golden, or if I were particularly deft at changing nappies, I might feel a little aggrieved, and certainly I could call in question any law that forbade a man to play the part of a woman or be a nursemaid. Some substantial public good would need to be shown to justify a legal decision enforceable by penal sanctions being uniformly based not on my

[3][*Au pair* is a system of exchange students who help with the children and housework.]

actual inability to fill the role required but only my supposed unsuitability on account of my sex. We demand a higher standard of cogency in arguments justifying what laws there should be than in those concerned only with individual decisions; and although this standard can be satisfied, often by admitting considerations of the public good, yet the arguments need to be adduced, because, in framing laws, we need to be sensitive to individual rights and careful about our criteria of relevance. Although it may be the case that a nurse is a better nurse for having the feminine touch, we hesitate to deem it absolutely essential; and although many more women than men have been good nurses, we do not believe that it must invariably be so. There are male nurses. We reckon it reasonable to prefer a woman in individual cases, but do not insist upon it in all cases by law. We are reluctant to impose severe legal disqualifications, but equally would hesitate to impose upon employers an obligation not to prefer women to play female parts or to be nurses or to join a family in an *au pair* capacity. For we recognize that a person's sex can reasonably be regarded as relevant to his or her suitability for particular posts, and that many institutions will operate on this basis, and are entitled to. I am justified in refusing to employ a male *au pair* girl or a female foreman, although if there are many males anxious to be looking after young children or many women anxious to supervise the work of others, it may be desirable on grounds of Humanity to establish special institutions in which they can fulfil their vocations. If we will not let Miss Amazon join the Grenadier Guards, let there be an ATS or WRAC for her to join instead.

...

The would-be female Stakhanovite is penalized by the law forbidding firms to employ female labour for sixty hours a week, just as the youthful entrepreneur is handicapped by his legal incapacity, as a minor, to pledge his credit except for the necessities of life, and the skilled racing motorist by the law forbidding him to drive, however safely, at more than seventy miles per hour. In each case the justification is the same: the restriction imposed on the individual, although real and burdensome, is not so severe as to outweigh the benefits that are likely to accrue in the long run to women in general, or to minors, or to motorists. It is in the nature of political society that we forgo some freedoms in order that either we ourselves or other people can secure some good. All we can in general demand is that our sacrifices should not be fruitless, and that if we give up some liberty or immunity it is at least arguable that it will be on balance for the best.

Arguments in politics are nearly always mixed, and involve appeals to different principles, according to how the question is construed. We can elucidate some canons of relevance for some of the principles which may be invoked. Where the principle is that of Universal Humanity, the reason "Because you are a woman" is always irrelevant to its general applicability, though it may affect the way it is specified. . . . When the principle invoked is that of Formal Equality (or Universalizability) the reason "Because you are a woman" cannot be dismissed out of hand as necessarily irrelevant. A person's sex is not a "mere fact," evidently and necessarily separate from all other facts, and such that it is immediately obvious that no serious argument can be founded upon it. Particularly with those roles that involve relationships with other people, and especially where those relationships are fairly personal ones, it is likely to matter whether it is a man or a woman that is chosen. When some principle of Justice is at stake, the criteria of relevance become fairly stringent. We are concerned only with the individual's actions, attitudes and abilities, and the reason "Because you are a woman" must either be integrally connected with matter in issue (as in "Why cannot I marry the girl I love?") or be reliably, although only contingently, connected with it (as in "Why cannot I get myself employed for sixty hours a week?"); and in the latter case we feel that Justice has been compromised, although perhaps acceptably so, if there is no way whereby an individual can prove she is an exception to the rule and be treated as such. As the interests of the individual become more peripheral, or can be satisfied in alternative ways that are available, the principle of justice recedes, and we are more ready to accept rules and institutions based on general principles of social utility or tradition, and designed only to fit the general case. It is legitimate to base public feeling on such differences as seem to be relevant, but the more a law or an institution is based on merely a contingent, and not an integral, concomitance, the more ready we should be to cater for exceptions.

With sufficient care we may be able to disentangle what is true in the feminists' contention from what is false. At least we should be able to avoid the dilemma, which seems to be taken for granted by most participants in the debate, that we must say that women either are in all respects exactly the same as men or else are in all respects different from, and inferior to, them, and not members of the same universe of discourse at all. I do not share Plato's feelings about sex. I think the sexes are different, and incomparable. No doubt, women are not quite as good as men, *in some respects:* but since men are not nearly as good as women in others, this carries with it no derogatory implication of uniform inferiority. Exactly what these differences are, and, indeed, what sort of differences they are, is a matter for further research; and exactly what bearing they should have in the application of the various principles we value in making up our mind about social matters is a matter for further philosophical thought. But without any further thought we can align our emotions with the proponents of Women's Lib on the most important issue of all. What angers them most is the depersonalization of women in the Admass society: and one cannot but sympathize with their protest against women being treated as mere objects of sexual gratification by men; but cannot avoid the conclusion that their arguments and activities in fact lead towards just that result which they deplore. If we are insensitive to the essential femininity of the female sex, we shall adopt an easy egalitarianism which, while denying that there are any genetic differences, allows us to conclude in most individual cases that women, judged by male standards of excellence, are less good than their male rivals. Egalitarianism ends by depersonalizing women and men alike.

JOYCE TREBILCOT

Sex Roles: The Argument from Nature

Joyce Trebilcot considers several arguments for the conclusion that society ought to encourage and foster differences in personality and career choices between the sexes because of natural psychological differences. These psychological characteristics are not exclusively associated with either sex, but merely somewhat correlated with sex—just as men are typically taller than women, although some women are taller than some men. Trebilcot's points apply directly to Steven Goldberg's views (see pages 196–204, this volume).

Supposing for the sake of argument that, as Goldberg claims, hormones cause personality differences between the sexes, does it follow that certain sex roles are "inevitable" and should be taught? First, if the roles are biologically determined, there will be no need for society to inculcate or enforce them. On the other hand, if they are partly a result of social conditioning, then the conditioning could be changed, so they are not inevitable. Even natural but undesirable differences can be overcome by appropriate conditioning.

Goldberg makes another argument based on "well-being": most women will be happier if trained not to challenge men for traditionally male roles. Trebilcot points out that the happiness gained, say, by women who would otherwise have aspired to be surgeons and failed, must be weighed against the happiness of women who would have been happier as surgeons—plus the loss of freedom to all and the loss of the skill of some potential surgeons.

Lucas's argument from efficiency is also treated. He claims it would be "easier" to exclude Miss Amazon from the army than to screen and assess all women applicants. While Trebilcot agrees that efficiency is valuable, she points out that a great deal of efficiency must be gained to outweigh the value of the liberty, justice, and equal opportunity lost. In short, she argues that showing there are psychological differences between the sexes would not be enough to lead to the conclusion that sex role assignment should be practiced.

Further Reading

S. M. FARBER and R. L. WILSON, eds., *The Potential of Woman* (New York: McGraw-Hill, 1963).

MATINA S. HORNER, "Fail: Bright Women," *Psychology Today*, 3 (1969), 36–38, 62.

I am concerned here with the normative question of whether, in an ideal society, certain roles should be assigned to females and others to males. In discussions of this issue, a great deal of attention is given to the claim that there are natural psychological differences between the sexes. Those who hold that at least some roles should be sex roles generally base their view primarily on an appeal to such natural differences, while many of those advocating a society without sex roles argue either that the sexes do not differ in innate psychological traits or that there is no evidence that they do.[1] In this paper I argue that whether there are natural psychological differences between females and males has little bearing on the issue of whether society should reserve certain roles for females and others for males.

Let me begin by saying something about the claim that there are natural psychological differences between the sexes. The issue we are dealing with arises, of course, because there are biological differences among human beings which are bases for designating some as females and others as males. Now it is held by some that, in addition to biological differences between the sexes, there are also natural differences in temperament, interests, abilities, and the like. In this paper I am concerned only with arguments which appeal to these psychological differences as bases of sex roles. Thus I exclude, for example, arguments that the role of jockey should be female because women are smaller than men or that boxers should be male because men are more muscular than women. Nor do I discuss arguments which appeal directly to the reproductive functions peculiar to each sex. If the physiological processes of gestation or of depositing sperm in a vagina are, apart from any psychological correlates they may have, bases for sex roles, these roles are outside the scope of the present discussion.

[1]For support of sex roles, see, for example, Aristotle, *Politics*, Book I (reprinted in this volume); and Erik Erikson, "Womanhood and the Inner Space," *Identity: Youth and Crisis* (New York: W. W. Norton & Co., 1968). Arguments against sex roles may be found, for example, in J. S. Mill, *The Subjection of Women*, and Naomi Weisstein, "Psychology Constructs the Female" (both reprinted in this volume).

It should be noted, however, that virtually all those who hold that there are natural psychological differences between the sexes assume that these differences are determined primarily by differences in biology. According to one hypothesis, natural psychological differences between the sexes are due at least in part to differences between female and male nervous systems. As the male fetus develops in the womb, the testes secrete a hormone which is held to influence the growth of the central nervous system. The female fetus does not produce this hormone, nor is there an analogous female hormone which is significant at this stage. Hence it is suggested that female and male brains differ in structure, that this difference is due to the prenatal influence of testicular hormone, and that the difference in brains is the basis of some later differences in behavior.[2]

A second view about the origin of allegedly natural psychological differences between the sexes, a view not incompatible with the first, is psychoanalytical. It conceives of feminine or masculine behavior as, in part, the individual's response to bodily structure. On this view, one's more or less unconscious experience of one's own body (and in some versions, of the bodies of others) is a major factor in producing sex-specific personality traits. The classic theories of this kind are, of course, Freud's; penis envy and the castration complex are supposed to arise largely from perceptions of differences between female and male bodies. Other writers make much of the analogies between genitals and genders: the uterus is passive and receptive, and so are females; penises are active and penetrating, and so are males.[3] But here we are concerned not with the etiology of allegedly natural differences between the sexes but rather with the question of whether such differences, if they exist, are grounds for holding that there should be sex roles.

That a certain psychological disposition is natural only to one sex is generally taken to mean in part that members of that sex are more likely to have the disposition, or to have it to a greater degree, than persons of the other sex. The situation is thought to be similar to that of height. In a given population, females are on the average shorter than males, but some females are taller than some males, as suggested by Figure 1. The shortest members of the population are all females, and the tallest are all males, but there is an area of overlap. For psychological traits, it is usually assumed that there is some degree of overlap and that the degree of overlap is different for different characteristics. Because of the difficulty of identi-

---

[2]See John Money and Anke A. Ehrhardt, *Man and Woman, Boy and Girl* (Baltimore: Johns Hopkins Press, 1972); also Steven Goldberg (reprinted in this volume).

[3]For Freud, see for example "Some Psychological Consequences of the Anatomical Distinctions between the Sexes," in *Sigmund Freud: Collected Papers,* ed. James Strachey (New York: Basic Books, 1959), vol. 5, pp. 186–97. See also Karl Stern, *The Flight from Woman* (New York: Farrar, Straus & Giroux, 1965), ch. 2; and Erikson.

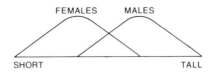

Figure 1

fying natural psychological characteristics, we have of course little or no data as to the actual distribution of such traits.

I shall not undertake here to define the concept of role, but examples include voter, librarian, wife, president. A broad concept of role might also comprise, for example, being a joker, a person who walks gracefully, a compassionate person. The genders, femininity and masculinity, may also be conceived as roles. On this view, each of the gender roles includes a number of more specific sex roles, some of which may be essential to it. For example, the concept of femininity may be construed in such a way that it is necessary to raise a child in order to be fully feminine, while other feminine roles—teacher, nurse, charity worker—are not essential to gender. In the arguments discussed below, the focus is on sex roles rather than genders, but, on the assumption that the genders are roles, much of what is said applies, *mutatis mutandis,* to them.

A sex role is a role performed only or primarily by persons of a particular sex. Now if this is all we mean by "sex role," the problem of whether there should be sex roles must be dealt with as two separate issues: "Are sex roles a good thing?" and "Should society enforce sex roles?" One might argue, for example, that sex roles have value but that, even so, the demands of individual autonomy and freedom are such that societal institutions and practices should not enforce correlations between roles and sex. But the debate over sex roles is of course mainly a discussion about the second question, whether society should enforce these correlations. The judgment that there should be sex roles is generally taken to mean not just that sex-exclusive roles are a good thing, but that society should promote such exclusivity.

In view of this, I use the term "sex role" in such a way that to ask whether there should be sex roles is to ask whether society should direct women into certain roles and away from others, and similarly for men. A role is a sex role then (or perhaps an "institutionalized sex role") only if it is performed exclusively or primarily by persons of a particular sex *and* societal factors tend to encourage this correlation. These factors may be of various kinds. Parents guide children into what are taken to be sex-appropriate roles. Schools direct students into occupations according to sex. Marriage customs prescribe different roles for females and males. Employers and unions may refuse to consider applications from persons of the "wrong" sex. The media carry tales of the happiness of those who conform and the suffering of the others. The law sometimes penalizes deviators. Individuals may ridicule and condemn role crossing and smile on conformity. Societal sanctions such as these are essential to the notion of sex role employed here.

I turn now to a discussion of the three major ways the claim that there are natural psychological differences between the sexes is held to be relevant to the issue of whether there should be sex roles.

1. INEVITABILITY

It is sometimes held that if there are innate psychological differences between females and males, sex roles are inevitable. The point of this argument is not, of course, to urge that there should be sex roles, but rather to show that the normative question is out of place, that there will be sex roles, whatever we decide. The argument assumes first that the alleged natural differences between the sexes are inevitable; but if such differences are inevitable, differences in behavior are inevitable; and if differences in behavior are inevitable, society will inevitably be structured so as to enforce role differences according to sex. Thus, sex roles are inevitable.

For the purpose of this discussion, let us accept the claim that natural psychological differences are inevitable. We assume that there are such differences and ignore the possibility of their being altered, for example, by evolutionary change or direct biological intervention. Let us also accept the second claim, that behavioral differences are inevitable. Behavioral differences could perhaps be eliminated even given the assumption of natural differences in disposition (for example, those with no natural inclination to a certain kind of behavior might nevertheless learn it), but let us waive this point. We assume then that behavioral differences, and hence also role differences, between the sexes are inevitable. Does it follow that there must be sex roles, that is, that the institutions and practices of society must enforce correlations between roles and sex?

Surely not. Indeed, such sanctions would be pointless. Why bother to direct women into some roles and men into others if the pattern occurs regardless of the nature of society? Mill makes the point elegantly in *The Subjection of Women:* "The anxiety of mankind to interfere in behalf of nature, for fear lest nature should not succeed in effecting its purpose, is an altogether unnecessary solicitude."[4]

It may be objected that if correlations between sex and roles are inevitable, societal sanctions enforcing these correlations will develop because

[4]Mill (p. 57, this volume).

people will expect the sexes to perform different roles and these expectations will lead to behavior which encourages their fulfillment. This can happen, of course, but it is surely not inevitable. One need not act so as to bring about what one expects.

Indeed, there could be a society in which it is held that there are inevitable correlations between roles and sex but institutionalization of these correlations is deliberately avoided. What is inevitable is presumably not, for example, that every woman will perform a certain role and no man will perform it, but rather that most women will perform the role and most men will not. For any individual, then, a particular role may not be inevitable. Now suppose it is a value in the society in question that people should be free to choose roles according to their individual needs and interests. But then there should not be sanctions enforcing correlation between roles and sex, for such sanctions tend to force some individuals into roles for which they have no natural inclination and which they might otherwise choose against.

I conclude then that, even granting the assumptions that natural psychological differences, and therefore role differences, between the sexes are inevitable, it does not follow that there must be sanctions enforcing correlations between roles and sex. Indeed, if individual freedom is valued, those who vary from the statistical norm should not be required to conform to it.

2. WELL-BEING

The argument from well-being begins with the claim that, because of natural psychological differences between the sexes, members of each sex are happier in certain roles than in others, and the roles which tend to promote happiness are different for each sex. It is also held that if all roles are equally available to everyone regardless of sex, some individuals will choose against their own well-being. Hence, the argument concludes, for the sake of maximizing well-being there should be sex roles: society should encourage individuals to make "correct" role choices.

Suppose that women, on the average, are more compassionate than men. Suppose also that there are two sets of roles, "female" and "male," and that because of the natural compassion of women, women are happier in female than in male roles. Now if females and males overlap with respect to compassion, some men have as much natural compassion as some women, so they too will be happier in female than in male roles. Thus, the first premise of the argument from well-being should read: Suppose that, because of natural psychological differences between the sexes, *most* women are happier in female roles and *most* men in male roles.

- The argument continues: If all roles are equally available to everyone, some of the women who would be happier in female roles will choose against their own well-being, and similarly for men.

Now if the conclusion that there should be sex roles is to be based on these premises, another assumption must be added—that the loss of the potential well-being resulting from societally produced adoption of unsuitable roles by individuals in the overlapping areas of the distribution is *less* than the loss that would result from "mistaken" free choices if there were no sex roles. With sex roles, some individuals who would be happier in roles assigned to the other sex perform roles assigned to their own sex, and so there is a loss of potential happiness. Without sex roles, some individuals, we assume, choose against their own well-being. But surely we are not now in a position to compare the two systems with respect to the number of mismatches produced. Hence, the additional premise required for the argument, that overall well-being is greater with sex roles than without them, is entirely unsupported.

Even if we grant, then, that because of innate psychological differences between the sexes members of each sex achieve greater well-being in some roles than in others, the argument from well-being does not support the conclusion that there should be sex roles. In our present state of knowledge, there is no reason to suppose that a sex role system which makes no discriminations within a sex would produce fewer mismatches between individuals and roles than a system in which all roles are open equally to both sexes.

3. EFFICIENCY

If there are natural differences between the sexes in the capacity to perform socially valuable tasks, then, it is sometimes argued, efficiency is served if these tasks are assigned to the sex with the greatest innate ability for them. Suppose, for example, that females are naturally better than males at learning foreign languages. This means that, if everything else is equal and females and males are given the same training in a foreign language, females, on the average, will achieve a higher level of skill than males. Now suppose that society needs interpreters and translators and that in order to have such a job one must complete a special training program whose only purpose is to provide persons for these roles. Clearly, efficiency is served if only individuals with a good deal of natural ability are selected for training, for the time and effort required to bring them to a given level of proficiency is less than that required for the less talented. But suppose that the innate ability in question is normally distributed within each sex and that the sexes overlap (see fig. 2). If we assume that

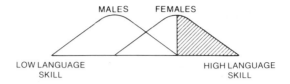

Figure 2

a sufficient number of candidates can be recruited by considering only persons in the shaded area, they are the only ones who should be eligible. There are no men in this group. Hence, although screening is necessary in order to exclude nontalented women, it would be inefficient even to consider men, for it is known that no man is as talented as the talented women. In the interest of efficiency, then, the occupational roles of interpreter and translator should be sex roles; men should be denied access to these roles, but women who are interested in them, especially talented women, should be encouraged to pursue them.

This argument is sound. That is, if we grant the factual assumptions and suppose also that efficiency for the society we are concerned with has some value, the argument from efficiency provides one reason for holding that some roles should be sex roles. This conclusion of course is only *prima facie.* In order to determine whether there should be sex roles, one would have to weigh efficiency, together with other reasons for such roles, against reasons for holding that there should not be sex roles. The reasons against sex roles are very strong. They are couched in terms of individual rights —in terms of liberty, justice, equality of opportunity. Efficiency by itself does not outweigh these moral values. Nevertheless, the appeal to nature, if true, combined with an appeal to the value of efficiency, does provide one reason for the view that there should be sex roles.

The arguments I have discussed here are not the only ones which appeal to natural psychological differences between the sexes in defense of sex roles, but these three arguments—from inevitability, well-being, and efficiency—are, I believe, the most common and the most plausible ones. The argument from efficiency alone, among them, provides a reason—albeit a rather weak reason—for thinking that there should be sex roles. I suggest, therefore, that the issue of natural psychological differences between women and men does not deserve the central place it is given, both traditionally and currently, in the literature on this topic.

It is frequently pointed out that the argument from nature functions as a cover, as a myth to make patriarchy palatable to both women and men. Insofar as this is so, it is surely worthwhile exploring and exposing the myth. But of course most of those who use the argument from nature take it seriously and literally, and this is the spirit in which I have dealt with it. Considering the argument in this way, I conclude that whether there should be sex roles does not depend primarily on whether there are innate psychological differences between the sexes. The question is, after all, not what women and men naturally are, but what kind of society is morally justifiable. In order to answer this question, we must appeal to the notions of justice, equality, and liberty. It is these moral concepts, not the empirical issue of sex differences, which should have pride of place in the philosophical discussion of sex roles.

CHRISTINE PIERCE

Natural Law Language and Women

Many authors have assigned roles or duties to women on the basis of what is "natural." Christine Pierce analyzes this general approach, separating two questions: (1) what do you mean when you call something "natural," and (2) are the things that are natural in this sense good?

"Natural" sometimes means "untouched by human invention" or "what most animals do." In these senses, what is natural is not necessarily good. Simply because air travel and umbrellas are "unnatural," along with birth control and appendectomies, we do not conclude that they are wrong. And if primates follow the law of the strongest or kill defective newborns, we do not conclude that people should, too.

Aristotle used "naturalness" in just the opposite way. According to him, women are naturally inferior because they lack part of the rational element that distinguishes humans from animals. So Aristotle assumed that it is what animals do not do—namely, reason—that is good. This results from his assumption that nature intended a certain "place" for everything—including women. Such talk of intentions and purposes makes sense only when we are investigating the actions of a person or other deliberate, rational agent. But nature is not a person doing everything for some intentional purpose. (Do rocks, sunspots, and earthquakes have a purpose?)

In short, Pierce shows the weakness of arguments based on what is "natural"—they can be adapted to support nearly any position. Yet even authors as liberated as John Stuart Mill and as recent as Senator Sam Ervin set out to investigate and draw conclusions from women's "natural" tendencies. What we need to discover, rather, is what arrangements are fair or good.

Further Reading

VIOLA KLEIN, *The Feminine Character: History of an Ideology* (London: Routledge & Kegan Paul, 1946).

LIONEL TIGER, *Men in Groups* (New York: Random House, 1969).

ASHLEY MONTAGU, *The Natural Superiority of Women* (London: George Allen & Unwin, Ltd., 1954).

"Nature" or "human nature" must be among the most enigmatic concepts ever used. Often, when the "natural" is invoked, we are left in the dark as to whether it is meant as an explanation, a recommendation, a claim for determinism, or simply a desperate appeal, as if the "natural" were some sort of metaphysical glue that could hold our claims or values together.

For centuries people have appealed to the "natural" to back up their moral and social recommendations. The ordinary uses of the term which everyone hears from time to time demonstrate that such efforts are still very much with us. We are told, for example, that suicide, birth control and homosexuality are wrong because they are unnatural. Now and then the use takes a positive form; motherhood is natural and hence the duty of women.

My major intent is to examine the language of "proper sphere," role, or function, showing its relationship to the language of natural law and pointing out problems in this kind of reasoning that are overlooked in the discussions of those who use this type of argument against women.

The following three examples characterize in a more extensive way the type of argument to be analyzed here. (1) in 1872, Myra Bradwell was refused admission to the Illinois bar by the state supreme court even though she had passed the bar entrance examination. Her suit, based upon the supposed right of every person, man or woman, to engage in any lawful employment for a livelihood, was denied. Justice Bradley, in his concurring opinion, opposed the idea that women might be attorneys on grounds that both God and nature disapprove.

> The civil law, as well as nature herself, has always recognized a wide difference in the respective spheres and destinies of man and woman. Man is, or should be, woman's protector and defender. The natural and proper timidity and delicacy which belongs to the female sex evidently unfits it for many of the occupations of civil life. The constitution of the family organization, which is founded in the divine ordinance, as well as in the nature of things, indicates the domestic sphere as that which properly belongs to the domain and functions of womanhood.[1]

A revised and expanded version of "Natural Law Language and Women," by Christine Pierce from *Woman in Sexist Society: Studies in Power and Powerlessness,* edited by Vivian Gornick and Barbara K. Moran, © 1971 by Basic Books, Inc., Publishers, New York. Research supported in part by a summer grant from the State University of New York Research Foundation.

[1] *Bradwell* v. *The State,* 83 U.S. 130, 141 (1872).

(2) In a statement denouncing abortion, Pope Pius XI assumed that nature assigns duties to women. "However much we may pity the mother whose health and even life is gravely imperiled in the performance of *the duty allotted to her by nature,* nevertheless what could ever be a sufficient reason for excusing in any way the direct murder of the innocent?"[2] (3) A paragraph from Étienne Gilson's commentary on Aquinas illustrates the incredible implications of a well-known view that identifies natural sexuality with the reproductive function. On this concept of nature, rape is preferable to masturbation.

> . . . To violate nature is to set oneself against God who has ordained nature. Now the worst way of violating nature is to carry corruption into its very principle. Fornication, rape, adultery, incest, respect nature's order in the performing of the sexual act. Unnatural vice, however, refuses to respect this order. The worst form of luxury is bestiality, and after it, sodomy, irregularities in the sexual act and onanism. . . . [3]

Rape, a violent action, is not recommended, but it is not as bad as consensual sodomy or interrupting heterosexual intercourse, because heterosexual rape allows for the possibility of fulfilling the purpose of sexuality, namely, procreation. At the very least, it seems somewhat peculiar to prefer sexual acts which are by definition unloving, violent abuses of persons to acts which need not be, and may be quite the contrary. Here we see the natural defined as function or purpose and applied to the sexual organs. It is assumed that procreation is the only purpose of sexual activity, and that fulfilling its function is what makes an act morally good and deviating from that function is what makes an act morally bad.

As a preface to analyzing these kinds of arguments, it is important to stress how difficult it is for anyone in any social or moral context to say what they mean by "natural" and why it recommends itself as good. Two distinct steps are involved here: defining what is meant by "natural" and arguing that what is natural is good. . . .

It is often assumed that the word "natural" has an automatic "plus" value tag which does not have to be argued for on independent grounds. In other words, it is taken for granted that if one persuades us that " 'X' is natural," he has also persuaded us that " 'X' is good." The Vatican's position on birth control reflects this: *Humanae Vitae* assumes that it is sufficient to point out that artificial means of birth control interrupt the

---

[2] *Encyclical Letter of Pope Pius XI on Christian Marriage,* St. Paul Editions (Boston, n.d.), p. 32. Emphasis added.

[3] Étienne Gilson, *The Christian Philosophy of Saint Thomas Aquinas,* trans. L. K. Shook (New York: Random House, 1956), p. 298.

natural order of things. The most significant question of all, "Why is 'natural order' a good thing?" is never asked. Apparently, what the "natural order" means in this case is that which will happen if untouched by human invention. This definition, however, yields absurd consequences if we try to use it as a prescription. If "natural order" is a good thing, and we must assume it is because we are told not to interrupt it, why isn't shaving a moral issue? Clearly, it is natural for hair to grow on a man's face, and shaving introduces an artificial means to disrupt the natural order of things.

One thing is evident: we cannot discuss whether the natural is good until we are able to state what we mean by the term. "Natural" can mean "untouched by human invention," but this use is not a coherent basis for normative judgments. A second meaning of "natural" sometimes applied to human beings is that human nature is everything that human beings do. As an explanation, this use is simply vacuous; if meant as a justification, however, it would justify everything. If things are morally right because they are natural, and if everything human beings do is natural, then everything human beings do is morally justified. The third and fourth meanings that I want to consider are particularly interesting, not only because of their relevance to arguments for women's inequality, but because both definitions are currently in use and yet clearly incompatible. Human nature is construed to be either what human beings have in common with the rest of the animal world or what distinguishes human beings from the rest of the animal world.

One of the most amusing efforts to make the third use work against women is the following comment by Mary Hemingway: "Equality, what does it mean? What's the use for it? I've said it before and I'll repeat: Women are second-class citizens and not only biologically. A female's first duty is to bear children and rear them. With the exception of a few fresh water fish, most animals follow this basic rule."[4] Unfortunately, the most obvious consequence of Hemingway's argument is that a few fresh water fish are immoral! What she meant to say, however, was that human duties somehow can be determined by observing animal behavior. *Prima facie,* it seems odd to claim that the meaningfulness of moral terminology could be derived from a realm to which moral vocabulary does not apply. We must insist that people who talk this way be able to make sense of it. What does it mean, for example, to say that nature intends for us to do certain things? We know what it means to say that "I intend to pack my suitcase," but what sense can it make to say that nature intends for us to do one thing rather than another? The above use of "natural" reduces to saying "this is what most animals do." To the extent that this is the meaning of the

4Mary Hemingway, *Look,* September 6, 1966, p. 66.

term, it will be hard to get a notion of value out of it. The fact that something happens a lot does not argue for or against it.

Interchanging words like "normal" and "natural" illustrates prejudice for the statistically prevalent as opposed to the unusual, the exception. The unusual *qua* unusual, however, cannot be ruled out as bad; it can be alternatively described as "deviant" or "original," depending on whether or not we like it. Nothing prevents describing the so-called sexual deviant as a sexual original except most people's inability to tolerate any unusual behavior in this area; hence, they use statistical concepts with bad connotations (unnatural, abnormal) to discuss it, instead of those with good connotations (original, exceptional).

The fourth meaning of "natural," that which distinguishes human beings from the rest of the (animal) world, reaches back to Plato. For Plato, to state the nature of any given class of things was to state the features of that class which distinguished it from all other classes of things. Although Plato did not claim that men and women have different natures, but rather referred to human beings as the class with the capacity to reason, his use of "natural" lends itself to the defining of classes of things according to function or role that is frequently used to restrict women. In order to understand how similar our way of talking and explaining things is to the Platonic view, it is first necessary to grasp how the latter has been historically conceived. An increased awareness of the natural law basis of the language of function should help us to be more critical of the language we take for granted, and to see what kinds of philosophical commitment we perhaps unwittingly make.

The Greek method of explanation for questions of the sort, "What is the nature of 'X'?" was teleological; explanations were given in terms of function, role, end or purpose, as opposed to mechanistic explanations. The difference between these explanations can easily be illustrated by comparing their answers to a simple question such as "What is a lawnmower?" A teleologist will explain: a lawnmower is something that is used to cut grass; a mechanist will explain about pulleys, plugs, and metal "teeth." Manufactured items lend themselves to the former type of explanation because hopefully we have in mind what the function of something is going to be before we start making any of it. Such explanation, however, is not so easily forthcoming for questions like, "What is the nature of human beings?" However, Plato was interested in this type of question; he wanted to explain the "natural" world. In this realm of nonmanufactured items, functions and roles are discovered, not created.

Although Plato thought he could answer the question concerning the nature of human beings, for the moment what concerns us is not the content of his answer, but the additional philosophical mileage we can expect from success in providing this type of answer. To be able to say what a thing is in terms of its function or purpose is simultaneously to set up standards for its evaluation. Once we can state the function of any "X," we can say what a good "X" is, or more precisely, we can say that "X" is good to the extent that it fulfills its function. We still have this use of "good" in English; we say, for example, that a good lawnmower is one that cuts grass well, that is, one that fulfills its function.

Plato's effort to apply this teleological framework to human beings consists of his functional analysis of the soul as reason, spirit, and desire. These are analogous to functioning units in the state, namely, philosopher-kings, soldiers, and artisans. Even as the function of the philosopher-king is to rule the state, implicit in the notion of reason as a function is the ability to rule, govern, or control the rest of the soul or personality. When anything does its work well, it is virtuous or excellent. In this case, when reason as well as every other functioning unit is working well and working together, the result is harmony or an order of soul to which Plato gives the name of the overarching virtue, justice. Reason, then, is the ordering principle; a good person is one who has an ordered soul, whose personality is controlled by reason.

Aristotle's agreement with both the teleological method and Plato's application of it to reason is evident when he says, "It is both natural and expedient for the body to be ruled by the mind, and for the emotional part of our natures to be ruled by that part which possesses reason, our intelligence."[5] But, for Aristotle, the soul's capacities vary for different classes of people. While the parts of the soul are present in women, slaves and children, "the slave has no deliberative faculty at all, the woman has, but it is without authority, and the child has, but it is immature."[6]

Plato may be the only philosopher to have held a doctrine of natural place which assigns social roles on the basis of individual merit rather than assigning places to whole classes of people as illustrated by the common-place statement, "woman's place is in the home." According to Plato, the nature (distinctive function) of human beings is reason, and a whole spectrum of rational abilities are distributed among human beings. One's nature, then, can be determined only by discovering one's talents, and, as Plato put it, "many women are better than many men in many things."[7] Aristotle believed the more familiar doctrine that whole classes of people —women, slaves—have their natural places: "as between male and female the former is by nature superior and the ruler, the latter inferior and subject."[8]

[5] Aristotle, *The Politics*, 1254b5 (trans. T. A. Sinclair), p. 25 in this volume.

[6] Aristotle, *The Politics*, 1260a13 (trans. Benjamin Jowett), p. 29 in this volume. Sinclair translates this passage: "the deliberative faculty in the soul is not present at all in a slave; in a female it is inoperative, in a child underdeveloped."

[7] Plato, *Republic*, 455d (trans. Allan Bloom). A full discussion of Plato's argument appears in my essay, "Equality: *Republic* V," *The Monist* 57:1, January, 1973.

[8] Aristotle, *The Politics*, 1254b14, p. 25 in this volume.

When the class of human beings is divided into men and women (or, perhaps better rendered, when women are not considered full human beings), the method of determining the essence of each often remains teleological, but for women the natural is no longer the rational but the biological. This type of move usually results in defining women as child-bearers and reserving rationally oriented roles for men. The biological interpretation of women's nature distorts the Platonic enterprise insofar as reproduction is not a function peculiar to human beings.

Assigning to women the same function as would be appropriate to a female of any species has serious consequences, since in citing the function or role of something, we are setting certain standards which it must measure up to in order to be called good. If we are suspicious of teleology, the quarrel is not with the fact that a use of "good" is generated by defining things in terms of function; the quarrel concerns what sort of "good" we are talking about. Are the standards referred to in maintaining that a good "X" is one that functions well moral standards or simply standards of efficiency? They are at least the latter; the worry is they are perhaps only that. When we say a good lawnmower is one that cuts grass well, we clearly mean good in the sense of efficient or effective. If, to take another example, we define poison in terms of its function, good poison is that which does an effective, that is, quick and fatal, job. The good referred to is clearly not moral good. However, this does not imply that a teleological or instrumental use of "good" could not also be a moral use.

There may be cases where the word "good" serves both functions. For example, when Lon Fuller, a Professor of Jurisprudence at Harvard Law School, defines good law as laws that are clear, public, consistent, he is claiming that such standards are necessary for moral, that is fair, laws as well as effective ones. Laws that are unclear, secret, and inconsistent are not only ineffective, but unjust. Although some jurisprudential scholars have argued against Fuller by maintaining that an instrumental use of good cannot be a moral use, there seems to be no *a priori* reason why a word cannot function simultaneously in more than one way. Granting this, the criticism of teleology is not as dramatic as some would have it. Morality based on teleology cannot be scrapped merely because we claim to have discovered that the teleological use of "good" is not a moral use but simply means that things are efficient. However, we must always be on guard to discover from context which use is intended since we can not assume that fulfilling a function or role is necessarily good in any moral sense.

For example, even if it is accepted that a good woman is one who fulfills her role, it may well be that "good" means nothing more than contributing to efficiency. Morton Hunt, in the May, 1970, issue of *Playboy,* argues against husband and wife sharing equally in all tasks (career and home) on the grounds that "when there is no specialization of function, there is inefficient performance. . . ."[9] Although specialization is supposedly one essential aspect of all successful human groups (the other being a system of leadership), it is quite conceivable that a group of two (as opposed to a large corporation) might not prize efficiency as its highest value.

Much depends upon what is meant by "success." Liberty or freedom of role choice may not be very "successful" if success is measured in terms of efficiency. Freedom has never been known for its efficiency; it is always getting in the way of the smooth operations of orderly systems. The conflict between freedom and efficiency can be illustrated by marriage, but is hardly confined to it. It may be inefficient for any one person (married, single, or living in a commune) to teach in a university, write articles, buy groceries, do karate, and demonstrate for political rights, but if a choice must be made between the freedom to do all these things and efficiency, the choice should at least be portrayed as a legitimate one.

Hunt argues not only that specific roles contribute to efficiency, but that they are (as opposed to unisex) attractive. "It feels good, and is productive of well-being, for man and woman to look different, smell different, act somewhat different."[10] He quotes Dr. Benjamin Spock to the effect that the sexes are "more valuable and more pleasing" to one another if they have "specialized traits and . . . roles to play for each other's benefit—gifts of function, so to speak, that they can give to each other." We cannot argue against the claim that specialization of function or role yields efficiency. We can, however, question the importance of efficiency; we can also ask, as we shall see later, efficient for whom? We cannot deny that many men and women find complementarity of role attractive. Some people even find inferiority attractive. Note once again the remarks of Mary Hemingway: "Equality! I didn't want to be Ernest's equal. I wanted him to be the master, to be the stronger and cleverer than I, to remember constantly how big he was and how small I was."[11] However, arguing that specific roles are efficient and attractive does not in and of itself determine who is to do what. Telling us in advance what woman's gift of function is going to be makes Hunt's argument typical of anti–women's liberation arguments that are couched in the language of role.

The *essential* content of woman's role is probably best characterized by the concept of "support"—a concept that usually does not get, but certainly deserves, much analysis. What do people mean by the "supportive role"? Why do they think it belongs to women? Hunt, after characterizing the roles of husband and wife as analogous to those of President and Speaker of the House respectively, concedes that "although the man is the

[9]Morton Hunt, "Up Against the Wall, Male Chauvinist Pig," *Playboy,* May, 1970, p. 209.

[10]*Ibid.,* p. 207. [Cf. Jaggar, this volume.]

[11]Hemingway, p. 66.

head, he owes much to his wife's managerial support."[12] To prove the value of support, he appeals to a remark once made by Senator Maurine Neuberger that her greatest single need as a senator was for a good "wife." Neuberger's comment certainly proves that the supportive role aids efficiency; it is undeniably easier to be a senator if one has someone to shake hands, smile with you on campaign posters, repeat your ideas to groups you have not time for, and answer your dinner invitations. That playing the supportive role aids efficiency cannot be questioned; however, the question remains efficient for whom? It must be remembered that efficiency only requires that *someone* play the supportive role, belong to the maintenance class, devote [his or her life] psychologically and physically to making sure that other people get done whatever they want done. As long as women as a class play supportive roles, they contribute to the efficiency of a power structure that excludes them from freedom of role choice.

Carried to the harshest extreme, slaves played a very important supportive role for their masters; from the masters' point of view, society was the more efficient and hence more desirable for it. Aristotle attests to the efficiency, if not the morality, of his view of natural arrangements when he says that slaves would not be needed if looms would weave by themselves.[13] In its weakest version, playing the supportive role can mean as little as the truism that everyone likes to be fussed over. What Hunt has in mind is something between the two and closer to the former, since he points to the current system as admittedly unfair, but more workable and satisfying than any other alternatives. Part of what he means by "supportive" can be gleaned from the fact that for the most part he is thinking in terms of cases involving children (although not all of his illustrations bear this out—for example, Neuberger). His perspective, then, centers around the social alternatives of the married woman. They are: the state may take care of the children, hired help may take care of the children, or we can introduce some notion of equality between men and women with regard to whatever tasks confront them, but this, as we have seen, will be inefficient.

Being an essentially pragmatic society, we often buy without question the latter half of the teleological framework: that good things are those that function well; we fail to scrutinize what we mean by "good." We easily overlook that having a function, even a so-called natural one, does not entail that those having it *ought* to use it. As we have seen, to use "X" when "X" is defined as functional is to have a good "X" in some sense of the word. We can explain what poison is by citing its function, but it does not necessarily follow that it ought (in any moral sense) to function. Having

[12]Hunt, p. 209.
[13]Politics, 1253b38.

children is also a natural function; whether it is good to make use of this function is a separate issue. Given our current population problems, we might well decide that childbearing is not good in either the moral or efficient use of that word.

One might, at this point, legitimately object that the well-being of human beings is more complicated than that of lawnmowers and poisons. If a lawnmower does not function well or is never used to cut grass, the lawnmower is not worse off for it. However, one might say, indeed Freudian conservatives have said, that the human being's biological potential is so integrated that when it is not realized, some kind of "maladjustment" or "unhappiness" results. Of course, some maintain that no such frustration ensues; obviously, to the extent that this is correct, there is no problem, and, for example, people can decide whether or not to have children on the basis of values already discussed (efficiency, morality) since their "happiness" or "adjustment" is not at stake.

However, if we accept the Freudian conservatives' view, we must apply it consistently. Freudians have also taught us that suppression of sexual and aggressive impulses was necessary for the development of civilization. Even though suppression may result in frustration, we are told that in some cases this is the price that must be paid to purchase other goals. It is certainly not a new observation that one pays in some way for everything that one gets. Certainly, in recent times, humanity has paid in increased anxiety, frustration, and, most probably, neuroses, for its advanced technological society. Freudians must allow the same perspective on the question of childbearing as on the questions of sexuality and aggressiveness. In the latter case, we realize that some sort of suppression, probably resulting in some unhappiness, is required for civilization and/or technology. Some women's deliberate suppression of their biological potential should be regarded as an enhancement of the civilized and rational aspects of experience. If there is some biological or psychological frustration involved in the suppression of biological potential, only the individual woman should decide how she wishes to balance her desire for biological "completion" and her desire to experience the world as an independent human being. To recognize the possibility of such unhappiness is not to condone social arrangements which intensify the either/or character of this choice, but to elucidate once again the importance of liberty, and to complicate values (liberty, morality, efficiency) by which we decide which units capable of functioning ought to function.

In the conclusion of his article, Hunt once more calls upon natural law, assuring us that we need not fear the eradication of all sex-role differences because "nothing as joyless and contrary to our instinct is likely to become the pattern of the majority."[14] The language of "instinct," a somewhat

---

[14]Hunt, p. 209.

modern way to refer to those things that we want to call "natural," is usually attached to some variation of philosophical determinism. "Instincts" are not considered to be matters of value choice, but a small class of desires that are somehow given. Some uses of "natural" lose their force without this built-in determinism; for example, excusing an action on the grounds that one was jealous, and "jealousy is only natural," will work only if the people listening accept the reasoning, "I couldn't help myself." If we do not buy the determinism, we do not buy the excuse.

Hunt's argument, and similar arguments from instinct, assume that that which is not the result of human effort is impervious to human control, since he moves from the claim that these instincts are "natural" (meaning by "natural," something that happens without our doing anything to bring it about) to the claim that they are unalterable. That is an empirical assumption which is extremely dubious; it would commit us to the position that, since gravity "naturally" keeps us on the ground, we could never raise ourselves off the ground. Natural instinct may be just as open to control through education and training as our response to gravity is to the technology of air travel. However, if we assume that the behavior related to instincts is unalterable and inevitable, we can guarantee much more than that their obliteration will not become "the pattern of the majority." As John Stuart Mill argued a hundred years ago in *The Subjection of Women,* if the "proper sphere" of women is naturally determined, there will be no need for social and legal coercion to insure that women stay in that sphere. We need not fear that women will do what they cannot do. There is no point in recommending that people desire what they inevitably will desire, so, insofar as we recommend that people adopt certain roles, we are assuming that those roles are, at least to some extent, items of choice. So, he cannot have it both ways: as soon as one uses a claim of naturalness to entail a claim of inevitability, one shows it to be inappropriate as a support for a recommendation to be natural.

In psychoanalytic literature, the notion of instinct is frequently replaced by that of unconscious desire. Freud, in his *New Introductory Lectures on Psycho-Analysis,* defined the unconscious as follows: ". . . We call a psychical process unconscious whose existence we are obliged to assume—for some such reason as that we infer it from its effects—but of which we know nothing."[15] In other words, the unconscious is not a thing, not some kind of container filled with desires that "drive" us to do this or that, but

---

[15]Sigmund Freud, *New Introductory Lectures on Psycho-Analysis* (1933), reprinted in E. Kuykendall, *Philosophy in the Age of Crisis* (New York: Harper & Row, 1970), p. 122. To philosophers the above sounds like the kind of move John Locke made when he posited the existence of material substance as an explanatory account for why collections of qualities regularly occur together. To the extent that the move is similar to Locke's, it is, of course, subject to the same types of criticisms.

rather an explanatory device, not itself empirically evident, but *needed* to explain certain behavior which is. "Needed," that is, in the sense that there are certain "effects" that defy explanation, that simply cannot be accounted for unless we posit an unconscious. For example, if people say they desire one thing, but act as if they desired the contrary, and we know they are not lying, we may be tempted to say that they are somehow unaware of what their "real" motivation is.

If Susan says she wants a career more than anything else in the world, but she does nothing all day except stay home and put on make-up, we are puzzled and desire an explanation. If she is not lying or frivolous, we still lack an explanation; anything, including childhood and gene structure, is fair game as far as possible explanations go. But if Leslie has spent eight years preparing for a career and assures a prospective employer that she is serious about it, she does not deserve as an answer: "I would like to believe you, my dear, but all women really desire to devote their lives to men and children. . . ." Such a remark is unwarranted because there are no "effects" in this case that need to be explained. (Of course, external evidence of competence, such as Ph.D.'s and M.D.'s, do help when one wants to be taken seriously. The undergraduate argument, "she only went to college to find a husband," does not seem so plausible when applied to Ph.D.'s. There simply has to be an easier way to get a husband!)

. . .

I have tried to show some of the muddles that language of the "natural" gets us into. Except in cases where the natural is defined in terms of purpose or function, it carries no automatic value tag, and in no case carries an automatic moral implication. After finding out what a person means by "natural," we then have to decide on independent grounds whether what is meant is in any sense good. For example, why is it good to do what animals do, or to avoid invented devices which interrupt what ordinarily happens? Why is what ordinarily happens considered to be a good thing? What is so good about order? Teleological uses of "natural" automatically set up an evaluative context; knowing the function of "X" makes it possible for us to evaluate "X" on grounds of functioning well. But as we have seen, teleological uses have to be morally evaluated: a good bomb is one that destroys, but is a good bomb morally good?

There is no reason to assume that the problem of evaluation would change because some things are created by persons and others are not. Many people, for example, argue that nature is good because God made it. This, of course, precipitates the old problem of evil. How can earthquakes and birth defects be good? The answer does not abandon the language of purpose, but rather tells us in Platonic fashion that all of "creation" functions for some good end; however, humans are incapable of knowing this end or purpose. Indeed, part of what it means to have faith is to believe that all natural (that is, created) purposes (in humans or otherwise) are good purposes, and work together toward some larger purpose. Since human beings cannot know this larger end, there is no way that they can evaluate it. This, however, does not eliminate the problem of evaluation. It does not eliminate the question, "In what sense are things that function well good?" It simply tells us that there is no cognitive answer, or more precisely, that only the faithful, after they have been faithful in believing the acceptability of God's answer, will receive an answer. The position comes to this: because we believe in God, we should believe that nature is good in some good sense.

Theological positions, however, in no way exempt us from either defining what we mean by "natural" or appraising it. Indeed, even if the ultimate evaluation is said to be a matter of faith, the task that Thomas Aquinas referred to as natural or rational theology (the spelling out of the ends of things that are imprinted on the natures of things) is something that human beings must be prepared to perform without divine assistance. This task brings us right back to the beginning of our inquiry, namely, what in the world do people mean when they say that " 'X' is natural"?

ONORA O'NEILL

How Do We Know
When Opportunities Are Equal?

*The strongest form of equality Bernard Williams distinguished was the ideal of
equal opportunity. Onora O'Neill attempts to explicate this ideal and finds two
different interpretations available.*

Formal equal opportunity *is the weaker version. On this view, equal
opportunity is attained if schools and employers ignore irrelevant characteristics,
such as sex and race, in admissions and hiring. This is like Williams's example
of the society which opens military careers to the poor, without taking into
consideration whether the undernourishment of the poor could nevertheless keep
them from qualifying. Mere formal equal opportunity takes the qualifications of
the candidates as given, even if they did not have the same chance to develop
those qualifications.*

Substantive equal opportunity *includes the background conditions under
which the candidates' qualifications developed. Unless women as a group have
the same statistical chance as men to become surgeons, equal opportunity in this
sense has not been attained, O'Neill says. This view requires such equalization
in achievement only between the* major *social groups, however. (It is not
required that the tone deaf be as well represented in orchestras as those with
perfect pitch, for example.) Nor is it necessary that every* individual *have the
same chance as every other, since native abilities may differ.*

*How far substantive equality should go is still a problem. If two groups have
different native abilities for a task, are equal* results *required? Is a society in
which half of the professional football players are not women lacking in equal
opportunity? Or what if we offer the same education and incentives to all, but
some groups work harder and benefit more from it than others do? At the
extreme, substantive equality would go too far if it required us to artificially
make all groups statistically alike in their resulting achievements.*

Further Reading

JOHN RAWLS, *A Theory of Justice* (Cambridge, Mass.: Harvard University Press, 1971), §14.

T. D. CAMPBELL, "Equality of Opportunity," *Proceedings of the Aristotelian Society*, 75 (1974–75), 51–68.

MICHAEL MARTIN, "Equal Education, Native Intelligence and Justice," *Philosophical Forum*, 6 (1974), 29–39.

JUDITH THOMSON, "Preferential Hiring," *Philosophy and Public Affairs*, 2 (1973), 364–84.

I shall start my argument from the very simple observation that "equal" is an incomplete predicate. If someone asks whether A and B are equal we have to ask "equal in which respect?" before we can answer the question. Once we know that we are being asked whether they are equal in height or weight or wealth or health we know which sorts of measurements and observations are relevant to answering the question. Yet when we are asked whether A and B are equal *in opportunity,* it is not at all obvious which measurements or observations are relevant to answering the question.

I believe that this unclarity has two separate sources. It is attributable in the first place to the fact that "equal in opportunity" is still an incomplete predicate; secondly to an ambiguity in the concept of "opportunity." I shall deal with these unclarities in turn, and hope in doing so to reach some substantive as well as some analytical conclusions.

To complete the predicate "equal in opportunity" we need only note that all opportunities are opportunities to do or enjoy some activity or benefit. Schematically any opportunity is an opportunity to do *x*—an opportunity to visit Tokyo or an opportunity to earn $20,000 or an opportunity to win a lottery. There are many sorts of opportunities whose equal distribution is not of particular concern to us. A society can choose to equalize the opportunity to live in a home fit for a hero or the opportunity to have a chicken in every pot, but the opportunities which these symbolize and which are usually thought important for a just society are mainly educational and occupational opportunities. An equal opportunity society does not have to offer each person exactly the same work, commodities, recreation, friends, and so on, but in a broad sense it is supposed to give each person an equal opportunity for educational and occupational attainment, where "attainment" is interpreted so as to cover both the learning or work and the credentials or pay that schools and jobs provide.

But when we complete the predicate "equal in opportunity" as "equal in opportunities for educational and occupational attainment" we are little the wiser about the criteria for attributing equal opportunities for such attainment. The problem is not merely that educational and occupational attainment may be harder to measure than height and weight, wealth and health. It lies rather in a systematic ambiguity in the criteria for judging when opportunities are equal. I shall call them respectively the formal and the substantive interpretation of equal opportunity. I shall spend no time investigating the grounds for preferring either of these interpretations; my aim is to disentangle them.

THE FORMAL INTERPRETATION OF "EQUAL IN OPPORTUNITY"

A familiar interpretation of equal opportunity sees two persons, A and B, as having equal opportunities in some respect if neither faces a legal or quasi-legal obstacle in doing something which the other does not face. Under this formal interpretation A and B can have equal opportunities with respect to x without being likely to enjoy x. Jencks and his associates start from this formal interpretation of equal opportunity; they describe it as the demand "that the rules determining who succeeds and who fails should be fair," and argue that "equal opportunity is not enough to ensure equal results."[1]

On this view, once the rules governing admissions to places of education, appointments to jobs and promotions are fair, a society is an equal opportunity society. If no classes of persons are debarred by law or the policies of medical schools and licensing bodies from qualifying and practicing as doctors, then all persons have equal opportunities to become doctors—even though it might turn out that a derisory number of women or blacks succeed in being doctors. If women are not barred from engineering school on account of their sex, then they have equal opportunity to become engineers—and the fact that very few do so cannot be attributed to any inequality of opportunity.

This formal interpretation of equal opportunity is part and parcel of the classical liberal tradition of political thought, in that it is mainly an extension of the idea of securing the equal liberties of all persons. Just as the removal of class, income, race and sex obstacles could make all persons able

---

[1]Christopher Jencks, *Inequality: A Reassessment of the Effect of Family and Schooling in America* (New York, 1972), p. 3 and p. 37.

to vote, hold property, serve on juries, hold office, and so on, so a removal of legal obstacles could open up places of education and employment to persons from all social groups. Where access to a place of education or a type of employment had to be restricted, selection procedures which took account not of social status, but of relevant qualifications, were devised. The career open to talents is a career entered by competitive examination.

The selection procedures devised to admit, employ and promote on "non-discriminating" criteria have generally produced results which were highly unequal in two respects. First they have produced societies whose members were extremely unequal in educational and occupational attainment whether measured by competence, credentials, income or status. This in itself is not worrying to liberals who regard the unequal results as justifiable if everyone had an equal opportunity to succeed. After all, selection procedures are needed in the first place only in societies where certain sorts of positions are fewer than the number of people wanting them, so candidates cannot all succeed. But the second type of unequal results of the supposedly "non-discriminating" selection procedures has worried liberals of certain sorts. For these selection procedures frequently lead to disproportionate success in some social groups and correspondingly disproportionate failure in others.

If such disproportion is to be justifiable according to liberals it must be the result only of the varying capacities and desires of those to whom the selection procedures are applied. So males might be justifiably underrepresented as nurses or secretaries if they lack the appropriate desires/capacities, and for the same reasons females might justifiably be underrepresented among executives and undertakers. Blacks might be underrepresented among upper income groups either unjustifiably because of the effects of legal obstacles at some earlier stage of their education and careers or justifiably because of different desires and capacities. In the view of the classical liberal a complete equality of opportunity will prevail when all remaining legal and quasi-legal obstacles to educational and occupational attainment have been eliminated, and when sufficient time has passed for the people who may once have been hindered by such obstacles to have died. Such an "equal opportunity society" would however not be characterized by equal incomes or equal property holdings or equal standards of living or of education. Nor need it be characterized by the proportionate representation of all social groups in all lines of activity and income strata. Equal opportunity in the formal sense does not ensure equal success or equal health or equal status but only the fair application of the rules governing the pursuit of such goods. This is the equality of opportunity of a competitive, meritocratic society, a society in which there are winners and losers, and in which winning appears often as merited by the winners and losing as deserved by the losers—for did they not all have equal opportunity to win?

While the liberals are not bothered by unequal educational and occupational attainments, many of them have been concerned that at least some of the disproportionate success and failure rates of certain social groups reflected more than capacities and desires and have often inferred from this that selection procedures have not yet been devised that are truly non-discriminating. Two types of response are commonly made to this problem. The narrower one is to claim that certain allegedly non-discriminating procedures are in fact culturally biased: for example I.Q. tests discriminate against children from certain backgrounds; employment agencies treat applicants of different sexes and races differently; promotions are often made on criteria other than on-the-job performance. These problems, and they are surely still common, are exactly the ones which the formal interpretation of equal opportunity is equipped to handle. A broader response to this problem is to look at a person's educational and occupational attainments over a longer stretch of time and hence to uncover a wider range of selection procedures which may have been discriminating. For example the disproportionately low representation of persons from poor families in college preparatory high school programs or of women in mathematics programs may be due to their lack of opportunity at an earlier stage of life and consequent redirection of their capacities and desires. They may have had access only to an inferior school with less financing, less varied curriculum and so on, or they may have had their aspirations and ambitions systematically belittled and questioned. If desires and capacities themselves have been produced or modified by earlier educational and occupational experiences, the justice of conferring success on their basis becomes questionable. Hence in the name of redressing past discrimination a limited sort of favoritism is often advocated: colleges and professional schools may set a lower admissions hurdle for certain sorts of applicants; employers may (at least apparently) make special efforts to employ persons from groups that are under-represented. Such moves mark a shift from a purely formal conception of equal opportunity towards a more substantive one, to which I shall now turn.

THE SUBSTANTIVE INTERPRETATION
OF "EQUAL IN OPPORTUNITY"

The one selection procedure which all agree is non-discriminating is the lottery. If each major social group had a number of tickets in a lottery proportionate to its representation in the population, then we would expect the prizes to be distributed to each major social group in the same proportion. The same proportion of women as of men, of blacks as of whites, of old as of young, would win the prizes. This situation provides the paradigm of the view which I shall call the substantive or actuarial interpretation of equality of opportunity. On this view opportunities for A and B with respect to x are to be regarded as equal not because neither faces legal or quasi-legal obstacles which the other does not face, but because they belong to social groups whose rates of success at obtaining x are equal. An equal opportunity society on the substantive view is one in which the success rates of all major social groups are the same. On the substantive interpretation of equal opportunity, preferential and quota admissions and hirings and promotions are justifiable not because they apply standards in a non-discriminating way (they don't) but because they confer equal (or at least less unequal) rewards.

On the substantive view of equal opportunity women have an equal opportunity to enter law school only if they are admitted in proportions appropriate to the number who apply, and their applications are not being deterred or reduced by any policy of the school so that the pool of applicants contains all women who wish to go to that law school. And on this view a company can truthfully claim to be an equal opportunity employer only if appropriate proportions of its jobs at all levels are held by workers from various minority groups, or, where this is not the case, there is evidence of serious attempts to recruit and promote members of the under-represented groups. A strong commitment to substantive equality of opportunity demands that any under-representation of some group in some line of employment/income group/educational group be due solely to the unmanipulated choice of members of that group. Substantive equality of opportunity is not breached if Hassidic Jews are under-represented among those who have Saturday jobs; it is breached if women are under-represented among those promoted to supervisory rank. In many cases it may be harder to tell when choices are unmanipulated.

A society which confers substantive or actuarial equal opportunity is very different from one which aims at equal results, such as equal incomes, equal education, equal health and welfare or equal standards of living. Substantively equal opportunity is achieved when the success rates of certain major social groups—such as the two sexes, various ethnic groups and perhaps various age groups—are equalized. It is not breached when there are large differences between the most and least successful members of these groups, provided that there are equally large differences between the most and least successful members of the other major social groups. It is not true in a society which aims at substantively equal opportunities that all individuals have the same chance of any given type of success. For individuals are all members of many differently defined groups, and substantive equal opportunity seeks only to equalize their chances of success *qua* members of certain major social groups; it seeks to eliminate inter-group differences, but not to alter intra-group ones. If A is a highly qualified woman, and B a slightly retarded man, then substantively equal opportunity would give them the same chance, *qua* woman and *qua* man, of earning, say, $20,000 a year, but it would not alter the fact that A has, *qua* highly qualified, a far greater chance of doing so. Substantively equal opportunity would yield equal results only if the groups whose success rates were to be equalized included all those groups consisting of a single person.

By and large a move from a formal to a substantive view of equal opportunity becomes controversial only when a scarce and widely coveted educational or occupational attainment is at issue. Nobody objects if the opportunity to enter second grade, which is almost universally available, results in a proportionate representation among all second graders of all social groups. And nobody objects because disproportionately many stee-plejacks are Mohawks or tries to gain proportionate representation for other groups. But if a substantive interpretation of equal opportunity to enter law school would result in a proportionate representation among law students and, later, lawyers of all social groups, then (given that not all groups have the same distribution of qualifications), there is likely to be considerable opposition to a move from a formal to a substantive interpretation of equal opportunity from members of groups which are disproportionately successful under the formal interpretation. In particular it has been urged that preferential and quota admissions and hiring policies which fail to prefer the more qualified will lead to a less competent performance and are both unjust and inefficient.

Advocates of preferential and quota admissions and hiring policies concede that a certain price in efficiency is (reasonably) incurred in pursuit of justice but claim that the price will not be high (at least for many jobs) since the relevance of job qualifications to job performance is often meager and, in any case, people grow on the job. In return they can point to certain longer run increases in efficiency which a break in favor of the disadvantaged might bring, for in the long run substantive equal opportunity maximizes the size of the pool of applicants for any position, affording the greatest choice among candidates. But they have a less ready answer on the question of justice. Some concede that an injustice is done to those better qualified candidates who are passed over, but contend that to do so is the only solution to the variation in the proportion of qualified candidates which past discrimination has produced in each social group. In the long run, it is supposed, the cumulative elimination of differential rates of attainment in different social groups at successive stages in their careers may eliminate the need for compensatory educational programs, preferential admissions and hiring and promotion. In the words of a defense brief in the *De Funis* case:

> our society cannot be completely color blind in the short term if we are to have a color blind society in the long term.

The substantive interpretation of equal opportunity builds on a central feature of the idea of opportunity. To have an opportunity to do x is to have a chance to do x, and for A and B to have an equal opportunity to do x is for them to be equally likely (*qua* members of certain reference classes) to do x. A substantively equal opportunity society equalizes the rate of educational and occupational attainment of all major social groups. If it wants *also* to demand certain prerequisites or qualifications for certain positions, then it has to ensure that these prerequisites and qualifications are met equally frequently by members of all social groups. Only so can the demands of meritocratic admissions, hiring and promotions be combined with substantively equal opportunities. This combination of demands makes a commitment to substantive equal opportunity an embarrassing position for liberals to take.

SUBSTANTIVELY EQUAL OPPORTUNITY
AND SELECTION PROCEDURES

The work of Jencks and his associates shows very clearly how enormous the task of equalizing the distribution of qualifications and competences in all social groups would be. Schools as we know them are hardly equipped for the task. Still, schools need not remain as we know them. Could not a more radical restructuring of education achieve just what the compensatory programs had in mind: a situation where all people are prepared to grasp the opportunities available for them, and so one in which the distribution of qualifications for educational and occupational success are equalized for all groups? If this were possible meritocratic selection procedures could be combined with substantive equality of opportunity, at least in the long run.

The evidence on such an issue is, of course, incomplete and any conclusion must be tentative. But it seems that an effective equalization of the distribution of handicaps would have to take control of children's lives to an extent not envisaged by school systems today. Children from each major social group would have to be given a distribution of health care, diet, socialization, consideration and respect, as well as of schooling, which would ensure the same distribution of competences: for the treatment of all groups would have to provide the same distribution of intra-group differences. But such a control of children's lives would not be acceptable to classical liberals or even probably to ordinary or woolly minded ones. Liberals of all sorts do not object to the control of children (within reason) but they are committed to respect the rights of parents and thereby to denouncing attempts to remove such rights and place the control of children in the hands of government agencies. Yet short of such measures it is difficult to see how equality of opportunity can ever be more than formal and from one standpoint a sham: a pretense that certain goods are equally accessible to persons of all backgrounds when in fact they are far more easily available to persons from some groups than others. A pretense, furthermore, which unfairly shifts the burden of failure and the pride of success onto those who have in the first place been denied or granted the advantages which enable people to win in the system of selection for success.

But it is not only liberals who will find some difficulty in accepting a complete program of engineering substantive equality of opportunity, by producing the same distribution of competences and incompetences in all social groups. The institutions needed to achieve these distributions end up imposing far more than substantive equality of opportunity: they demand actual equality of attainment at earlier stages of a career as the only basis for substantive equality achieved on meritocratic principles at later stages. To use meritocratic principles at later stages we would have to avoid them at earlier stages—lest any group end up disproportionately likely to succeed or fail on these selection procedures. Something it seems must give: either we abandon a commitment to meritocratic selection procedures within the schools and so can engineer some substantive equality of attainment which in turn can be the basis for a stage of substantive equality of opportunity; or we use meritocratic selection procedures from early on in the educational/career ladder, produce different proportions of different competences in different social groups and will not later be able to combine substantive equality of opportunity with meritocratic selection procedures. The option which is closed is that of consistently using meritocratic selection procedures and yet expecting all social groups to develop the same distribution of competences and so to have substantively equal opportunities at later stages of their careers. This point does not depend on assuming that different social groups differ genetically and so that their performance will diverge under meritocratic selection; it depends only on the assumption that different social groups differ and so will have different success rates on various selection tests, and that a succession of such tests, where success in earlier ones earns privileges in preparation for later ones, will produce quite sharply divergent success rates.

Under competitive, meritocratic selection procedures substantive equality of opportunity is an inherently transitory phenomenon. For it presupposes a uniform distribution of competence among members of each major social group which could only have been produced by an imposed distribution of treatment, i.e. by social institutions in which opportunity is no issue. But it leads to a diversity of attainment, which will be reflected in different abilities to grasp future opportunities, and so to a diminution of substantive equality of opportunity. Only a society whose various social groups have lost their diversity and consistently turn out to have the same distribution of competences could remain a substantively equal opportunity society over a long period.

I don't believe that this means that there is no choice in these matters, but rather that there are many choices. The task is to balance liberty against both equality and efficiency, and there are many ways of doing so. If we want both liberty and short run efficiency then we must choose competitive selection procedures and settle for formal equal opportunity. If we want to retain liberty but are willing to sacrifice some short run efficiency then we can equalize the occupational attainments of different social groups to the extent we wish to by selection procedures which disregard competence to some extent and aim at proportionate representation of all major social groups. All selection procedures would require quotas to be met; success and failure would depend on social origin as well as competence; substantive equality of opportunity would be institutionalized. If we want to have short and long run efficiency and a considerable range of equalities, the price must be paid in liberty. We can combine meritocratic selection procedures with various sorts of equality if we choose to minimize differential rewards for different attainments. If incomes and wealth and prestige were more equal the pain of failure and joy of success would be lessened, and though there would (given meritocratic selection procedures) be no substantive equality of opportunity, this might be compensated for by more equal results. The lives of the successful and unsuccessful would be more similar.

Apart from these three pure policies there is possible any number of interim or combination policies. For example one might choose to sacrifice some efficiency or some liberty at some stages of an educational system in return for a less glaringly uneven distribution of competences with the consequence that a subsequent application of meritocratic selection procedures would, while still producing an inegalitarian society, produce less divergent success rates for different major social groups. Policies which tend in this direction, i.e. towards substantive equal opportunity, include compensatory educational programs, the abolition of tracking and acceleration, the extension of open admissions. Or one could choose to bypass substantive equality of opportunity in favor of some increase in equality of results with a sacrifice of liberty but not of efficiency. Policies which tend in this direction include income redistribution; ensuring more equal access to good schools, good medical care, good transportation.

Affirmative action plans are among the mildest of such compromise policies. They try to achieve somewhat greater substantive equality of opportunity without sacrificing either liberty or efficiency. Although affirmative action plans may set target employment goals, these are not enforced,[2] provided employers show that they have made good faith efforts to meet them. Affirmative action in a context in which candidates from certain social groups are hardly ever successful in practice achieves no more than formal equality of opportunity, by requiring selection procedures to disregard certain traditional but irrelevant "qualifications." An employer who has filed an affirmative action plan is committed to tip evenly balanced scales in favor of a candidate from an under-represented group. But this degree of "favoritism" does not require any sacrifice of efficiency either in the short or in the long run: no more qualified candidate was available. Nor can it be regarded as an injustice to the unsuccessful candidates, whose qualifications were not superior to those of the successful candidate. In spite of this, candidates from groups accustomed to favoritism may resent its loss. Preferential and quota admissions, hiring and promotion are rather stronger policies aiming at greater substantive equality of opportunity at the expense of some sacrifices of liberty and efficiency. But these policies too hardly threaten the whole system of differential rewards and meritocratic selection procedures. Candidates from any major social group are still ranked on the basis of their qualifications, but candidates from different major social groups may not be ranked against one another. The result may be that some groups of successful candidates are on average less qualified than others. This may involve at least short run sacrifices of efficiency, but the impact of this sacrifice can vary greatly in its seriousness. Most jobs can be adequately filled by a great range of candidates and the penalty for having less than the best is not great, though there are exceptions, such as neurosurgeons and pilots, whose rarity may be suggested by the frequency with which the same examples recur in discussions. Further most qualifications are imperfect predictors of job performance; there are enormous numbers of positions for which the main qualification is to be appointed to them. Preferential and quota policies also pass over some candidates with superior qualifications. But if these qualifications are in some measure the result of earlier special treatment, rather than of intrinsic merit, then the injustice of failing to reward these candidates further is slight. It amounts only to a refusal to allow those who have won earlier races headstarts in later races.

SUBSTANTIVELY EQUAL OPPORTUNITIES
AND EQUAL RESULTS

An increase in substantive equality of opportunity is the avowed goal of many reforms in educational and employment practices in the U.S. today. I have argued that the cost of such reforms in terms of efficiency

[2]Cf. Gertrude Ezorsky, "Fight over University Women," *The New York Review of Books,* Vol. XXI, 8, May 1974.

may be relatively slight, and that the injustice to those whose qualifications are passed over is not great if qualifications are capacities and desires conferred by earlier success. But the justice of substantively equal opportunities should also be looked at from the point of view of the results it produces.

In principle substantive equality of opportunity could be produced without any overall decrease in the inequality of results. The distribution of income, wealth, education and prestige could remain as sharply pyramidal as in a society without substantively equal opportunity. The difference would be that each segment of the pyramid would contain the same proportion of persons from each major social group. Yet if there are grounds for objecting to unequal results for different groups, are there not also grounds for objecting to unequal results for different individuals? Is privilege conferred on the qualified less objectionable than privilege conferred by race, sex, or social background? This raises deeper considerations about efficiency and incentives, and about the grounds of obligation, than I intend to handle here. I shall note only that practice may go further than principle. The actuarial basis of substantively equal opportunity is neutral on the justifiability of unequal results. But a society which tries to equalize the success rates for different major social groups may set up powerful incentives for conferring more equal results on all individuals.

The educational arrangements needed to combine substantively equal opportunities with some concern for qualifications and efficiency must produce the same distribution of competences in each social group. Hence access to certain sorts of training could not be limited to any one social group. The exclusiveness of institutions which are *de facto* (let alone *de jure*) segregated by race, ethnic background or sex would be eliminated. It does not follow that the heritability of success and failure would be eliminated; but it would at least be reduced. Social groups and families would be less able to ensure the success of their members than they could in a society in which success and failure rates differ in different groups, and this provides the successful with a powerful incentive for making even failure tolerable.

LISA NEWTON

Reverse Discrimination as Unjustified

Equal opportunity has not existed in our society in the past. Should we now favor the groups previously discriminated against, to correct this situation? This is the issue of preferential treatment, also known as reverse discrimination.

Lisa Newton opposes preferential treatment. Her ideal of equality is that of equal citizenship, of equality under the laws. Formal equality alone dictates that the laws should not make special considerations for special groups. If the laws cannot make such exceptions, she argues, then they cannot make exceptions for previously disadvantaged groups, either, without violating equal opportunity. Thus, formal equal opportunity alone appears to rule out preferential treatment.

Another argument Newton advances is that everyone is a member of some group which can demand to be favored. This amounts to a challenge to Onora O'Neill to clarify the notion of equal opportunity applying to the "major social groups." Newton also asks what quantity of preferential treatment will be considered sufficient to compensate the wronged group. And cannot the previously favored group then claim that compensation is due to it in turn, as the disadvantaged party under the reverse discrimination? By these arguments, Newton concludes that reverse discrimination cannot be justified.

Further Reading

JAMES W. NICKEL, "Discrimination and Morally Relevant Characteristics," *Analysis,* 32 (1972), 146–50.

J. L. COWAN, "Inverse Discrimination," *Analysis,* 33 (1972), 10–12.

MICHAEL BAYLES, "Reparations to Wronged Groups," *Analysis,* 33 (1972), 182–84.

PAUL W. TAYLOR, "Reverse Discrimination and Compensatory Justice," *Analysis,* 33 (1973), 177–82.

MICHAEL BAYLES, "Compensatory Reverse Discrimination in Hiring," *Social Theory and Practice,* 2 (1973), 301–12.

WILLIAM T. BLACKSTONE, "Reverse Discrimination and Compensatory Justice," *Social Theory and Practice,* 3 (1975), 253–88.

I have heard it argued that "simple justice" requires that we favor women and blacks in employment and educational opportunities, since women and blacks were "unjustly" excluded from such opportunities for so many years in the not so distant past. It is a strange argument, an example of a possible implication of a true proposition advanced to dispute the proposition itself, like an octopus absent-mindedly slicing off his head with a stray tentacle. A fatal confusion underlies this argument, a confusion fundamentally relevant to our understanding of the notion of the rule of law.

Two senses of justice and equality are involved in this confusion. The root notion of justice, progenitor of the other, is the one that Aristotle[1] assumes to be the foundation and proper virtue of the political association. It is the condition which free men establish among themselves when they "share a common life in order that their association bring them self-sufficiency"—the regulation of their relationship by law, and the establishment, by law, of equality before the law. Rule of law is the name and pattern of this justice; its equality stands against the inequalities—of wealth, talent, etc.—otherwise obtaining among its participants, who by virtue of that equality are called "citizens." It is an achievement—complete, or, more frequently, partial—of certain people in certain concrete situations. It is fragile and easily disrupted by powerful individuals who discover that the blind equality of rule of law is inconvenient for their interests. Despite its obvious instability, Aristotle assumed that the establishment of justice in this sense, the creation of citizenship, was a permanent possibility for men and that the resultant association of citizens was the natural home of the species. At levels below the political association, this rule-governed equality is easily found; it is exemplified by any group of children agreeing together to play a game. At the level of the political association, the attainment of this justice is more difficult, simply because the stakes are so much higher for each participant. The equality of citizenship is not something that happens of its own accord, and without the expenditure of a fair amount of effort it will collapse into the rule of a powerful few over an apathetic many. But at least it has been achieved,

[1] *Nicomachean Ethics,* Book V, Chapter 6; *Politics,* Book I, Chapter 2 [reprinted in this volume] and Book III, Chapter 1.

at some times in some places; it is always worth trying to achieve, and eminently worth trying to maintain, wherever and to whatever degree it has been brought into being.

...

The moral ideal of equality should be recognized as logically distinct from the condition (or virtue) of justice in the political sense. Justice in this sense exists *among* a citizenry, irrespective of the number of the populace included in that citizenry. Further, the moral ideal is parasitic upon the political virtue, for "equality" is unspecified; it means nothing until we are told in what respect that equality is to be realized. In a political context, "equality" is specified as "equal rights"—equal access to the public realm, public goods and offices, equal treatment under the law—in brief, the equality of citizenship. If citizenship is not a possibility, political equality is unintelligible. The ideal emerges as a generalization of the real condition and refers back to that condition for its content.

Now, if justice (Aristotle's justice in the political sense) is equal treatment under law for all citizens, what is injustice? Clearly, injustice is the violation of that equality, discriminating for or against a group of citizens, favoring them with special immunities and privileges or depriving them of those guaranteed to the others. When the southern employer refuses to hire blacks in white-collar jobs, when Wall Street will only hire women as secretaries with new titles, when Mississippi high schools routinely flunk all blacks boys above ninth grade, we have examples of injustice, and we work to restore the equality of the public realm by ensuring that equal opportunity will be provided in such cases in the future. But of course, when the employers and the schools *favor* women and blacks, the same injustice is done. Just as the previous discrimination did, this reverse discrimination violates the public equality which defines citizenship and destroys the rule of law for the areas in which these favors are granted. To the extent that we adopt a program of discrimination, reverse or otherwise, justice in the political sense is destroyed, and none of us, specifically affected or not, is a citizen, a bearer of rights—we are all petitioners for favors. And to the same extent, the ideal of equality is undermined, for it has content only where justice obtains, and by destroying justice we render the ideal meaningless. It is, then, an ironic paradox, if not a contradiction in terms, to assert that the ideal of equality justifies the violation of justice; it is as if one should argue, with William Buckley, that an ideal of humanity can justify the destruction of the human race.

Logically, the conclusion is simple enough: all discrimination is wrong *prima facie* because it violates justice, and that goes for reverse discrimination too. No violation of justice among the citizens may be justified (may overcome the *prima facie* objection) by appeal to the ideal of equality, for that ideal is logically dependent upon the notion of justice. Reverse discrimination, then, which attempts no other justification than an appeal to equality, is wrong. But let us try to make the conclusion more plausible by suggesting some of the implications of the suggested practice of reverse discrimination in employment and education. My argument will be that the problems raised there are insoluble, not only in practice but in principle.

We may argue, if we like, about what "discrimination" consists of. Do I discriminate against blacks if I admit none to my school when none of the black applicants are qualified by the tests I always give? How far must I go to root out cultural bias from my application forms and tests before I can say that I have not discriminated against those of different cultures? Can I assume that women are not strong enough to be roughnecks on my oil rigs, or must I test them individually? But this controversy, the most popular and well-argued aspect of the issue, is not as fatal as two others which cannot be avoided: if we are regarding the blacks as a "minority" victimized by discrimination, what is a "minority"? And for any group— blacks, women, whatever—that has been discriminated against, what amount of reverse discrimination wipes out the initial discrimination? Let us grant as true that women and blacks were discriminated against, even where laws forbade such discrimination, and grant for the sake of argument that a history of discrimination must be wiped out by reverse discrimination. What follows?

First, are there other groups which have been discriminated against? For they should have the same right of restitution. What about American Indians, Chicanos, Appalachian Mountain whites, Puerto Ricans, Jews, Cajuns, and Orientals? And if these are to be included, the principle according to which we specify a "minority" is simply the criterion of "ethnic (sub) group," and we're stuck with every hyphenated American in the lower-middle class clamoring for special privileges for *his* group—and with equal justification. For be it noted, when we run down the Harvard roster, we find not only a scarcity of blacks (in comparison with the proportion in the population) but an even more striking scarcity of those second-, third-, and fourth-generation ethnics who make up the loudest voice of Middle America. Shouldn't they demand *their* share? And eventually, the WASPs will have to form their own lobby, for they too are a minority. The point is simply this: there is no "majority" in America who will not mind giving up just a bit of their rights to make room for a favored minority. There are only other minorities, each of which is discriminated against by the favoring. The initial injustice is then repeated dozens of times, and if each minority is granted the same right of restitution as the others, an entire area of rule governance is dissolved into a pushing and shoving match between self-interested groups. Each works to catch the public eye and political popularity by whatever means of advertising and power politics lend themselves to the effort, to capitalize as much as possible on temporary popularity until the restless mob picks another group to feel sorry for. Hardly an edifying spectacle, and in the long run no one can benefit: the pie is no larger—it's just that instead of setting up and enforcing rules for getting a piece, we've turned the contest into a free-for-all, requiring much more effort for no larger a reward. It would be in the interests of all the participants to reestablish an objective rule to govern the process, carefully enforced and the same for all.

Second, supposing that we do manage to agree in general that women and blacks (and all the others) have some right of restitution, some right to a privileged place in the structure of opportunities for a while, how will we know when that while is up? How much privilege is enough? When will the guilt be gone, the price paid, the balance restored? What recompense is right for centuries of exclusion? What criterion tells us when we are done? Our experience with the Civil Rights movement shows us that agreement on these terms cannot be presupposed: a process that appears to some to be going at a mad gallop into a black takeover appears to the rest of us to be at a standstill. Should a practice of reverse discrimination be adopted, we may safely predict that just as some of us begin to see "a satisfactory start toward righting the balance," others of us will see that we "have already gone too far in the other direction" and will suggest that the discrimination ought to be reversed again. And such disagreement is inevitable, for the point is that we could not *possibly* have any criteria for evaluating the kind of recompense we have in mind. The context presumed by any discussion of restitution is the context of rule of law: law sets the rights of men and simultaneously sets the method for remedying the violation of those rights. You may exact suffering from others and/or damage payments for yourself if and only if the others have violated your rights; the suffering you have endured is not sufficient reason for them to suffer. And remedial rights exist only where there is law: primary human rights are useful guides to legislation but cannot stand as reasons for awarding remedies for injuries sustained. But then, the context presupposed by any discussion of restitution is the context of preexistent full citizenship. No remedial rights could exist for the excluded; neither in law nor in logic does there exist a right to *sue* for a standing to sue.

From these two considerations, then, the difficulties with reverse discrimination become evident. Restitution for a disadvantaged group whose rights under the law have been violated is possible by legal means, but restitution for a disadvantaged group whose grievance is that there was no law to protect them simply is not. First, outside of the area of justice defined by the law, no sense can be made of "the group's rights," for no law recognizes that group or the individuals in it, qua members, as bearers of rights (hence *any* group can constitute itself as a disadvantaged minority in some sense and demand similar restitution). Second, outside of the area of protection of law, no sense can be made of the violation of rights (hence the amount of the recompense cannot be decided by any objective criterion). For both reasons, the practice of reverse discrimination undermines the foundation of the very ideal in whose name it is advocated; it destroys justice, law, equality, and citizenship itself, and replaces them with power struggles and popularity contests.

IRVING THALBERG

Reverse Discrimination and the Future

Lisa Newton discussed a compensatory *approach to preferential treatment; Irving Thalberg argues that it is not past wrongs but future justice that should be our main concern. He presents a* teleological, *or goal-directed, defense of preferential treatment.*

Thalberg considers a hypothetical society, R, with two subgroups: K' is a group which was discriminated against in the past but has somehow managed to have equal attainments, employment, power, and prestige today; K" is a different group which was never discriminated against but, for some reason for which its members were not responsible, is now at a low level of welfare and power. Suppose we had the resources to aid only one of these groups. Thalberg reasons that we would help K" rather than K', if forced to make this choice. In this way, he concludes that the proper place to look for a justification of preferential treatment is at the future consequences in terms of equality which it would produce, rather than at compensation for past wrongs.

Thalberg also rebuts several of Newton's specific points. In particular, he argues that even the group previously favored (for example, white males) would eventually benefit rather than suffer from preferential treatment of others, since they would in the long run live in a more just and equal society.

Further Reading

James W. Nickel, "Preferential Policies in Hiring and Admissions: A Jurisprudential Approach," *Columbia Law Review,* 75 (1975), 534–58.

George Sher, "Justifying Reverse Discrimination in Employment," *Philosophy and Public Affairs,* 4 (1975), 159–70.

Lawrence Crocker, "Preferential Treatment," in M. V. Braggin, F. Elliston, and J. English, eds., *Feminism and Philosophy* (Totowa, N.J.: Littlefield, Adams, 1977).

Richard Wasserstrom, "The University and the Case for Preferential Treatment," *American Philosophical Quarterly,* 13 (1976), 165–70.

I. MISLEADING MODELS FOR THIS SORT OF POLICY

I want to reach a clearer understanding of what it is to engage in reverse discrimination, and especially of what is *not* involved. I emphasize the negative thrust of my inquiry because many philosophers, along with most polemicists, uncritically equate "affirmative action" and similar measures with old-fashioned Jim Crow practices and traditional sexism—even with the feudal caste system![1] My analytical task would be easier if detractors of the programs in question agreed to relinquish the perjorative label, "reverse discrimination." But one can hardly ask them to forego this terminological advantage. They realize that when one comes to decide for or against some course of action, it will make a difference how one specifies the action, and what models the specification will bring to mind. Incidentally, besides suggesting parallels with *Apartheid* and patriarchy, the tag "reverse discrimination" can also sound menacingly vindictive. Thus one writer, after parading "the evils . . . that will result from reverse discrimination," goes on to declare: "Compensatory edicts are none other than . . . primitive, pre-moral *lex talionis* in disguise."[2] An equally widespread but curious belief, perhaps due to our use of terms like "compensation" and "reparation," is that the programs we are considering should somehow "make up for" or "undo" antecedent injustices—whether or not such programs "even the score."

I shall devote most of my analytical energy to questioning this latter assumption, and more generally to challenging our fixation on the past when we discuss this topic. This obsession is excusable, for what analogies encourage us to approve of preferential treatment of a group? First there is the person who is entitled to indemnification for injuries resulting from another's negligent, reckless or wilful misconduct. Then there are people who deserve compensation because they suffered from illegal state action, or from unofficial action which state agencies made no effort to stop. For example, many public school teachers who were summarily discharged, or hounded from their jobs, during the McCarthy era, have since been reinstated, with back pay and seniority. Recently I came across a newspaper report of a Florida man who was "held fourteen years in a state mental hospital for a crime authorities say he did not commit." The article continues: "The Florida House last week voted [him] $75,000 compensation for being 'victimized by our society.' "[3] In all these paradigmatic instances, some previous harm or illegality is the source of entitlement.

Reprinted with omissions by permission of G. P. Putnam's Sons and Irving Thalberg from *Women and Philosophy* edited by Carol C. Gould and Marx W. Wartofsky. Copyright © 1976 by Carol C. Gould and Marx W. Wartofsky.

[1]Virginia Black, "The Erosion of Legal Principles in the Creation of Legal Policies," *Ethics*, 84 (1974), 93, 109, 112.

[2]Ibid., p. 114; see also p. 107.

[3]*Chicago Sun-Times*, 22 April 1974, p. 44.

This creates philosophical perplexity, however. Among those groups in the U.S.A. which appear to have the strongest *prima facie* claim upon special treatment—Native Americans, Black Americans, Chicanos, women generally—you find individuals who have escaped indignities. In fact, some have prospered. Yet it will often raise the status of these groups if such "lucky" members receive the same advantages as certified victims. Our model cases provide no illumination here. How could a fortunate member of some downtrodden group have a right to reparations—and for what injury or miscarriage of justice? If we are going to make any case for the kind of policy toward groups which is stigmatized as "reverse discrimination," we will have to build our concept of it from other materials.

One usable analogy might be the favored treatment of ex-colonies by the European powers which exploited them. A minor practical snag with this is that American womankind, Blacks and so on lack corporate status. Who are their official representatives, negotiators, policy-makers and treasurers? Even the majority of Native Americans have left their various tribes of origin. Should reverse discrimination be directed toward individuals from these groups? That would leave former oppressors at the helm, still making all the crucial decisions—this time, of course, for the benefit of their erstwhile victims. It would be equally paternalistic if the general government selected the organizations of women, Blacks, Chicanos and Native Americans to negotiate on reparations for each group. So perhaps the ex-colony model will be germane only when the formerly oppressed convince themselves and others that they have gotten organized.

I shall not pursue that line of inquiry, but I should draw out one of its implications. If we think in terms of ex-colonies, having leaders with both *de facto* and *de jure* authority, then perhaps we will not conceive of reverse discrimination as a oneway, *noblesse oblige* gesture of charity and atonement. Instead we might see an interaction. Some militants dramatize such reciprocity by saying: "This is a stickup; we've come for what's ours!" I assume that they use the word "stickup," rather than declare that they are standing up for their human rights, and are going to take power over their own lives, because the oppressor has demonstrated better comprehension of armed robbery. In any case, my point is that instead of assuming that its beneficiaries are merely passive recipients of handouts, we should conceive of reverse discrimination as a process of mutual adjustment. The oppressor transfers to the oppressed the control he held over their destiny.

Before we try to capture other important dimensions of this process, I should warn readers that even when I use words like "duty" and "obligation," my approach will be teleological. That is, I shall look for goals one might have, and results one might be seeking, when one demands or dispenses special treatment. Although I feel more comfortable with a "consequentialist" analysis, I do not mean to rule out deontological accounts of reverse discrimination—perhaps based on some duty to make amends to a group for injustice suffered by some of its members. At all events, when I investigate what it is to engage in reverse discrimination, I am giving the sort of action-theoretical analysis which I think will mesh with the concerns of consequentialists in ethics.

II. AN ABSTRACT FORMULATION OF THE PROBLEM

A schematic fable will help me develop my alternative to the standard conception. We should imagine a readily identifiable class K of citizens within society R. K has met with brutal, widespread and prolonged oppression during former times. Agencies of R's government either helped inflict, or made no attempt to halt these inequities. The results are what you would expect. Present-day members of K are virtually absent from the political hierarchy, and are over-represented on the lower rungs of R's economic ladder. They crowd welfare rolls and prison cells. Psychologically speaking, even Ks who did not experience indignities often seem hindered from developing their potential by conscious or unconscious feelings of incompetence, self-hatred, and fear of success. These self-defeating attitudes of Ks seem to be bound up with their sometimes repressed awareness that they belong to a once subjugated group. Thus, although we can suppose that discrimination against K has somehow ended, K is in a sorry plight, by comparison with other classes of R.

From this sketchy account, might it follow, on intuitively plausible moral or legal principles, that all surviving members of K are now entitled to special benefits, to make up for the humiliations previously imposed upon their group? I am not interested in the "realist's" question whether any known society would ever be likely to make amends to K. Nor do I wish to investigate how high a priority this goal should have for R. I am concerned with what is owed to K, and why.

More important from a conceptual standpoint, I am not asking whether members of K who have suffered *personally* from bias have a right to compensation—perhaps in the form of preferential hiring and other advantages. Such an "individualized" policy might be difficult to carry out,[4] and it has been sadly neglected in practice. However, remedial action for the benefit of an individual who endured unjust treatment is well understood and philosophically uncontroversial.

The enterprise I want to clarify is trickier. My question is whether Ks generally deserve advantages now because of the grossly unfair way their fellow citizens dealt with most Ks in the past. A somewhat analogous problem would be this. Evidently a disabled war veteran should get the nod in employment, within certain limits, because of the sacrifices he

---

[4]See Boris I. Bittker, *The Case for Black Reparations* (New York: Random House, 1973).

actually made on behalf of society R. But what about unscathed ex-servicemen who got "soft" assignments? Should they also be favored, in any way, on the grounds that most people in the military forces have suffered?

Returning to class K, here is a more specific version of our query: to what extent do R's legislators, judges and administrative officials have a duty—however unacknowledged by them—to bestow advantages upon members of K, and to demand similar compensatory action by nongovernmental institutions—commercial, financial, educational, cultural? For instance: should it be legally permissible, or even mandatory, that political candidacies, cushy administrative posts, corporate directorships, managerial jobs in business and industry, research grants and facilities, scholarships to elite schools, patronage for artists, membership in key labor unions, and so on, be reserved for a representative number of people from K? Do Ks deserve these benefits only from those institutions which contributed to the oppression of their group? And how much will it take to pay the debt owed K? Naturally no K will be forced to accept these privileges.

III. INITIAL REACTIONS

However we settle these questions of detail, we will encounter a general complaint: why must non-Ks pay the price of atonement? Presumably most non-Ks have nothing to make amends for, having neither wronged a member of K, nor having gained from the group's degradation. How then can we justify the unfair treatment of non-Ks who are more qualified? They will be passed over for jobs and other opportunities because of favoritism toward Ks who, through no fault of their own, now have less talent and experience. Paradoxically, past discrimination against K seems to be offered as a reason for doing the same injustice to other groups now. But if unequal treatment of people because of the group they belong to was wrong then, how could it be a method for restoring justice today?

What is more, two kindred lines of argument seem to reduce the policy of favoritism to an absurdity. First, where can we stop? Won't every citizen of R fall into some grouping or other which has encountered some degree of prejudice? Consequently everyone is entitled to the advantages reserved for Ks, and Ks should not be singled out.[5] But suppose we are partial to Ks alone. Then a second line of argument is that we will oppress non-Ks by discriminating against them. The qualified non-Ks who lose out because Ks receive preferential treatment will become a new deprived class,

---

[5]Lisa Newton, "Reverse Discrimination as Unjustified," *Ethics,* 83 (1973), 311. [Reprinted in this volume.]

sooner or later, with a valid claim to similar restitution. So eventually we will have to turn and discriminate against qualified Ks. This never-ending see-saw will surely hinder R from establishing the very sort of lawfulness, impartiality, and equal opportunity which it wrongly denied to group K in former times. Here is how Lisa Newton formulates this second line of reasoning:

> Just as the previous discrimination did, this reverse discrimination violates the public equality which defines citizenship and destroys the rule of law for the areas in which these favors are granted ... [J]ustice is destroyed, and none of us, specifically affected or not, is a citizen, a bearer of rights—we are all petitioners for favors.[6]

IV. A POINT ABOUT THE FUTURE

I propose to redirect the whole controversy before it loses its heat. Broadly speaking, my intention is to counteract the emphasis that nearly all participants have, understandably enough, given to the past. One noteworthy exception is Bernard Boxill. He distinguishes between reparations for a past injustice and such compensatory measures as those I listed above. Then he boldly asserts:

> The characteristic of compensatory programs is that they are essentially "forward looking"; by that I mean that such programs are intended to alleviate disabilities which stand in the way of some *future* good, *however* these disabilities may have come about. Thus, the history of injustices suffered by black and colonial people is quite irrelevant to their right to compensatory treatment. What is strictly relevant to this is that such compensatory treatment is necessary if some future goods such as increased happiness, equality of incomes, and so on, are to be secured. To put it another way, given the contingency of causal connections, the present condition of black and colonial people could have been produced in any one of a very large set of different causal sequences. Compensation is concerned with remedying the present situation however it may have been produced; and to know the present situation, and how to remedy it, it is not, strictly speaking, necessary to know just how it was brought about, or whether it was brought about by injustice.[7]

I find no argument in Boxill's admirably concise paper to support his contention that "the history of injustices suffered by black and colonial people is quite irrelevant to their right to compensatory treatment." Before I go on to sketch a rationale, which I think also applies to women, I should

---

[6]Newton, p. 157. See Black, pp. 94f, 110f.
[7]Bernard Boxill, "The Morality of Reparation," *Social Theory and Practice,* 2 (1972), 117.

quote the only other philosopher who alludes to long-term social goals we might have when we contemplate favoritism toward an oppressed group. Michael D. Bayles remarks briefly:

> The ideal is a society based upon non-discrimination and equality of opportunity. Compensatory reverse discrimination aids in bringing about that society, for it helps remove the vestiges of previous discrimination. And by raising the status of members of the minority group denied equality of opportunity, it helps ensure that the next generation does not suffer a similar denial.[8]

My own outlook is that we can deal with worries like those of Newton about the unfairness of reverse discrimination, and see how little resemblance it need have to old-style racism and sexism, if we investigate more fully Boxill's "future goods" and Bayles's notion of status raising. To begin with, how can we explain why it is—or ought to be—more germane to look ahead, rather than estimate the mistreatment that a group has endured in the past? A two-stage fantasy may elucidate my view. First, against all historical precedent, imagine another group K'. Its members were, until a short time ago, liable to dreadful persecution and bias simply because they belonged to K'. Nevertheless at present, members of K' somehow manage to occupy as many influential and satisfying roles as people from other classes within R. Our second leap of imagination, inspired by Boxill, is then to compare K' with another group K"—perhaps defined by gender, color, language, religion, national origin or sexual proclivities—which has never met with discrimination. Yet although K" was never oppressed, most of its members are toward the bottom of the socio-economic-political pecking order, and unlikely to rise as things are presently arranged. That is, they identify themselves as members of K", but nobody in R has wronged them because of their identity. Nor is their plight due to genetic deficiencies, to some common psychological trait like sloth, or to a self-perpetuating but hallowed "culture of poverty." More positively, there might be quite different explanations why particular members of K" have fared badly, and why they will continue to do so if conditions do not alter. But perhaps there is no general account of why all K"s are in relative misery. I could elaborate the situation of K" in a vain attempt to satisfy hard-headed realists; but I think we have a sufficiently clear picture of groups K' and K" to disentangle the backward and the forward-looking concerns which may have blended in our original group K.

My test question is straightforward. Suppose we agree that reverse discrimination might be worth trying as a social measure in R; that our

---

[8]Michael D. Bayles, "Compensatory Reverse Discrimination in Hiring," *Social Theory and Practice,* 2 (1973), 309.

resources are enough for one group only; and that K' and K" would probably advance about the same distance from their current position: then which should we favor—and for what reasons? As I said at the outset, we are not concerned with the obvious merits of restitution to individual victims of injustice—to members of K' who have suffered personally. The issue is which whole group most deserves special treatment, resulting in privileges for any of its members. If past indignities alone counted, or figured as a prerequisite for reverse discrimination, we would dismiss K". Yet are we not inclined to give K" the nod? If so, then remediable current distress is a more decisive factor than unmerited past inequities—even though history tells us that the latter usually cause the former. My fable also suggests that we might justify reverse discrimination although the group we propose to favor has escaped oppression altogether.

Of course it is fanciful to contrast "past inequities" and "current misery." This brings me to a subnary point about overemphasizing the past. If we look realistically at the cases we are most familiar with—women generally, Native Americans, Black Americans, Chicanos—we are reminded that barriers and humiliations are not things of the past. It is misleading for Bayles to write of mere "vestiges of previous discrimination"—as if bias had practically disappeared and we only have to treat the injuries it has left. One philosophical contributor has remarked briefly on this. In a sentence-long footnote, J. W. Nickel recognizes that "discrimination against blacks is [not] a thing of the past."[9] Why do I think it vital to sear this fact into our consciousness? Otherwise, if we happen not to be from a downtrodden group, or if we happen to be token members who "made it"—perhaps the hard way—we might forget the urgency of that distress which reverse discrimination is suited to palliate. We might misconceive the situation as having to do exclusively with effects of earlier injustice, not noticing the dark shadow that oppression still casts upon the lives and minds of many of our fellow citizens. From the standpoint of analytic philosophy, we should also realize that one primary source and object of oppressed people's unhappiness may be the fact that they must accept indignities which others do not have to face. They are distressed over their second-class status.[10]

V. COMPARING INJUSTICES

Now we should turn our attention to oppressors, to non-participating beneficiaries of oppression and to innocent bystanders. If we institute reverse discrimination, will their fate be on a par with the sufferings of

---

[9]James W. Nickel, "Discrimination and Morally Relevant Characteristics," *Analysis,* 32 (1972), 114.

[10]See John Rawls, *A Theory of Justice* (Cambridge, Mass.: Harvard University Press, 1971), pp. 535ff, 546.

people from K or K"? As we saw, Newton would apparently equate the injustice toward Ks in the past, and the effect of reverse discrimination upon everyone else in times to come. My second major point is that this forecast is unjustifiably grim. Would non-members of K or K" be barred altogether and permanently from government, professions, corporate power, elite universities and so on—as Ks were? Would they be deprived of protection against violence and insults from hostile fellow citizens? Would they have no recourse against high-handed police, courts, welfare agencies, hospitals, banks, realtors? Would they be arbitrarily dislodged from positions which they had managed to reach in spite of prejudice— as Black locomotive engineers and firemen were by racist unions in the 1940s?[11] Would victims of reverse discrimination be conditioned into dependency by the child-rearing and educational system, and the media, as women and most non-white Americans have been? Unfairness would occur, but not of these types. So the injustices of old-fashioned and reverse discrimination are not equivalent. And similarly for economic and "status" deprivations. When Ks or K"s receive preferential treatment, other people who are more qualified for jobs and the like will have to wait. Instead of getting all the goodies, they will receive a fair share. They will achieve power and wealth, but at a reduced rate. The suffering this entails will be a genuine misfortune, as well as an injustice. But it does not compare with the misery of those whom reverse discrimination is supposed to upgrade.

In fact, I wonder if more qualified citizens face only injustice and diminished happiness. I would enlarge my foregoing second point by asking whether non-members of K or K" might actually derive some benefits if even vestigial discrimination against Ks should come to an end, and if Ks or K"s achieve socio-economic-political parity with their erstwhile betters. In times gone by, I suppose most well-off people did not see themselves as losing because of their complicity with a caste system. But if in the future they start making comparisons, perhaps they will regard the more egalitarian order as a source of happiness, not only a loss of former advantages. So we should not overlook the possibility that today's oppressors and neutrals may in the future admit that reverse discrimination has a silver lining to it.

---

[11]See *Steele* v. *L. & N. Railway Co.*, 323 U.S. 192 (1944); and *Railroad Trainmen* v. *Howard*, 343 U.S. 768 (1951).

THOMAS E. HILL, JR.

Servility and Self-Respect

The second ideal of equality Bernard Williams discussed was that of respect for each person as a human being having equal rights and moral worth with every other person. This aspect of equality includes having respect for oneself as a human being, too, and for one's own rights. Thomas E. Hill, Jr., describes a particular form of the lack of self-respect—servility—and tries to demonstrate why this is morally objectionable.

Self-respect should not be confused with holding a high opinion of oneself and one's abilities. One might realize that one has less intelligence, wealth, or education than others and still believe one has an equal right to vote, have a fair trial, or receive equal pay for equal work. These rights are part of one's equality as a moral person and do not depend on other traits which may be unequal.

People often claim that it is morally acceptable not to demand one's rights. One could refuse to vote or to ask for a jury trial, for example, even when this refusal is to one's disadvantage. Hill argues against this that refusing to stand up for one's rights and take what is due in our moral system shows a lack of respect for that system. He cites Kant's position that right actions are those done purely out of a respect for the moral law.

Individuals who are servile, that is, who refuse to accept what is due to them, show a lack of respect for themselves as moral persons. Hill reasons that such behavior, which disrespects our system of moral rules, is not optional but actually wrong.

Further Reading

VIRGINIA HELD, "Reasonable Progress and Self-Respect," *The Monist,* 57 (1973), 12–27.

ALIX NELSON, "How I Learned to Stop Being Grateful and Stand Up for My Rights," *Ms.,* 2 (June 1973), 40–44.

LYNNE BELAIEF, "Self-Esteem and Humanity," *Philosophy and Phenomenological Research,* 36 (1975), 25–43.

Several motives underlie this paper. In the first place, I am curious to see if there is a legitimate source for the increasingly common feeling that servility can be as much a vice as arrogance is. There seems to be something morally defective about the Uncle Tom and the submissive housewife; and yet, on the other hand, if the only interests they sacrifice are their own, it seems that we should have no right to complain. Secondly, I have some sympathy for the now unfashionable view that each person has duties to himself as well as to others. It does seem absurd to say that a person could literally violate his own rights or owe himself a debt of gratitude, but I suspect that the classic defenders of duties to oneself had something different in mind. If there are duties to oneself, it is natural to expect that a duty to avoid being servile would have a prominent place among them. . . .

I

Three examples may give a preliminary idea of what I mean by *servility*. Consider, first, an extremely deferential black, whom I shall call the *Uncle Tom*. He always steps aside for white men; he does not complain when less qualified whites take over his job; he gratefully accepts whatever benefits his all-white government and employers allot him, and he would not think of protesting its insufficiency. He displays the symbols of deference to whites, and of contempt towards blacks: he faces the former with bowed stance and a ready "Sir" and "Ma'am"; he reserves his strongest obscenities for the latter. Imagine, too, that he is not playing a game. He is not the shrewdly prudent calculator, who knows how to make the best of a bad lot and mocks his masters behind their backs. He accepts without question the idea that, as a black, he is owed less than whites. He may believe that blacks are mentally inferior and of less social utility, but that is not the crucial point. The attitude which he displays is that what he values, aspires for, and can demand is of less importance than what whites value, aspire for, and can demand. He is far from the picture book's carefree, happy servant, but he does not feel that he has a right to expect anything better.

Another pattern of servility is illustrated by a person I shall call the *Self-Deprecator*. Like the Uncle Tom, he is reluctant to make demands. He says nothing when others take unfair advantage of him. When asked for his preferences or opinions, he tends to shrink away as if what he said should make no difference. His problem, however, is not a sense of racial inferiority but rather an acute awareness of his own inadequacies and failures as an individual. These defects are not imaginary: he has in fact done poorly by his own standards and others'. But, unlike many of us in the same situation, he acts as if his failings warrant quite unrelated mal-

Reprinted with omissions from *The Monist*, 57 (1973), 87–104, by permission of the author and *The Monist*.

treatment even by strangers. His sense of shame and self-contempt makes him content to be the instrument of others. He feels that nothing is owed him until he has earned it and that he has earned very little. He is not simply playing a masochist's game of winning sympathy by disparaging himself. On the contrary, he assesses his individual merits with painful accuracy.

A rather different case is that of the *Deferential Wife.* This is a woman who is utterly devoted to serving her husband. She buys the clothes *he* prefers, invites the guests *he* wants to entertain, and makes love whenever *he* is in the mood. She willingly moves to a new city in order for him to have a more attractive job, counting her own friendships and geographical preferences insignificant by comparison. She loves her husband, but her conduct is not simply an expresson of love. She is happy, but she does not subordinate herself as a means to happiness. She does not simply defer to her husband in certain spheres as a trade-off for his deference in other spheres. On the contrary, she tends not to form her own interests, values, and ideals; and, when she does, she counts them as less important than her husband's. She readily responds to appeals from Women's Liberation that she agrees that women are mentally and physically equal, if not superior, to men. She just believes that the proper role for a woman is to serve her family. As a matter of fact, much of her happiness derives from her belief that she fulfills this role very well. No one is trampling on her rights, she says; for she is quite glad, and proud, to serve her husband as she does.

Each one of these cases reflects the attitude which I call servility.[1] It betrays the absence of a certain kind of self-respect. What I take this attitude to be, more specifically, will become clearer later on. It is important at the outset, however, not to confuse the three cases sketched above with other, superficially similar cases. In particular, the cases I have sketched are not simply cases in which someone refuses to press his rights, speaks disparagingly of himself, or devotes himself to another. A black, for example, is not necessarily servile because he does not demand a just wage; for, seeing that such a demand would result in his being fired, he might forbear for the sake of his children. A self-critical person is not necessarily servile by virtue of bemoaning his faults in public; for his behavior may be merely a complex way of satisfying his own inner needs quite independent of a willingness to accept abuse from others. A woman need not be servile

---

[1]Each of the cases is intended to represent only one possible pattern of servility. I make no claims about how often these patterns are exemplified, nor do I mean to imply that only these patterns could warrant the labels "Deferential Wife," "Uncle Tom," etc. All the more, I do not mean to imply any comparative judgments about the causes or relative magnitude of the problems of racial and sexual discrimination. One person, e.g. a self-contemptuous woman with a sense of racial inferiority, might exemplify features of several patterns at once; and, of course, a person might view her being a woman the way an Uncle Tom views his being black, etc.

whenever she works to make her husband happy and prosperous; for she might freely and knowingly choose to do so from love or from a desire to share the rewards of his success. If the effort did not require her to submit to humiliation or maltreatment, her choice would not mark her as servile. There may, of course, be grounds for objecting to the attitudes in these cases; but the defect is not servility of the sort I want to consider. It should also be noted that my cases of servility are not simply instances of deference to superior knowledge or judgment. To defer to an expert's judgment on matters of fact is not to be servile; to defer to his every wish and whim is. Similarly, the belief that one's talents and achievements are comparatively low does not, by itself, make one servile. It is no vice to acknowledge the truth, and one may in fact have achieved less, and have less ability, than others. To be servile is not simply to hold certain empirical beliefs but to have a certain attitude concerning one's rightful place in a moral community.

II

Are there grounds for regarding the attitudes of the Uncle Tom, the Self-Deprecator, and the Deferential Wife as morally objectionable? Are there moral arguments we could give them to show that they ought to have more self-respect? None of the more obvious replies is entirely satisfactory.

One might, in the first place, adduce utilitarian considerations. Typically the servile person will be less happy than he might be. Moreover, he may be less prone to make the best of his own socially useful abilities. He may become a nuisance to others by being overly dependent. He will, in any case, lose the special contentment that comes from standing up for one's rights. A submissive attitude encourages exploitation, and exploitation spreads misery in a variety of ways. These considerations provide a *prima facie* case against the attitudes of the Uncle Tom, the Deferential Wife, and the Self-Deprecator, but they are hardly conclusive. Other utilities tend to counterbalance the ones just mentioned. When people refuse to press their rights, there are usually others who profit. There are undeniable pleasures in associating with those who are devoted, understanding, and grateful for whatever we see fit to give them—as our fondness for dogs attests. Even the servile person may find his attitude a source of happiness, as the case of the Deferential Wife illustrates. There may be comfort and security in thinking that the hard choices must be made by others, that what I would say has little to do with what ought to be done. Self-condemnation may bring relief from the pangs of guilt even if it is not deliberately used for that purpose. On balance, then, utilitarian considerations may turn out to favor servility as much as they oppose it.

For those who share my moral intuitions, there is another sort of reason for not trying to rest a case against servility on utilitarian considerations. Certain utilities seem irrelevant to the issue. The utilitarian must weigh them along with others, but to do so seems morally inappropriate. Suppose, for example, that the submissive attitudes of the Uncle Tom and the Deferential Wife result in positive utilities for those who dominate and exploit them. Do we need to tabulate *these* utilities before conceding that servility is objectionable? The Uncle Tom, it seems, is making an error, a moral error, quite apart from consideration of how much others in fact profit from his attitude. The Deferential Wife may be quite happy; but if her happiness turns out to be contingent on her distorted view of her own rights and worth as a person, then it carries little moral weight against the contention that she ought to change that view. Suppose I could cause a woman to find her happiness in denying all her rights and serving my every wish. No doubt I could do so only by nonrational manipulative techniques, which I ought not to use. But is this the only objection? My efforts would be wrong, it seems, not only because of the techniques they require but also because the resultant attitude is itself objectionable. When a person's happiness stems from a morally objectionable attitude, it ought to be discounted. That a sadist gets pleasure from seeing others suffer should not count even as a partial justification for his attitude. That a servile person derives pleasure from denying her moral status, for similar reasons, cannot make her attitude acceptable. These brief intuitive remarks are not intended as a refutation of utilitarianism, with all its many varieties; but they do suggest that it is well to look elsewhere for adequate grounds for rejecting the attitudes of the Uncle Tom, the Self-Deprecator, and the Deferential Wife.

. . .

III

Why, then, is servility a moral defect? There is, I think, another sort of answer which is worth exploring. The first part of this answer must be an attempt to isolate the objectionable features of the servile person; later we can ask why these features are objectionable. As a step in this direction, let us examine again our three paradigm cases. The moral defect in each case, I suggest, is a failure to understand and acknowledge one's own moral rights. I assume, without argument here, that each person has moral rights. Some of these rights may be basic human rights; that is, rights for which a person needs only to be human to qualify. Other rights will be derivative and contingent upon his special commitments, institutional affiliations, etc. Most rights will be *prima facie* ones; some may be absolute. Most can be waived under appropriate conditions; perhaps some cannot. Many rights can be forfeited; but some, presumably, cannot. The servile person does not, strictly speaking, violate his own rights. At least in our paradigm cases he fails to acknowledge fully his own moral status because he does not fully understand what his rights are, how they can be waived, and when they can be forfeited.

The defect of the Uncle Tom, for example, is that he displays an attitude that denies his moral equality with whites. He does not realize, or apprehend in an effective way, that he has as much right to a decent wage and a share of political power as any comparable white. His gratitude is misplaced; he accepts benefits which are his by right as if they were gifts. The Self-Deprecator is servile in a more complex way. He acts as if he has forfeited many important rights which in fact he has not. He does not understand, or fully realize in his own case, that certain rights to fair and decent treatment do not have to be earned. He sees his merits clearly enough, but he fails to see that what he can expect from others is not merely a function of his merits. The Deferential Wife *says* that she understands her rights vis-à-vis her husband, but what she fails to appreciate is that her consent to serve him is a valid waiver of her rights only under certain conditions. If her consent is coerced, say, by the lack of viable options for women in her society, then her consent is worth little. If socially fostered ignorance of her own talents and alternatives is responsible for her consent, then her consent should not count as a fully legitimate waiver of her right to equal consideration within the marriage. All the more, her consent to defer constantly to her husband is not a legitimate setting aside of her rights if it results from her mistaken belief that she has a moral duty to do so. (Recall: "The *proper* role for a woman is to serve her family.") If she believes that she has a *duty* to defer to her husband, then, whatever she may say, she cannot fully understand that she has a *right* not to defer to him. When she says that she freely gives up such a right, she is confused. Her confusion is rather like that of a person who has been persuaded by an unscrupulous lawyer that it is legally incumbent on him to refuse a jury trial but who nevertheless tells the judge that he understands that he has a right to a jury trial and freely waives it. He does not really understand what it is to have and freely give up the right if he thinks that it would be an offense for him to exercise it.

Insofar as servility results from moral ignorance or confusion, it need not be something for which a person is to blame. ... Suppose, however, that our servile persons come to know their rights but do not substantially alter their behavior. Are they not still servile in an objectionable way?

· · ·

The answer, I think, should depend upon why the deferential role is played. If the motive is a morally commendable one, or a desire to avert dire consequences to oneself, or even an ambition to set an oppressor up for a later fall, then I would not count the role player as servile. The Uncle Tom, for instance, is not servile in my sense if he shuffles and bows to keep the Klan from killing his children, to save his own skin, or even to buy time while he plans the revolution. Similarly, the Deferential Wife is not servile if she tolerates an abusive husband because he is so ill that further strain would kill him, because protesting would deprive her of her only means of survival, or because she is collecting atrocity stories for her book against marriage. If there is fault in these situations, it seems inappropriate to call it *servility*. The story is quite different, however, if a person continues in his deferential role just from laziness, timidity, or a desire for some minor advantage. He shows too little concern for his moral status as a person, one is tempted to say, if he is willing to deny it for a small profit or simply because it requires some effort and courage to affirm it openly. A black who plays the Uncle Tom merely to gain an advantage over other blacks is harming them, of course; but he is also displaying disregard for his own moral position as an equal among human beings. Similarly, a woman throws away her rights too lightly if she continues to play the subservient role because she is used to it or is too timid to risk a change. A Self-Deprecator who readily accepts what he knows are violations of his rights may be indulging his peculiar need for punishment at the expense of denying something more valuable. In these cases, I suggest, we have a kind of servility independent of any ignorance or confusion about one's rights. The person who has it may or may not be blameworthy, depending on many factors; and the line between servile and nonservile role playing will often be hard to draw. Nevertheless, the objectionable feature is perhaps clear enough for present purposes: it is a willingness to disavow one's moral status, publicly and systematically, in the absence of any strong reason to do so.

· · ·

IV

The objectionable feature of the servile person, as I have described him, is his tendency to disavow his own moral rights either because he misunderstands them or because he cares little for them. The question remains: why should anyone regard this as a moral defect? After all, the rights which he denies are his own. He may be unfortunate, foolish, or even distasteful; but why *morally* deficient? One sort of answer, quite different from those reviewed earlier, is suggested by some of Kant's remarks. Kant held that servility is contrary to a perfect nonjuridical duty to oneself.[2] To say that the duty is perfect is roughly to say that it is stringent, never overridden by other considerations (e.g., beneficence). To say that the duty is nonjuridical is to say that a person cannot legitimately be coerced to comply. Although Kant did not develop an explicit argument for this view, an argument can easily be constructed from materials which reflect the spirit, if not the letter, of his moral theory. The argument which I have in mind is prompted by Kant's contention that respect for persons, strictly speaking, is respect for moral law.[3] If taken as a claim about all sorts of respect, this seems quite implausible. If it means that we respect persons only for their moral character, their capacity for moral conduct, or their status as "authors" of the moral law, then it seems unduly moralistic. My strategy is to construe the remark as saying that at least one sort of respect for persons is respect for the rights which the moral law accords them. If one respects the moral law, then one must respect one's own moral rights; and this amounts to having a kind of self-respect incompatible with servility.

The premises for the Kantian argument, which are all admittedly vague, can be sketched as follows:

First, let us assume, as Kant did, that all human beings have equal basic human rights. Specific rights vary with different conditions, but all must be justified from a point of view under which all are equal. Not all rights need to be earned, and some cannot be forfeited. Many rights can be waived but only under certain conditions of knowledge and freedom. These conditions are complex and difficult to state; but they include something like the condition that a person's consent releases others from obligation only if it is autonomously given, and consent resulting from underestimation of one's moral status is not autonomously given. Rights can be objects of knowledge, but also of ignorance, misunderstanding, deception, and the like.

Second, let us assume that my account of servility is correct; or, if one prefers, we can take it as a definition. That is, in brief, a servile person is one who tends to deny or disavow his own moral rights because he does not understand them or has little concern for the status they give him.

---

[2] See Immanuel Kant, *The Doctrine of Virtue,* Part II of *The Metaphysics of Morals,* ed. by M. J. Gregor (New York: Harper & Row, 1964), pp. 99–103; Prussian Academy edition, Vol. VI, pp. 434–37.

[3] Immanuel Kant, *Groundwork of the Metaphysics of Morals,* ed. by H. J. Paton (New York: Harper & Row, 1964), p. 69; Prussian Academy edition, Vol. IV, p. 401; *The Critique of Practical Reason,* ed. by Lewis W. Beck (New York: Bobbs-Merrill, 1956), pp. 81, 84; Prussian Academy edition, Vol. V, pp. 78, 81. My purpose here is not to interpret what Kant meant but to give a sense to his remark.

Third, we need one formal premise concerning moral duty, namely, that each person ought, as far as possible, to respect the moral law. In less Kantian language, the point is that everyone should approximate, to the extent that he can, the ideal of a person who fully adopts the moral point of view. Roughly, this means not only that each person ought to do what is morally required and refrain from what is morally wrong but also that each person should treat all the provisions of morality as valuable—worth preserving and prizing as well as obeying. One must, so to speak, take up the spirit of morality as well as meet the letter of its requirements. To keep one's promises, avoid hurting others, and the like, is not sufficient; one should also take an attitude of respect towards the principles, ideals, and goals of morality. A respectful attitude towards a system of rights and duties consists of more than a disposition to conform to its definite rules of behavior; it also involves holding the system in esteem, being unwilling to ridicule it, and being reluctant to give up one's place in it. The essentially Kantian idea here is that morality, as a system of equal fundamental rights and duties, is worthy of respect, and hence a completely moral person would respect it in word and manner as well as in deed. And what a completely moral person would do, in Kant's view, is our duty to do so far as we can.

The assumptions here are, of course, strong ones, and I make no attempt to justify them. They are, I suspect, widely held though rarely articulated. In any case, my present purpose is not to evaluate them but to see how, if granted, they constitute a case against servility. The objection to the servile person, given our premises, is that he does not satisfy the basic requirement to respect morality. A person who fully respected a system of moral rights would be disposed to learn his proper place in it, to affirm it proudly, and not to tolerate abuses of it lightly. This is just the sort of disposition that the servile person lacks. If he does not understand the system, he is in no position to respect it adequately. This lack of respect may be no fault of his own, but it is still a way in which he falls short of a moral ideal. If, on the other hand, the servile person knowingly disavows his moral rights by pretending to approve of violations of them, then, barring special explanations, he shows an indifference to whether the provisions of morality are honored and publicly acknowledged. This avoidable display of indifference, by our Kantian premises, is contrary to the duty to respect morality. The disrespect in this second case is somewhat like the disrespect a religious believer might show towards his religion if, to avoid embarrassment, he laughed congenially while nonbelievers were mocking the beliefs which he secretly held. In any case, the servile person, as such, does not express disrespect for the system of moral rights in the obvious way by violating the rights of others. His lack of respect is more subtly manifested by his acting before others as if he did not know or care about his position of equality under that system.

The central idea here may be illustrated by an analogy. Imagine a club, say, an old German dueling fraternity. By the rules of the club, each member has certain rights and responsibilities. These are the same for each member regardless of what titles he may hold outside the club. Each has, for example, a right to be heard at meetings, a right not to be shouted down by the others. Some rights cannot be forfeited: for example, each may vote regardless of whether he has paid his dues and satisfied other rules. Some rights cannot be waived: for example, the right to be defended when attacked by several members of the rival fraternity. The members show respect for each other by respecting the status which the rules confer on each member. Now one new member is careful always to allow the others to speak at meetings; but when they shout him down, he does nothing. He just shrugs as if to say, "Who am I to complain?" When he fails to stand up in defense of a fellow member, he feels ashamed and refuses to vote. He does not deserve to vote, he says. As the only commoner among illustrious barons, he feels that it is his place to serve them and defer to their decisions. When attackers from the rival fraternity come at him with swords drawn, he tells his companions to run and save themselves. When they defend him, he expresses immense gratitude—as if they had done him a gratuitous favor. Now one might argue that our new member fails to show respect for the fraternity and its rules. He does not actually violate any of the rules by refusing to vote, asking others not to defend him, and deferring to the barons, but he symbolically disavows the equal status which the rules confer on him. If he ought to have respect for the fraternity, he ought to change his attitude. Our servile person, then, is like the new member of the dueling fraternity in having insufficient respect for a system of rules and ideals. The difference is that everyone ought to respect morality whereas there is no comparable moral requirement to respect the fraternity.

The conclusion here is, of course, a limited one. Self-sacrifice is not always a sign of servility. It is not a duty always to press one's rights. Whether a given act is evidence of servility will depend not only on the attitude of the agent but also on the specific nature of his moral rights, a matter not considered here. Moreover, the extent to which a person is responsible, or blameworthy, for his defect remains an open question. Nevertheless, the conclusion should not be minimized. In order to avoid servility, a person who gives up his rights must do so with a full appreciation for what they are. A woman, for example, may devote herself to her husband if she is uncoerced, knows what she is doing, and does not pretend that she has no decent alternative. A self-contemptuous person may decide not to press various unforfeited rights but only if he does not take the attitude that he is too rotten to deserve them. A black may demand less than is due to him provided he is prepared to acknowledge that no one has a right to expect this of him. Sacrifices of this sort, I suspect, are extremely rare. Most people, if they fully acknowledged their rights, would not autonomously refuse to press them.

An even stronger conclusion would emerge if we could assume that some basic rights cannot be waived. . . .

Even if there are no specific rights which cannot be waived, there might be at least one formal right of this sort. This is the right to some minimum degree of respect from others. No matter how willing a person is to submit to humiliation by others, they ought to show him some respect as a person. By analogy with self-respect, as presented here, this respect owed by others would consist of a willingness to acknowledge fully, in word as well as action, the person's basically equal moral status as defined by his other rights. To the extent that a person gives even tacit consent to humiliations incompatible with this respect, he will be acting as if he waives a right which he cannot in fact give up. To do this, barring special explanations, would mark one as servile.

· · ·

Kant suggests that duties to oneself are a precondition of duties to others. On our account of servility, there is at least one sense in which this is so. Insofar as the servile person is ignorant of his own rights, he is not in an adequate position to appreciate the rights of others. Misunderstanding the moral basis for his equal status with others, he is necessarily liable to underestimate the rights of those with whom he classifies himself. On the other hand, if he plays the servile role knowingly, then, barring special explanation, he displays a lack of concern to see the principles of morality acknowledged and respected and thus the absence of one motive which can move a moral person to respect the rights of others. In either case, the servile person's lack of self-respect necessarily puts him in a less than ideal position to respect others. Failure to fulfill one's duty to oneself, then, renders a person liable to violate duties to others. This, however, is a consequence of our argument against servility, not a presupposition of it.

III

The Popular Debate

SAM J. ERVIN, JR.

The Equal Rights Amendment

Senator Sam Ervin makes an argument against the Equal Rights Amendment on grounds of the natural functions of the sexes. He cites physiological, functional, and psychological differences which make women more suited to bearing and raising children and maintaining the home; men more suited to providing a livelihood. Because these differences are natural and relevant, he reasons, they cannot be abolished by passing a constitutional amendment. He believes that even feminists would not want to prohibit laws that work to women's advantage.

Ervin's use of the term functional *deserves special attention. He first cites muscular strength and child-bearing as physiological and functional differences. Next he reasons that laws should not ignore such differences. But eventually, housekeeping and earning a livelihood are included as functional differences between the sexes which the laws should take into consideration. He has moved from the natural differences in strength and reproduction to drawing the same conclusions about homemaking and careers. His notion of "functional" difference is sufficiently vague and flexible that it could be used to support any differences we find already existing in social roles. (The reader might also consider whether similar arguments could be constructed to support racism.)*

Ervin also assumes, like Steven Goldberg, that what is natural for the sexes is either inevitable or good. But as Christine Pierce showed earlier, many natural things can be changed by reason and not all natural things are good.

Further Reading

BARBARA BROWN, THOMAS I. EMERSON, GAIL FALK, and ANNE E. FREEDMAN, "The Equal Rights Amendment: a Constitutional Basis for Equal Rights for Women," *Yale Law Journal,* 80 (1970–71), 871–985.

LEO KANOWITZ, *Women and the Law: The Unfinished Revolution* (Albuquerque: University of New Mexico Press, 1969).

HAMIDA BOSMAJIAN and HAIG BOSMAJIAN, *This Great Argument: The Rights of Women* (Reading, Mass.: Addison-Wesley, 1972).

Mr. Chairman, the objective of those who advocate the adoption of the equal rights amendments S.J. Res. 8 and 9 and H.J. Res. 208 is a worthy one. It is to abolish unfair discriminations which society makes against women in certain areas of life. No one believes more strongly than I that discriminations of this character ought to be abolished and that they ought to be abolished by law in every case where they are created by law.

Any rational consideration of the advisability of adopting the Equal Rights Amendment raises these questions:

1. What is the character of the unfair discriminations which society makes against women?

2. Does it require an amendment to the Constitution of the United States to invalidate them?

3. If so, would the Equal Rights Amendment constitute an effective means to that end?

It is the better part of wisdom to recognize that discriminations not created by law cannot be abolished by law. They must be abolished by changed attitudes in the society which imposes them.

From the many conversations I have had with advocates of the Equal Rights Amendment since coming to the Senate, I am convinced that many of their just grievances are founded upon discriminations not created by law, and that for this reason the Equal Rights Amendment will have no effect whatsoever in respect to them.

. . .

FUNCTIONAL DIFFERENCES BETWEEN MEN AND WOMEN

While I believe that any unfair discriminations which the law has created against women should be abolished by law, I have the abiding conviction that the law should make such distinctions between them as are reasonably necessary for the protection of women and the existence and development of the race.

I share completely this recent observation by Mr. Bernard Swartz: "Use of the law in an attempt to conjure away all the differences which do exist between the sexes is both an insult to the law itself and a complete disregard of fact."

From "The Equal Rights Amendment: An Atomic Mousetrap," speech before the House Judiciary Committee, 23 March 1971. Reprinted by permission of Senator Ervin.

Let us consider for a moment whether there be a rational basis for reasonable distinctions between men and women in any of the relationships or undertakings of life.

When He created them, God made physiological and functional differences between men and women. These differences confer upon men a greater capacity to perform arduous and hazardous physical tasks. Some wise people even profess the belief that there may be psychological differences between men and women. To justify their belief, they assert that women possess an intuitive power to distinguish between wisdom and folly, good and evil.

To say these things is not to imply that either sex is superior to the other. It is simply to state the all important truth that men and women complement each other in the relationships and undertakings on which the existence and development of the race depend.

The physiological and functional differences between men and women empower men to beget and women to bear children, who enter life in a state of utter helplessness and ignorance, and who must receive nurture, care, and training at the hands of adults throughout their early years if they and the race are to survive, and if they are to grow mentally and spiritually. From time whereof the memory of mankind runneth not to the contrary, custom and law have imposed upon men the primary responsibility for providing a habitation and a livelihood for their wives and children to enable their wives to make the habitations homes, and to furnish nurture, care, and training to their children during their early years.

In this respect, custom and law reflect the wisdom embodied in the ancient Yiddish proverb that God could not be everywhere, so he made mothers. The physiological and functional differences between men and women constitute the most important reality. Without them human life could not exist.

For this reason, any country which ignores these differences when it fashions its institutions and makes its laws is woefully lacking in rationality.

Our country has not thus far committed this grievous error. As a consequence, it has established by law the institutions of marriage, the home, and the family, and has adopted some laws making some rational distinctions between the respective rights and responsibilities of men and women to make these institutions contribute to the existence and advancement of the race.

It may be that times are changing and more and more women will leave the home to compete in the business and professional community. However, I would like to call the Committee's attention to the remarks of Professor Phil Kurland of the University of Chicago Law School on this point. He said:

Times have changed in such a way that it may well be possible for the generation of women now coming to maturity, who had all the opportunities for education afforded to their male peers and who had an expectation of opportunities to put education to the same use as their male peers, to succeed in a competitive society in which all differences in legal rights between men and women were wiped out. There remains a very large part of the female population on whom the imposition of such a constitutional standard would be disastrous. There is no doubt that society permitted these women to come to maturity not as competitors with males but rather as the bearers and raisers of their children and the keepers of their homes. There are a multitude of women who still find fulfillment in this role. In the eyes of some, this may be unfortunate, but it is true. It can boast no label of equality now to treat the older generations as if they were their own children or grandchildren. Certainly the desire to open opportunities to some need not be bought at the price of removal of legal protections from others.

. . .

THE DESTRUCTIVE POTENTIALITY
OF THE HOUSE-PASSED EQUAL RIGHTS AMENDMENT

The Congress and the legislatures of the various states have enacted certain laws based upon the conviction that the physiological and functional differences between men and women make it advisable to exempt or exclude women from certain arduous and hazardous activities in order to protect their health and safety.

Among federal laws of this nature are the Selective Service Act, which confines compulsory military service to men; the acts of Congress governing the voluntary enlistments in the armed forces of the nation which restrict the right to enlist for combat service to men; and the acts establishing and governing the various service academies which provide for the admission and training of men only.[1]

Among the state laws of this kind are laws which limit hours during which women can work, and bar them from engaging in occupations particularly arduous and hazardous such as mining.[2]

If the Equal Rights Amendment should be interpreted by the Supreme Court to forbid any legal distinctions between men and women, all existing and future laws of this nature would be nullified.

The common law and statutory law of the various states recognize the reality that many women are homemakers and mothers, and by reason of the duties imposed upon them in these capacities, are largely precluded

[1][All these laws have since been changed—Ed.]

[2][Most of these laws, and the following ones Senator Ervin mentions, had not been changed, as of 1976—Ed.]

from pursuing gainful occupations or making any provision for their financial security during their declining years. To enable women to do these things and thereby make the existence and development of the race possible, these state laws impose upon husbands the primary responsibility to provide homes and livelihoods for their wives and children, and make them criminally responsible to society and civilly responsible to their wives if they fail to perform this primary responsibility. Moreover, these state laws secure to wives dower and other rights in the property left by their husbands in the event their husbands predecease them in order that they may have some means of support in their declining years.

If the Equal Rights Amendment should be interpreted by the Supreme Court to forbid any legal distinctions between men and women, it would nullify all existing and all future laws of this kind.

There are laws in many states which undertake to better the economic position of women. I shall cite only one class of them, namely, the laws which secure to women minimum wages in many employments in many states which have no minimum wage laws for men, and no other laws relating to the earnings of women.

If the Equal Rights Amendment should be interpreted by the Supreme Court to prohibit any legal distinctions between men and women, it would nullify all existing and future laws of this kind.

In addition there are federal and state laws and regulations which are designed to protect the privacy of males and females. Among these laws are laws requiring separate restrooms for men and women in public buildings, laws requiring separate restrooms for boys and girls in public schools, and laws requiring the segregation of male and female prisoners in jails and penal institutions.

Moreover, there are some state laws which provide that specified institutions of learning shall be operated for men and other institutions of learning shall be operated for women.

If the Equal Rights Amendment should be interpreted by the Supreme Court to forbid legal distinctions between men and women, it would annul all existing laws of this nature, and rob Congress and the states of the constitutional power to enact any similar laws at any time in the future.

I do not believe that the advocates of the Equal Rights Amendment wish to nullify laws which are adopted for the protection of women and for the promotion of the highest interest of society.

RUTH BADER GINSBURG

Equal Opportunity,
Free from Gender-Based Discrimination

Ruth Bader Ginsburg opposes part of Sam Ervin's position. She argues from examples that the laws instituted to protect women—and hence, in Ervin's eyes, to work to their advantage—actually work to their disadvantage. Some cases are obvious: prohibiting women from entering certain professions or denying equal fringe benefits to a woman's dependents. More subtle are privileges under law which free women from some of the obligations of citizenship. If women do not have to serve on juries or pay a poll tax when they do not vote, they are not equal citizens. Citizenship carries responsibilities as well as rights.

Viewed in isolation, special protective laws for women seem obviously unnecessary. If mining or serving alcohol is dangerous or demoralizing, why should not the law protect men from these consequences, too? It seems either all or none should be protected with minimum wages and maximum hours. But in the context of actual legislation, the issue is not so simple, because the courts have consistently withdrawn such protections rather than extend them to men. In many states, for example, women cannot be required to work compulsory overtime hours, but men can. So working women have often opposed the Equal Rights Amendment on the grounds that it would withdraw this protection from them rather than extending it to men too.

The position Ginsburg defends is fairly limited. She agrees with Alison Jaggar that women do not need special "female rights." At first glance, at least, this seems to be incompatible with her call for temporary reverse discrimination to rectify the injustices of the past. The equal treatment Ginsburg advocates is akin to Plato's ideal, treating each individual according to his or her relevant capacities, disregarding traits of the other groups he or she may belong to.

Further Reading

Bradwell v. *The State,* 16 Wall 130, 21 L.Ed. 442 (1872).

Mueller v. *Oregon,* 208 U.S. 412, 28 S.Ct. 324, 52 L.Ed 392 (1908).

Goesaert v. *Cleary,* 335 U.S. 464, 69 S.Ct. 198, 98 L.Ed.2d 163 (1948).

State v. *Hunter,* 208 Ore. 282, 300 P.2d 455 (1956).

Reed v. *Reed,* 404 U.S. 71, 92 S.Ct. 251, 30 L.Ed.2d 225 (1971).

My remarks will focus on *Equal Opportunity, Free from Gender-Based Discrimination.* "Women's rights" seems to me less clearly descriptive of our concern; that label has been used by advocates of sharp lines between the sexes, as well as by feminists who champion equal opportunity for women and men. For example, opponents of the Equal Rights Amendment assert that the amendment will destroy "the wonderful rights women have." Proponents, on the other hand, claim that the supposed favors conferred or forced on women serve ultimately to keep them "in their place," and to insulate man's world from women's competition.

Is there a middle ground? At least one of our Supreme Court Justices indicated last year his belief that there is. In an informal discussion with Harvard students, Justice Stewart remarked that women occupy the best of all possible legal worlds: They have the right to challenge laws that discriminate against them, and at the same time, to preserve laws that discriminate in their favor. Apart from a remedy specifically drawn to rectify past discrimination in a particular setting, however, it is difficult, perhaps impossible, to identify any legislative measure for women only that would aid in terminating, rather than perpetuating sex discrimination.

Consider these examples of laws once thought by jurists to protect women or to discriminate in women's favor.

In 1922, the Supreme Court approved a state license fee exemption accorded women operators of hand laundries employing only women. The exemption terminated if the female boss hired a man to work on the premises. Earlier, in 1873 and again in 1894, the Court had upheld prohibitions against women's admission to the bar. Some thought that a favor— women were to be spared the foul language and noxious atmosphere sometimes encountered in the courtroom. The same rationale was used through the 60's to keep women off juries. In 1948, the Supreme Court upheld a prohibition against women working behind a bar. Again, chivalrous gentlemen described this as a favor—women needed protection from barroom brawls. These decisions conveyed a rather clear message: Women may be favored in their place in occupations deemed suitable to them; but they may be disfavored, indeed barred, when the occupation ranks as a male preserve.

A speech reprinted in full from *The Key Reporter,* 3, no. 4 (Summer, 1974), 2–4, by permission of the author and The United Chapters of Phi Beta Kappa.

In 1937, the Court approved this differential on access to the ballot box: Men in the state in question had to pay poll tax for every year since they attained their majority; women were spared the tax for years in which they refrained from voting. Was this a "woman's right," or did it signify that women were regarded as less than fully responsible members of the community?

Compare the similar "right" still conferred on women by New York and several other states with respect to service on juries. Best of all possible worlds: women may serve if they so desire, but need not serve if that is their preference. In 1970, a NYS trial judge addressed himself to the issue of automatic exemption of women from jury service. The case involved a woman engaged in a controversy with her landlord. She complained that the exemption deprived her of a jury of her peers, since excusing women for the asking tends to produce predominantly male juries. The judge said in his published opinion: Don't complain to me. Your lament should be addressed to the state of womanhood that prefers cleaning and cooking, rearing of children and television soap operas, bridge and canasta, the beauty parlor and shopping to [civic responsibility].

So much for the image projected by a person with a right, but no corresponding responsibility.

Finally, recall the "wonderful rights" women once had as protection from untoward working conditions. In nations that never proceeded on the assumption that female, but not male workers needed protection, Norway for example, Worker Protective Acts covered men and women together from the start. One of the supposed protections thrust on women in the United States was featured in an equal pay case decided by the Supreme Court on June 3, 1974. The job in question, inspecting glass, was once regarded as women's work. When the company opened a night shift, in the 1920's, it could not hire women, for state laws protected women from working after 10:00 P.M. So men were sought for the night shift and, to attract them to the job, they were offered twice the pay women were receiving.

Similar examples of old-style "women's rights" abound, but perhaps these suffice to illustrate a point made by Sarah Grimke, noted feminist and abolitionist, over a century ago. Addressing an all-male legislature in 1837, she said: I ask no favors for my sex. All I ask of our brethren is that they take their feet off our necks.

Favors rarely come without exacting a price.

Consider this case in point. During a marriage that tragically ended after three years, the wife, a school teacher, was the principal breadwinner. The husband, starting up a business in the couple's home, incidentally attended to most of the housekeeping chores. Her annual income was approximately $10,000; his, $3,000. In the summer of 1972, the wife died in childbirth.

The young widower, struggling to care for his infant, to maintain his home, and to secure employment, applied to Social Security for survivor's benefits he thought due to him under his wife's account. That benefit, he was informed, is owed only to a widow. Indeed, it is specifically labelled a "Mother's Benefit," not a parent's benefit. On December 14, 1973, a federal district court recognized the fundamental unfairness of this scheme. It held that the exclusion of widowed fathers from benefits discriminates against men and children who have lost their wives and mothers, but perhaps primarily against gainfully employed women, who contribute to Social Security as much as their male counterparts, but whose labor secures less protection for their families.

Do women need special favors because, as child bearers, they perform a function no man can accomplish? In January 1974, it appeared that new light was dawning in the Supreme Court on this issue. The Court held that a pregnant school teacher could not be denied the right to work if the teacher's physician thought her fully fit to do so. Far from being placed on a pedestal, women in the job market have been penalized for pregnancy. With few exceptions, they have been denied fringe benefits granted to others with physical conditions that occasion a period of temporary disability. In 1972, the Equal Employment Opportunity Commission issued guidelines declaring generally that for job-related purposes, pregnancy must be treated as any other temporary disability. A number of state and federal courts and other authorities arrived at the same conclusion: They found no reason in logic or fairness to distinguish disability due to childbirth from other temporary disabilities. However, the Supreme Court adhered to an old line here. In June, 1974, six of the justices held that it was not a denial of equal protection to exclude pregnant women, along with institutionalized drug addicts, from a state's income protection program for disabled workers.

To summarize, only those who have failed to learn the lessons of the past can regard old-style "women's rights" as a viable system. Rather, as Sarah Grimke urged, women must have the same rights and responsibilities as men if they are to achieve equal opportunity, free from genderbased discrimination. Some important steps in the new direction have been taken by our legislatures and courts over the past decade.

The Supreme Court has begun to strike down some sex lines in the law once accepted as in the nature of things. For example, last term the Court declared unconstitutional a military fringe benefit scheme that worked like this: A married male member of the military received a substantial housing allowance, regardless of the dependency of his spouse; a female member was denied this allowance even if she was the family's principal breadwinner. The female member qualified only if she supplied over half her husband's support.

The plaintiffs were Sharron and Joseph Frontiero. Sharron was a Lieutenant in the Air Force; Joseph, a full-time student. Sharron's income covered nearly three-fourths of the family's budget. But Joseph's G.I. Bill checks took care of just over half his expenses (or just over one-fourth of the family's expenses)—hence, no housing allowance for the Frontieros. In their complaint, the Frontieros, like the young widower in the case just described, charged double-edged discrimination. Sharron was denied an allowance paid to similarly situated males; Joseph was denied benefits granted automatically for similarly situated females.

The law in question represented a common statutory arrangement. For example, as the young widower's case illustrates, a husband's earnings bring fringe benefits to his family under social security and other employment-related programs; a wife's earnings generally have not. Some thought the Supreme Court's *Frontiero* decision signalled the end for such differentials. But on April 24, 1974, the Court retrenched. Six of the Justices held a state property tax exemption for "widows only" permissible.

Justice Douglas who wrote the opinion for the majority declared the gender classification acceptable so long as the legislature could come up with some reason for it. Just a day earlier, Justice Douglas had declared that so far as race is concerned any state sponsored preference to one over another is unconstitutional. Some commentators consider him wrong on both counts. However, he made one point that is unassailable: The main purpose of the equal protection clause was to end racial discrimination. Sex discrimination was no concern of the framers of the equal protection guarantee.

Constitutional litigation with respect to sex discrimination is thus retarded by historic fact. The tools pressed into service by feminist lawyers are the due process and equal protection clauses of the Constitution. But one thing is perfectly clear: neither the Fifth nor the Fourteenth Amendment was designed with women in mind. As to the original understanding of the framers of the Constitution, consider Thomas Jefferson's appraisal:

> Were our state a pure democracy there would still be excluded from our deliberations women, who, to prevent deprivation of morals or ambiguity of issues, should not mix promiscuously in gatherings of men.

And when the Fourteenth Amendment was adopted, Congress rejected Susan B. Anthony's pleas for a specific guarantee that women and men stand as equals before the law. Recall that at that time in our nation's history, total political silence was imposed on women—they could not vote or hold office, and if they married they could not contract or hold property except under their husband's aegis.

Since present constitutional guarantees were not framed with a view toward eradication of gender-based discrimination, for over half a century, feminists of both sexes have urged ratification of an Equal Rights Amendment. What was once a distant dream is now a near-reality. Thirty-three states have ratified the ERA since its approval by Congress in 1972; these states represent the vast majority of the nation's population. The ERA, now top priority of the League of Women Voters and supported by the AFL-CIO, seems destined to become part of our fundamental law in time for the nation's bicentennial.[1]

The ERA, like the due process and equal protection clauses, restricts governmental action. Unless action by government is implicated, constitutional guarantees of even-handed treatment do not control conduct in the private sector. However, Congress as well as state and local legislatures, and executives at every level of government, have made equal opportunity, and eradication of gender-based discrimination, the responsibility of private as well as public employers.

No fanfare marked the beginning of the new-style statutory rights given to women. In 1963, Congress mandated equal pay for equal work, a proposition that has universal appeal, at least in principle. (Practice continues to lag far behind.) In itself enactment of the Equal Pay Act was hardly an innovation. The ILO had adopted a convention on the subject in 1951; France had insisted in 1958 that an equal pay provision be included in the Rome Treaty that launched the EEC. Moreover, some have been sold on the equal pay principle by the argument that if the employer must pay men and women the same wage, the employer will, of course, prefer to hire men.

But the next year, a more significant development occurred: sex was included, along with race, religion and national origin, in Title VII of the Civil Rights Act of 1964. Title VII was not drafted with women in mind. Indeed, the category "sex" was added by floor amendment—not by a proponent of equal rights, but by a Congressman who sought thereby to defeat the entire bill. His tactic backfired. Complaints of sex discrimination under Title VII have been substantial from the start, and the charges mount higher each season. Probably the most potent weapon against employment discrimination, especially as strengthened by 1972 amendments, Title VII protects women and men against discrimination in hiring, firing, and all terms and conditions of employment. The notion underlying the race and sex discrimination prohibitions of Title VII is this: each person is entitled to be judged on the basis of his or her individual capacity; a visible and immutable biological characteristic—one that bears no necessary relation to ability—may not be used to foreclose individual opportunity.

[1][It failed to pass in time—Ed.]

Consistent with Title VII's nondiscrimination mandate, Presidential Executive Orders have been issued barring sex discrimination by the Government itself, all its agencies, and all those who contract with the Government. In 1972, Congress enacted the first comprehensive ban on assistance to educational institutions that discriminate on the basis of sex, Title IX of the Education Amendments of 1972.

A number of state and local governments have adopted measures comparable to the Federal Executive Orders, Equal Pay Act and Title VII.

It may be appropriate to conclude these comments with observations on two particularly sensitive points. First, does affirmative action required by anti-discrimination laws imply reverse discrimination? Second, are women equipped to pursue equality, or will this route, as Lionel Tiger and some others fear, prove harmful to women and their daughters? As to affirmative action, discrimination in the job market has been the traditional pattern—discrimination in favor of white males, and sometimes a narrower subspecies of that broad class. That pattern, of course, must be terminated. But when an employer traditionally has acted on the basis of a gender characteristic, by hiring only males, gender must be taken into account in order to undo what has been done. Otherwise, the effects of past discrimination will be perpetuated long into the future. Consider a not so hypothetical case in point: police women seek to take the exam for promotion to police sergeant. They are barred for lack of patrol duty experience. Why did they lack this experience? Because patrol jobs are closed to women. Affirmative action is called for in this situation—to provide women with the training needed (and up to now denied them) to qualify for sergeants' jobs.

Last year, a Yonkers, N.Y., Rotarian had the last word when members of the National Organization for Women spoke at a meeting of his club.

> I'm a firm believer in nature. If women were intellectually equal to men, wouldn't equality have come about one thousand years ago?

The answer, of course, is that few women had even an outside chance until the era in which we are living. But in the one thousand years of concern to the Rotarian, most women worked harder in their place than men or women do in the jobs they hold today. Before the mass production age, women's lives were crowded with economic as well as reproductive activity. Women labored to supply the market with food and goods now machine cultivated or manufactured. This activity, coupled with shorter adult life spans and the constant burden of childbearing, explain the historic phenomenon. Inferior intellectual equipment? The Rotarian would be chagrined to discover that women now outscore men on aptitude tests for the study of law—a profession traditionally typed as male. Physically inferior? The life insurance specialists tell us otherwise.

Could it be that the Rotarian's question and others like it, cover an underlying fear? The matter was put this way by Susan Brownmiller in a journal for business executives:

> A mediocre man . . . will suffer the pinch most sharply. No longer will he be assured a comfortable berth. . . . He stands to be displaced . . . by top-flight women on their way up and he will be under assault from equally mediocre women who are perhaps a shade more aggressive or sociable or better connected. Mediocre women have a right to equal treatment too.

I leave it to you to judge whether there is more than a kernel of truth in that comment.

Twin features of contemporary life have combined to make new-style women's rights an idea that is here to stay: curtailed population goals and reduction of necessary home-centered activity. These factors have created an atmosphere in which women and men, who are not so captivated by traditional roles, can create new traditions by their actions, if artificial barriers are removed, and avenues of opportunity held open to them. Until very recently, the law has cast its weight on the side of the status quo, providing support for traditional sex-role allocations, and deterring deviations from the historic pattern. But change is in the wind—the law has begun to provide a stimulus toward a society in which members of both sexes are free to pursue their individual talents. With ratification of the equal rights amendment, my hope and expectation is that the law will develop on course in the new direction.

STEVEN GOLDBERG

The Inevitability of Patriarchy

*Physiological differences may cause psychological differences between the sexes.
Steven Goldberg presents a sophisticated argument from the fact of hormonal
differences between males and females to the conclusion that women should be
socialized to accept male dominance and not to challenge men for traditional
male roles.*

*The main steps in his reasoning are as follows. The male hormone
testosterone, present even before birth, has been shown to cause aggressive
behavior. Aggressiveness leads to the dominance of men in all known societies.
The male domination of any society's most sought-after positions is inevitable;
the few exceptions are irrelevant. Raising girls to strive for these positions,
which they have little or no chance to attain, would simply lead to their failure
and unhappiness as adults. So it is better to channel all children into those
social roles in which they can be expected to succeed. Hence consideration of sex
is relevant in assigning roles.*

*Assessing the correctness of Goldberg's scientific claims is something we must
leave to scientists (see Naomi Weisstein, in this volume). But we can assume
that his premises are true, for the sake of the argument, and examine whether
his conclusions about socialization follow from them. Consider the following
parallel reasoning: "Height is determined by genes and hormones. In virtually
all societies, the tall dominate over the short. Even if 10 percent of the
population were exceptions, this would be irrelevant. Therefore, we should
condition short children to accept the dominance of the tall and not to strive for
positions of power and leadership." If this conclusion does not follow from the
assumptions about height, then Goldberg's conclusion does not follow from the
analogous assumptions about sex.*

Further Reading

L. M. Terman and Leona Tyler, "Psychological Sex Differences," in *A
Manual of Child Psychology*, L. Carmichael, ed. (New York: John Wiley,
1954), pp. 1064–1114.

John Money and Anke A. Ehrhardt, *Man and Woman, Boy and Girl* (Baltimore: Johns Hopkins Press, 1972).

S. N. Levine, "Sex Differences in the Brain," *Scientific American,* 214 (April 1966), 84–90.

THE UNIVERSALITY OF PATRIARCHY

The definitions of patriarchy and male dominance used in this book, while they are similar to the orthodox anthropological definitions, will be meant to connote no more than is stated here. Patriarchy is any system of organization (political, economic, religious, or social) that associates authority and leadership primarily with males and in which males fill the vast majority of authority and leadership positions. Patriarchy refers only to suprafamilial levels of organization; authority in familial and dyadic relationships is described by the term *male dominance.* Patriarchy is universal. For all the variety different societies have demonstrated in developing different types of political, economic, religious, and social systems, there has never been a society that has failed to associate authority and leadership in these areas with men. No anthropologist contests the fact that patriarchy is universal. Indeed, of all social institutions there is probably none whose universality is so totally agreed upon. . . .

MALE DOMINANCE DEFINED AND DISCOVERED

Male dominance refers to the *feeling* acknowledged by the emotions of both men and women that the woman's will is somehow subordinate to the male's and that general authority in dyadic and familial relationships, in whatever terms a particular society defines authority, ultimately resides in the male. I realize that this is not the most graceful way of defining male dominance, but it is the most accurate. As was the case with patriarchy, male dominance is universal; no society has ever failed to conform its expectations of men and women, and the social roles relevant to these expectations, to the feeling of men and women that it is the male who "takes the lead." This book will attempt to demonstrate that every society accepts the existence of these feelings, and conforms to their existence by socializing children accordingly, because every society must.

For all but a very few societies the presence of male dominance is apparent from the customs of deference so well documented by the anthropologists. It is important to bear in mind, however, that dominance and deference refer to the *feelings* that come into play in male-female and familial relationships. Anthropologists tend to discuss such feelings in terms of their manifestations in customs of deference because, among other reasons, the inconcreteness of feelings makes it difficult to deal with them in any other way. . . .

The voluminous writings of the feminists attest to the fact that, despite the virtual absence of customs of deference in American society, the feelings and emotional expectations that underpin the customs of every other society affect our behavior as surely as these feelings affect the behavior of the men and women of every other society. . . . Thus the feminist novelist objects to the fact that it is somehow the male who "takes the lead" in endless numbers of situations as varied as crossing streets and choosing friends. The husband tends to "tell" ("my husband told me to take the TV to the repair shop") while the wife tends to "ask" ("my wife asked me to take the TV to the repair shop"). To be sure, women do, as these novelists acknowledge, have a great deal of power in that they make decisions in many areas, but it is the *feeling* that the husband *lets* them make such decisions (that he delegates authority, that he "allows") that annoys the feminist and that is the evidence of the presence of male dominance. . . .

MALE ATTAINMENT OF HIGH-STATUS ROLES AND POSITIONS

Occasionally one who attempts to deny the universality of male dominance will mimic those who claim the existence of a matriarchy: he will not actually name a society whose institutions do not acknowledge male dominance but will merely make vague reference to unnamed societies. He knows that, if he were to be specific, reference to the ethnographic materials on the society he named would show that, while it was perhaps matrilineal or matrilocal, the society's institutions conformed to patriarchy and male dominance as much as, or more than, do ours.

More often, however, he invokes societies such as the Bamendas, the Hopi, the Iroquois, the Mbuti Pygmies, the Nayar, certain Philippine groups, the people of the Kibbutz, or even the fictitious Amazons. These alleged exceptions are merely societies that associate with women *tasks* or *functions* that *we* associate with men. These are not exceptions to the universality of male dominance, for—in addition to the fact that dominance-deference refers to the *feelings* of men and women in every society that authority resides in the male, feelings that are reflected in the expectations of male and female behavior in every society—male dominance in no way precludes the possibility that any task or function which we (as uninvolved outsiders) may choose to emphasize can be seen to be served by women in one society or another. As was the case with customs of deference, what is important here is the attitudes of the members of the society in question. In every society, whatever the particular tasks performed by women, the members feel that women do "women's tasks" (as defined by the particular society) either because only women are biologically capable of the tasks or because men serve functions that are more crucial to the society's survival. *Every society gives higher status to male roles than to the nonmaternal roles of females.* To put it another, and I believe more illuminating, way: *in every society males attain the high-status (nonmaternal) roles and positions and perform the high-status tasks, whatever those tasks are.* Margaret Mead has written:

> In every known human society, the male's need for achievement can be recognized. *Men may cook, or weave or dress dolls or hunt hummingbirds, but if such activities are appropriate occupations of men, then the whole society, men and women alike, votes them as important. When the same occupations are performed by women, they are regarded as less important.* [1]

A woman who is older, wealthier, from a higher class or "better" family, more intelligent, or more educated than a particular male may be given authority over that male and perhaps she may even feel dominance over him, but she will have less status and authority than an equivalent male and she will feel deference toward him. Thus in some societies the older woman whose husband has died rules the family, and the presence of an educated, wealthy woman will make the less wealthy and educated male experience feelings of insecurity. *But whatever variable one chooses, authority, status, and dominance within each stratum rest with the male in contacts with equivalent females.*

Men do not merely fill most of the roles in high-status areas, they also fill the high-status roles in low-status areas. The higher the level of power, authority, status, prestige, or position—whether the area be economic, occupational, political, or religious—the higher the percentage of males. Thus the percentage of women in the work force in the United States has risen by 75 percent since 1900, but the percentage of women in the high-status area of medicine has declined during this period. In the Soviet Union, where medicine has a far lower status than it does in the United

---

[1]Margaret Mead, *Male and Female* (New York: William Morrow, 1949), p. 168. Emphasis added. As we shall see, one need not postulate a male "need to achieve" any greater than that of the female to explain why men attain the high-status roles in every society; the male aggression advantage is enough to explain why high-status roles and positions are always attained primarily by men and why every society associates its (nonmaternal) high-status roles with men.

States, the majority of all doctors are women, but as one ascends from the level of practical medicine to the levels of authority the percentage of males rises until, at the top, males constitute the overwhelming majority.[2]

Of all the *tasks* one might think of or choose to emphasize, virtually every one, with the exception of those related to protection, fighting, and political authority, is associated with women in one society or another,[3] but in every society it is the roles filled by men that are given high status. None of this, of course, denies that in every society it is women who are responsible for the care and rearing of the young, the single most important function served in any society or in nature itself. Just as patriarchy, male dominance, and male attainment of high-status roles and positions are universal, so is the association of nurturance and emotional socialization with the woman universal, and these female roles are, in some societies, given the highest of status.

. . .

TESTOSTERONE AND AGGRESSION

The hormonal etiology of aggression is exceedingly complex. It is a gross oversimplification, at best, to speak merely in terms of hormone levels. The male hormone is not, in itself, "aggressive." The biological aggression of which we shall speak is a function of an interaction between the fetally prepared central nervous system and the later presence of endogenous testosterone. This explains the possibility of the rare exceptional species in which the effect of testosterone in the male is the reverse of that in humans and in which the female is more aggressive than the male. It is by no means clear that there are any such exceptions at all among mammals. Certainly there are none in the species closely related to man. It has been suggested that the golden hamster is the single experimental exception to the development of sexual differences in aggression outlined here,[4] but this has recently been brought into question.[5] Even if the female hamster is

[2]See William J. Goode, *World Revolution and Family Patterns* (New York: Free Press of Glencoe, 1963), pp. 57–66.

[3]While there are no exceptions in these three spheres (every society's military and leadership functions are served primarily by men), it should be noted for the record that in the mid-nineteenth century the army of Dahomey included a corps of female warriors (different authors estimate their percentage of the total number of warriors as being between 5 and 15 percent) and that at one time Iroquoian women served a vital political function in selecting male leaders (though women were not permitted to lead).

[4]C. H. Phoenix, et al., "Sexual Differentiation as a Function of Androgenic Stimulation," in *Perspectives in Reproduction and Sexual Behavior*, M. Diamond, ed. (Bloomington: Indiana University Press, 1969), pp. 33–49.

[5]Leonore Tiefer, "Gonadal Hormones and Mating Behavior in the Adult Golden Hamster," *Hormones and Behavior*, 1 (1970). If Dr. Tiefer's suggestion is correct and the hamster differs only in mating behavior but not in fighting, then our discussion of hamsters is irrelevant and there are no genuine exceptions at all.

more aggressive than the male, this does not indicate an unwarranted selectivity on our part when we consider the mouse, the rat, and all the other animals for which aggression is associated primarily with the male, as analogues of the human male and exclude the hamster. For, unlike the mouse, rat, and other experimental animals, the hamster female is also larger than the male. This would seem a good indication that the entire CNS (Central Nervous System)-hormonal development of the hamster is the reverse of that in the other experimental animals so that, if one wants to consider the hamster, rather than the other animals, as analogous in its development to humans, he must indicate not only that the human female is more aggressive than the human male but also that she is larger.

With all this in mind, I refer the reader to a number of experiments that indicate beyond a shadow of a doubt that, at least among rats, mice, and many other mammals, testosterone is related not only to sexual differentiation but to aggression itself. In paired tests, females treated with exogenous testosterone during the crucial neonatal period will develop an aggression as adults, if appropriately hormonally treated as adults, equal to that of the male who receives neonatal testosterone stimulation of the CNS endogenously from his own testis. Females treated with androgen on the tenth day following birth will, as adults, demonstrate an aggression, dominance, propensity for fighting, and willingness to fight greater than that of the normal female, but less than that of neonatally treated females or normal males. . . .

HUMAN AGGRESSION

Aggression in human beings is not, of course, as easily described as it is in rats, but for our purposes this fact offers no difficulty; this book does not purport to describe the specific nature of human social aggression, but merely to demonstrate that the hormonal differences between men and women will inevitably manifest themselves in certain societal institutions. I use *aggression* only as a convenient hypothetical term, a nexus which flows from hormones and to which certain societal institutions conform. The reader is free to substitute *the X factor, male behavior,* or any other term that represents an element that flows from specifiable hormonal factors and that determines the limits of specifiable social institutions (patriarchy, male dominance, and male attainment of high-status roles and positions). Likewise, the reader is free to perceive the reality I refer to as a "male-female difference in the capacity for aggression" as a difference in the level of the threshold at which "aggressive" and "dominance" behavior is released. (In one respect the paradigm which envisions a sexual difference in threshold is superior to the paradigm which sees a difference in capacity: one might suggest that the ferocity with which a mother defends her endangered infant demonstrates that the female has a capacity for aggression equal to that of the male. I do not think that such behavior is "aggression" in any meaningful sense, but even if it is the same thing as aggression such female behavior demonstrates only that the environmental threat to her child is sufficient to reach the high threshold at which a female's aggression is released. We would then ask why, if there is no physiological difference between males and females that is relevant to aggression, male aggression is released at a much lower level, i.e., why does a much less threatening stimulus release male aggression so much more easily?) In any case, all that is necessary for the theory presented here is that there is a physiologically generated difference between males and females which engenders in males, to a greater degree or more easily than in females, the behavior to which the social institutions we discuss conform.

This is not, as it might seem at quick glance, tautological, because each of the two elements (the biological and the social) is specified, defined, and described without reference to the other. Thus I use *aggression* as one might use *strength* in an explanation of why young boys are socialized toward boxing prowess and young girls away from it. Greater adult male muscularity engenders greater male "strength," which makes the male a better boxer than the female, so that it is inevitable that boxing champions will be men, boxing will be associated with men, and small children will be socialized accordingly. Similarly, it will be argued, the male hormonal system engenders a greater male "aggression" that results in a male superiority at attaining roles and positions given high status (except when men are biologically incapable of playing a role) so that it is inevitable that positions and roles of leadership and status will be attained by men, and small children will be socialized accordingly.

. . . *The thesis put forth here is that the hormonal renders the social inevitable.*

. . .

THE IRRELEVANCE OF EXCEPTIONS

Whenever a biologist speaks of men and women he is speaking in virtually absolute terms. For all intents and purposes every human being begins life as either a genetic male or a genetic female. When a biologist speaks of masculine and feminine characteristics he is almost always speaking in the statistical terms of probability. When one deals with probability of any sort he expects exceptions. The biological nature of height is not brought into question by the fact that some women are taller than some men or by the fact that within-sex differences in height are much greater than the between-sex differences in height. Few genetic females have testosterone levels approaching that which would be normal for a male; a woman whose testosterone level is even half that of a normal male displays undeniable signs of hirsuteness and general virilization. But even if 10 percent of all women had higher testosterone levels than 10 percent of all men one would not be led to the conclusion that the parameters of hormone distribution by sex are irrelevant any more than he would say that the fact that there are some six-foot women and five-foot men disproves the biological nature of human height. . . .

SOCIALIZATION'S CONFORMATION TO BIOLOGICAL REALITY

Socialization is the process by which society prepares children for adulthood. The way in which its goals conform to the reality of biology is seen quite clearly when we consider the method in which testosterone generates male aggression (testosterone's serially developing nature). Preadolescent boys and girls have roughly equal testosterone levels, yet young boys are far more aggressive than young girls. Eva Figes has used this observation to dismiss incorrectly the possibility of a hormone-aggression association.[6] Now it is quite probable that the boy is more aggressive than the girl for a purely biological reason. We have seen that it is simplistic to speak simply in terms of hormone levels and that there is evidence of male-female differences in the behavior of infants shortly after birth (when differential socialization is not a plausible explanation of such differences). The fetal alteration of the boy's brain by the testosterone that was generated by his testes has probably left him far more sensitive to the aggression-related properties of the testosterone that is present during boyhood than the girl, who did not receive such alteration. But let us for the moment assume that this is not the case. This does not at all reduce the importance of the hormonal factor. For even if the boy is more aggressive than the girl only because the society allows him to be, the boy's socialization still flows from society's acknowledging biological reality. Let us consider what would happen if girls have the same innate aggression as boys and if a society did not socialize girls away from aggressive competitions. Perhaps half of the third-grade baseball team would be female. As many girls as boys would frame their expectations in masculine values and girls would develop not their feminine abilities but their masculine ones. During adolescence, however, the same assertion of the male chromosomal program that causes the boys to grow beards raises their testosterone level, and their potential for aggression, to a level far above that of the adolescent woman. If society did not teach young girls that beating boys at competitions was unfeminine (behavior inappropriate for a woman), if it did not

---

[6]Eva Figes, *Patriarchal Attitudes* (Greenwich, Conn.: Fawcett World, 1971), p. 8.

socialize them away from the political and economic areas in which aggression leads to attainment, these girls would grow into adulthood with self-images based not on succeeding in areas for which biology has left them better prepared than men, but on competitions that most women could not win. If women did not develop feminine qualities as girls (assuming that such qualities do not spring automatically from female biology) they then would be forced to deal with the world in the aggressive terms of men. They would lose every source of power their feminine abilities now give them and they would gain nothing. . . .

DISCRIMINATION OF A SORT

If one is convinced that sexual biology gives the male an advantage in aggression, competitiveness, and dominance, but he does not believe that it engenders in men and women different propensities, cognitive aptitudes, and modes of perception, and if he considers it discrimination when male aggression leads to attainment of position even when aggression is not relevant to the task to be performed, then the unavoidable conclusion is that discrimination so defined is unavoidable. . . .

NAOMI WEISSTEIN

Psychology Constructs the Female

The psychological differences which Steven Goldberg (not to mention Aristotle, Sam Ervin, Jean Jacques Rousseau, etc.) cites are the subject matter of psychology and, generally, biology. Naomi Weisstein rigorously examines the evidential basis of current theories. The evidence consistently shows that whatever views the researchers antecedently held about the psychology of women were generally found confirmed in their research. The prevalence of bias, especially in psychology, is striking.

The relevance of citing the behavior of various animals to determine what is natural for humans is also examined. Three main problems with that approach are (1) that humans need not imitate animals in all ways (for example, we use language); (2) that human behavior is more malleable than that of animals; and (3) that some animal can be found which exhibits almost any practice one wishes to justify in humans.

In short, psychological studies have been biased, the relevance of animal behavior is questionable, and humans have never been available for study in contexts where sex differences were not taught or enforced by the culture. In this situation, we cannot know the limitations of human variability and to what extent distinctions in personality and role between the sexes are natural or inevitable.

Further Reading

ELEANOR MACCOBY and CAROL JACKLIN, eds., *The Psychology of Sex Differences* (Stanford, Ca.: Stanford University Press, 1974).

JUDITH BARDWICK, *Psychology of Women* (New York: Harper & Row, 1971).

It is an implicit assumption that the area of psychology that concerns itself with personality has the onerous but necessary task of describing the limits of human possibility. Thus, when we are about to consider the liberation of women, we naturally look to psychology to tell us what "true" liberation would mean: what would give women the freedom to fulfill their own intrinsic natures?

Psychologists have set about describing the true nature of women with a certainty and a sense of their own infallibility rarely found in the secular world. Bruno Bettelheim tell us that "we must start with the realization that, as much as women want to be good scientists or engineers, they want first and foremost to be womanly companions of men and to be mothers."[1] Erik Erikson, upon noting that young women often ask whether they can "have an identity before they know whom they will marry, and for whom they will make a home," explains somewhat elegiacally that "much of a young woman's identity is already defined in her kind of attractiveness and in the selectivity of her search for the man (or men) by whom she wishes to be sought. . . ." Mature womanly fulfillment, for Erikson, rests on the fact that a woman's ". . . somatic design harbors an 'inner space' destined to bear the offspring of chosen men, and with it, a biological, psychological, and ethical commitment to take care of human infancy."[2] Some psychiatrists even see the acceptance of woman's role by women as a solution to societal problems. "Woman is nurturance," writes Joseph Rheingold, a psychiatrist at Harvard Medical School, ". . . anatomy decrees the life of a woman . . . when women grow up without dread of their biological functions and without subversion by feminist doctrine, and therefore enter upon motherhood with a sense of fulfillment and altruistic sentiment, we shall attain the goal of a good life and a secure world in which to live it."[3]

These views from men who are assumed to be experts reflect, in a surprisingly transparent way, the cultural consensus. They not only assert that a woman is defined by her ability to attract men, but they see no alternative definitions. They think that the definition of a woman in terms of a man is the way it should be; and they back it up with psychosexual incantation and biological ritual curses. A woman has an identity if she is attractive enough to obtain a man, and thus, a home; for this will allow her to set about her life's task of "joyful altruism and nurturance." A woman's *true* nature is that of a happy servant.

Business certainly does not disagree. If views such as Bettelheim's and Erikson's do indeed have something to do with real liberation for women, then seldom in human history has so much money and effort been spent

[1]B. Bettelheim, "The Commitment Required of a Woman Entering a Scientific Profession in Present-day American Society," in *Woman and the Scientific Professions,* an MIT Symposium on American Women in Science and Engineering (Cambridge, Mass., 1965).

[2]E. Erikson, "Inner and Outer Space: Reflections on Womanhood," *Daedalus* 93 (1964).

[3]J. Rheingold, *The Fear of Being a Woman* (New York: Grune & Stratton, 1964), p. 714.

on helping a group of people realize their true potential. Clothing, cosmetics, and home furnishings are multimillion dollar businesses. If you do not like investing in firms that make weaponry and flaming gasoline, then there is a lot of cash in "inner space." Sheet and pillowcase manufacturers are anxious to fill this inner space:

> Mother, for a while this morning, I thought I wasn't cut out for married life. Hank was late for work and forgot his apricot juice and walked out without kissing me, and when I was all alone I started crying. But then the postman came with the sheets and towels you sent, that look like big bandana handkerchiefs, and you know what I thought? That those big red and blue handkerchiefs are for girls like me to dry their tears on so they can get busy and do what a housewife has to do. Throw open the windows and start getting the house ready, and the dinner, maybe clean the silver and put new geraniums in the box. *Everything to be ready for him when he walks through that door.* [4]

Of course, it is not only the sheet and pillowcase manufacturers, the cosmetics industry, and the home furnishings salesmen who profit from and make use of the cultural definitions of men and women. The example above is blatantly and overtly pitched to a particular kind of sexist stereotype: the child nymph. But almost all aspects of the media are normative, that is, they have to do with the ways in which beautiful people, or just folks, or ordinary Americans, or extraordinary Americans should live their lives. They define the possible, and the possibilities are usually in terms of what is male and what is female.

It is an interesting but limited exercise to show that psychologists and psychiatrists embrace these sexist norms of our culture, that they do not see beyond the most superficial and stultifying conceptions of female nature, and that their ideas of female nature serve industry and commerce so well. Just because it is good for business does not mean it is wrong. What I will show is that it is wrong; that there is not the tiniest shred of evidence that these fantasies of servitude and childish dependence have anything to do with women's true potential; that the idea of the nature of human possibility which rests on the accidents of individual development of genitalia, on what is possible today because of what happened yesterday, on the fundamentalist myth of sex-organ causality, has strangled and deflected psychology so that it is relatively useless in describing, explaining, or predicting humans and their behavior. It then goes without saying that present psychology is less than worthless in contributing to a vision that could truly liberate—men as well as women.

The central argument of my essay, then, is this. Psychology has nothing

---

[4]Fieldcrest advertisement in the *New Yorker*, 1965. Italics added.

to say about what women are really like, what they need and what they want, essentially because psychology does not know. I want to stress that this failure is not limited to women; rather, the kind of psychology that has addressed itself to how people act and who they are has failed to understand in the first place why people act the way they do, and certainly failed to understand what might make them act differently.

These psychologists, whether engaged in academic personality research or in clinical psychology and psychiatry, make the central assumption that human behavior rests on an individual and inner dynamic, perhaps fixed in infancy, perhaps fixed by genitalia, perhaps simply arranged in a rather immovable cognitive network. But this assumption is rapidly losing ground as personality psychologists fail again and again to get consistency in the assumed personalities of their subjects.[5] Meanwhile, the evidence is accumulating that what a person does and who he believes himself to be will in general be a function of what people around him expect him to be, and what the overall situation in which he is acting implies that he is. Compared to the influence of the social context within which a person lives, his or her history and traits, as well as biological make-up, may simply be random variations, noise superimposed on the true signal that can predict behavior.

Some academic personality psychologists are at least looking at the counter-evidence and questioning their theories; no such corrective is occurring in clinical psychology and psychiatry. Freudians and neo-Freudians, Adlerians and neo-Adlerians, classicists and swingers, clinicians and psychiatrists simply refuse to look at the evidence against their theory and practice. And they support their theory and their practice with stuff so transparently biased as to have absolutely no standing as empirical evidence.

To summarize: psychology has failed to understand what people are and how they act because (1) psychology has looked for inner traits when it should have been noting social context; and (2) theoreticians of personality have generally been clinicians and psychiatrists, and they have never considered it necessary to offer evidence to support their theories.

THEORY WITHOUT EVIDENCE

Let us turn to the second cause of failure first: the acceptance by psychiatrists and clinical psychologists of theory without evidence. If we inspect the literature of personality, it is immediately obvious that the bulk of it is written by clinicians and psychiatrists whose major support for their theories is "years of intensive clinical experience." This is a tradition

---

[5] J. Block, "Some Reasons for the Apparent Inconsistency of Personality," *Psychological Bulletin* 70 (1968), pp. 210–22.

started by Freud. His "insights" occurred during the course of his work with his patients. Now there is nothing wrong with such an approach to theory *formulation;* a person is free to make up theories with any inspiration that works: divine revelation, intensive clinical practice, a random numbers table. However, he is not free to claim any validity for his theory until it has been tested and confirmed. But theories are treated in no such tentative way in ordinary clinical practice. Consider Freud. What he thought constituted evidence fell short of the most minimal conditions of scientific rigor. In *The Sexual Enlightenment of Children,* the classic document that is supposed to demonstrate empirically the existence of a castration complex and its connection to a phobia, Freud based his analysis on the reports of the father of the little boy, himself in therapy, and a devotee of Freudian theory.[6] I really do not have to comment further on the contamination in this kind of evidence. It is remarkable that only recently has Freud's classic theory on the sexuality of women—the notion of the double orgasm—been actually tested physiologically and found just plain wrong. Now those who claim that fifty years of psychoanalytic experience constitute evidence enough of the essential truths of Freud's theory should ponder the robust health of the double orgasm. Did women, until Masters and Johnson,[7] believe they were having two different kinds of orgasm? Did their psychiatrists cow them into reporting something that was not true? If so, were there other things they reported that were also not true? Did psychiatrists ever observe anything different from what their theories had led them to believe? If clinical experience means anything at all, surely we should have been done with the double-orgasm myth long before the Masters and Johnson studies.

But certainly, you may object, "years of intensive clinical experience" are the only reliable measure in a discipline that rests for its findings on insights, sensitivity, and intuition. The problem with insight, sensitivity, and intuition is that they can confirm for all time the biases that one started out with. People used to be absolutely convinced of their ability to tell which of their number were engaging in witchcraft. All it required was some sensitivity to the workings of the devil.

. . .

THE SOCIAL CONTEXT

Since clinical experience and tools can be shown to be worse than useless when tested for consistency, efficacy, agreement, and reliability, we can safely conclude that theories of a clinical nature advanced about women are also worse than useless. I want to turn now to the second major

[6]S. Freud, *The Sexual Enlightenment of Children* (New York: Collier Books, 1963).
[7]W. H. Masters and V. E. Johnson, *Human Sexual Response* (Boston: Little, Brown, 1966).

point in my essay: even when psychological theory is constructed so that it may be tested, and rigorous standards of evidence are used, it has become increasingly clear that in order to understand why people do what they do, and certainly in order to change what people do, psychologists must turn away from the theory of the causal nature of the inner dynamic and look to the social context within which individuals live.

Before examining the relevance of this approach for the question of women, let me first sketch the groundwork for this assertion. In the first place, it is clear that personality tests never yield consistent predictions;[8] a rigid authoritarian on one measure will be an unauthoritarian on the next. But the reason for this inconsistency is only now becoming clear; it seems overwhelmingly to have much more to do with the social situation in which the subject finds himself than with the subject himself.

In a series of brilliant experiments, R. Rosenthal and his coworkers have shown that if one group of experimenters has one hypothesis about what they expect to find, and another group of experimenters has the opposite hypothesis, both groups will obtain results in accord with their hypotheses.[9] The results obtained are not due to mishandling of data by biased experimenters; rather, the bias of the experimenter somehow creates a changed environment in which subjects actually act differently. For instance, in one experiment subjects were to assign numbers to pictures of men's faces, with high numbers representing the subject's judgment that the man in the picture was a successful person, and low numbers representing the subject's judgment that the man in the picture was an unsuccessful person. One group of experimenters was told that the subjects tended to rate the faces high; another group of experimenters was told that the subjects tended to rate the faces low. Each group of experimenters was instructed to follow precisely the same procedure: they were required to read to subjects a set of instructions and to *say nothing else.* For the 375 subjects run, the results showed clearly that those subjects who performed the task with experimenters who expected high ratings gave high ratings, and those subjects who performed the task with experimenters who expected low ratings gave low ratings. How did this happen? The experimenters all used the same words, but something in their conduct made one group of subjects do one thing, and another group of subjects do another thing.

The concreteness of the changed conditions produced by expectation is a fact, a reality: even in two separate studies with animal subjects, those

---

[8]Block, "Apparent Inconsistency."

[9]R. Rosenthal and L. Jacobson, *Pygmalion in the Classroom: Teacher Expectation and Pupil's Intellectual Development* (New York: Holt, Rinehart & Winston, 1968); R. Rosenthal, *Experimenter Effects in Behavioral Research* (New York: Appleton-Century-Crofts, 1966).

experimenters who were told that rats learning mazes had been especially bred for brightness obtained better learning from their rats than did experimenters believing their rats to have been bred for dullness.[10] In a very recent study Rosenthal and Jacobson extended their analysis to the natural classroom situation.[11] Here, they tested a group of students and reported to the teacher that some among the students tested "showed great promise." Actually, the students so named had been selected on a random basis. Some time later, the experimenters retested the group of students: those students whose teachers had been told that they were "promising" showed real and dramatic increments in their I.Q.'s as compared to the rest of the students. Something in the conduct of the teachers toward those whom the teachers believed to be the "bright" students made those students brighter.

Thus, even in carefully controlled experiments and with no outward or conscious difference in behavior, the hypotheses we start with will influence the behavior of the subject enormously. These studies are extremely important when assessing the validity of psychological studies of women. Since it is beyond doubt that most of us start with notions about the nature of men and women, the validity of a number of observations of sex differences is questionable, even when these observations have been made under carefully controlled conditions. Second, and more important, the Rosenthal experiments point quite clearly to the influence of social expectation. In some extremely important ways, people are what you expect them to be, or at least they behave as you expect them to behave. Thus, if women, according to Bettelheim, want first and foremost to be good wives and mothers, it is extremely likely that this is what Bruno Bettelheim and the rest of society want them to be.

· · ·

BIOLOGICALLY BASED THEORIES

Two theories of the nature of women, which come not from psychiatric and clinical tradition, but from biology, can be disposed of now with little difficulty. The first biological theory of sex differences argues that since females and males differ in their sex hormones, and sex hormones enter the brain, there must be innate differences in nature.[12] But this argument

[10]R. Rosenthal and K. L. Fode, "The Effect of Experimenter Bias on the Performance of the Albino Rat," unpublished manuscript (Cambridge: Harvard University, 1960); R. Rosenthal and R. Lawson, "A Longitudinal Study of the Effects of Experimenter Bias on the Operant Learning of Laboratory Rats," unpublished manuscript (Cambridge: Harvard University, 1961).

[11]Rosenthal and Jacobson.

[12]D. A. Hamburg and D. T. Lunde, "Sex Hormones in the Development of Sex Differences in Human Behavior," in E. Maccoby, ed., *The Development of Sex Differences* (Stanford: Stanford University Press, 1966), pp. 1–24.

only tells us that there are differences in physiological state. The problem is whether these differences are at all relevant to behavior. Recall that Schachter and Singer have shown that a particular physiological state can itself lead to a multiplicity of felt emotional states and outward behavior, depending on the social situation.[13] The second theory is a form of biological reductionism: sex-role behavior in some primate species is described, and it is concluded that this is the natural behavior for humans. Putting aside the not insignificant problem of observer bias (for instance, H. Harlow of the University of Wisconsin, after observing differences between male and female rhesus monkeys, quotes Lawrence Sterne to the effect that women are silly and trivial and concludes that "men and women have differed in the past and they will differ in the future"),[14] there are a number of problems with this approach.

The most general and serious problem is that there are no grounds to assume that anything primates do is necessary, natural, or desirable in humans, for the simple reason that humans are not nonhumans. For instance, it is found that male chimpanzees placed alone with infants will not "mother" them. Jumping from hard data to ideological speculation researchers conclude from this information that *human* females are necessary for the safe growth of human infants. Following this logic, it would be as reasonable to conclude that it is quite useless to teach human infants to speak since it has been tried with chimpanzees and it does not work.

One strategy that has been used is to extrapolate from primate behavior to "innate" human preference by noticing certain trends in primate behavior as one moves phylogenetically closer to humans. But there are great difficulties with this approach. When behaviors from lower primates are directly opposite to those of higher primates, or to those one expects of humans, they can be dismissed on evolutionary grounds—higher primates and/or humans grew out of that kid stuff. On the other hand, if the behavior of higher primates is counter to the behavior considered natural for humans, while the behavior of some lower primate is considered natural for humans, the higher primate behavior can be dismissed also on the grounds that it has diverged from an older, prototypical pattern. So either way, one can select those behaviors one wants to prove as innate for humans. In addition, one does not know whether the sex-role behavior

[13]S. Schachter and J. E. Singer, "Cognitive, Social and Physiological Determinants of Emotional State," *Psychological Review* 69 (1962).

[14]H. F. Harlow, "The Heterosexual Affectional System in Monkeys," *The American Psychologist* 17 (1962).

exhibited is dependent on the phylogenetic rank or on the environmental conditions (both physical and social) under which different species live.

Is there then any value at all in primate observations as they relate to human females and males? There is a value but it is limited: its function can be no more than to show some extant examples of diverse sex-role behavior. It must be stressed, however, that this is an extremely limited function. The extant behavior does not begin to suggest all the possibilities, either for nonhuman primates or for humans. Bearing these caveats in mind, it is nonetheless interesting that if one inspects the limited set of existing nonhuman primate sex-role behaviors, one finds, in fact, a much larger range of sex-role behavior than is commonly believed to exist. Biology appears to limit very little; the fact that a female gives birth does not mean, even in nonhumans, that she necessarily cares for the infant (in marmosets, for instance, the male carries the infant at all times except when the infant is feeding).[15] Natural female and male behavior varies all the way from females who are much more aggressive and competitive than males (for example, Tamarins) and male "mothers" (for example, Titi monkeys, night monkeys, and marmosets), to submissive and passive females and male antagonists (for example, rhesus monkeys).[16]

But even for the limited function that primate arguments serve, the evidence has been misused. Invariably, only those primates have been cited that exhibit exactly the kind of behavior that the proponents of the biological basis of human female behavior wish were true for humans. Thus, baboons and rhesus monkeys are generally cited: males in these groups exhibit some of the most irritable and aggressive behavior found in primates, and if one wishes to argue that females are naturally passive and submissive, these groups provide vivid examples. There are abundant counterexamples, such as those mentioned above; in fact, in general a counterexample can be found for every sex-role behavior cited, including, male "mothers." The presence of counterexamples has not stopped florid and overarching theories of the natural or biological basis of male privilege from proliferating. For instance, there have been a number of theories dealing with the innate incapacity of human males for monogamy. Here, as in most of this type of theorizing, baboons are a favorite example, probably because of their fantasy value: the family unit of the hamadryas baboon, for instance, consists of a highly constant pattern of one male and a number of females and their young. And again, the counterexamples, such as the invariably monogamous gibbon, are ignored.

[15]G. D. Mitchell, "Paternalistic Behavior in Primates," *Psychological Bulletin* 71 (1969).

[16]All these are lower-order primates, which makes their behavior with reference to humans unnatural, or more natural; take your choice.

An extreme example of this maiming and selective truncation of the evidence in the service of a plea for the maintenance of male privilege is a recent book, *Men in Groups,* by a man who calls himself Tiger.[17] The central claim of this book is that females are incapable of honorable collective action because they are incapable of "bonding" as in "male bonding." What is male bonding? Its surface definition is simple: "a particular relationship between two or more males such that they react differently to members of their bonding units as compared to individuals outside of it."[18] If one deletes the word male, the definition, on its face, would seem to include all organisms that have any kind of social organization. But this is not what Tiger means. For instance, Tiger asserts that because females are incapable of bonding, they should be restricted from public life. Why is bonding an exclusively male behavior? Because, says Tiger, it is seen in male primates. All male primates? No, very few male primates. Tiger cites two examples where male bonding is seen: rhesus monkeys and baboons. Surprise, surprise. But not even all baboons: as mentioned above, the hamadryas social organization consists of one-male units; so does that of the Gelada baboon.[19] The great apes do not go in for male bonding much either. The male bond is hardly a serious contribution to scholarship; one reviewer for *Science* has observed that the book "shows basically more resemblance to a partisan political tract than to a work of objective social science," with male bonding being "some kind of behavioral phlogiston."[20]

. . . In summary, primate arguments can tell us very little about our innate sex-role behavior; if they tell us anything at all, they tell us that there is no one biologically natural female or male behavior and that sex-role behavior in nonhuman primates is much more varied than has previously been thought.

CONCLUSION

In brief, the uselessness of present psychology with regard to women is simply a special case of the general conclusion: one must understand social expectations about women if one is going to characterize the behavior of women.

[17]L. Tiger, *Men in Groups* (New York: Random House, 1969). M. Schwarz-Belkin, "Les Fleurs du Mal," in *Festscript for Gordon Piltdown* (New York: Ponzi Press, 1914), claims that the name was originally *Mouse,* but this may be a reference to an earlier L. Tiger (putative).

[18]*Ibid.,* pp. 19–20.

[19]Mitchell, "Paternalistic Behavior."

[20] M. H. Fried, "Mankind Excluding Woman," review of Tiger's *Men in Groups, Science* 165 (1969), p. 884.

How are women characterized in our culture and in psychology? They are inconsistent, emotionally unstable, lacking in a strong conscience or superego, weaker, nurturant rather than productive, intuitive rather than intelligent, and, if they are at all "normal," suited to the home and the family. In short, the list adds up to a typical minority-group stereotype of inferiority:[21] if women know their place, which is in the home, they are really quite lovable, happy, childlike, loving creatures. In a review of the intellectual differences between little boys and little girls, Eleanor Maccoby has shown that there are no intellectual differences until about high school, or, if there are, girls are slightly ahead of boys.[22] In high school girls begin to do worse on a few intellectual tasks, such as arithmetic reasoning, and beyond high school the achievement of women now measured in terms of productivity and accomplishment drops off even more rapidly. There are a number of other, nonintellectual tests which show sex differences; I chose the intellectual differences since it is seen clearly that women start becoming inferior. It is useless to talk about women being different but equal; all of the tests I can think of have a "good" outcome and a "bad" outcome. Women usually end up at the "bad" outcome. In light of social expectations about women, what is surprising is not that women end up where society expects they will; what is surprising is that little girls do not get the message that they are supposed to be stupid until high school; and what is even more remarkable is that some women resist this message even after high school, college, and graduate school.

My essay began with remarks on the task of discovering the limits of human potential. Psychologists must realize that it is they who are limiting discovery of human potential. They refuse to accept evidence if they are clinical psychologists, or, if they are rigorous, they assume that people move in a context-free ether, with only their innate dispositions and their individual traits determining what they will do. Until psychologists begin respecting evidence and until they begin looking at the social contexts within which people move, psychology will have nothing of substance to offer in this task of discovery. I do not know what immutable differences exist between men and women apart from differences in their genitals; perhaps there are some other unchangeable differences; probably there are a number of irrelevant differences. But it is clear that until social expectations for men and women are equal, until we provide equal respect for both men and women, our answers to this question will simply reflect our prejudices.

[21]H. M. Hacker, "Women as a Minority Group," *Social Forces* 30 (1951).
[22]E. Maccoby, *The Development of Sex Differences*.

MICHAEL LEVIN

Vs. Ms.

Michael Levin presents some reasons for rejecting the feminists' proposed terms chairperson *and* Ms., *and for retaining* chairman, Miss, *and* Mrs. *Not only are the new terms awkward and unpoetic, but they make us self-conscious about the way we speak. If language is to convey our thoughts effectively, we must not be forced to choose our words so carefully; they should come to us unconsciously, Levin argues.*

To the view that English terms such as chairman *embody an outlook in which women cannot be chairmen, he points out that it is perfectly consistent and grammatical to say, "A woman is the chairman." Some philosophers, such as Ludwig Wittgenstein, have held the opposite position, though: that subtle nuances of language embody an entire world view.*

As for Ms., *Levin offers a biological argument. Reproduction would be hindered, he claims, if one sex did not take the role of "aggressor" in initiating sexual encounters, the other the role of "accepter." Since in humans, males are the aggressors, they need to know the availability status of prospective mates. The distinction between* Miss *and* Mrs. *conveys this information, he says. Since women are the accepters, they do not need the corresponding information; hence the ubiquitous* Mr.

Further Reading

ELIZABETH LANE BEARDSLEY, "Referential Genderization," *Philosophical Forum*, 5 (1973–74), 285–93.

WILLIAM SUTTON, "Sexual Fairness in Language," Document #ED–089–301 (Educational Resources Information Center, 1974).

JANICE MOULTON, "The Myth of the Neutral 'Man,'" in *Feminism and Philosophy*, M. Braggin, F. Elliston, and J. English, eds. (Totowa, N.J.: Littlefield, Adams, 1977).

As a member of Academia, the Maginot Line in the war of good sense against Women's Liberation, I have noticed a new disturbing manifestation of that movement's influence: the warping of language to suit the ideological conceptions of the new feminism. My colleagues are becoming chairpersons and he/she's. Ms.'s abound. Every memo contains such terms, tacit sermons on or boosts for feminism. These ugly neologisms have lately spread to the media. The progeny of the Pepsi Generation are the Pepsi People, who feel free. If you listen closely, not only have newspersons replaced newsmen, but TV football commentators have taken to referring to the "people" on the offensive line. One suspects unpublicized ukases from the network executives.

Like all bullies, the new feminists are attacking their easiest target—language. And make no mistake, language is under attack. Women's Lib has already shown itself willing to debase language, with its inaccurate talk of rape as a "political" crime (where were the caucuses and ultimata?) and housewifery as "prostitution." This effort to mutilate English further under the banner of "desexizing" language is altogether pernicious. Efforts to legislate linguistic change in line with a special world view have the net effect of making us unendurably *self-conscious* about our own language. Such a state of mind is profoundly unsupportable. Language is the vehicle of thought, and in an important sense we must be unconscious of our choice of words if we are to express our thoughts. When we become entangled with decisions about how to speak we lose contact with the reality our speech is directed to. Surely the most uncomfortable moments of life are marked precisely by the need to think what to say: emotional scenes, awkward first dates, diplomatic negotiations with the boss. When things go smoothly we don't think about what words to use. They come.

Women's Lib is succeeding in making everybody self-conscious about his use of language. Again, listen to your local commentator. There is a small but perceptible hesitation as he chooses his pronouns to describe, say, the average consumer. He? She? He or She? He finally opts for "the average person" and tries to avoid pronominal constructions. Editorial decisions about pronouns become tedious, since they come at hundreds per day. He does not yet love Big Sister.

It might be hoped that this imposition on our thinking process will eventually collapse of its own onerousness. Nonetheless, as Justice Holmes remarked, the mode in which the inevitable comes to pass is effort, so part of the process of lifting this burden of self-consciousness must be the opposition of those who resent oppression. Women have the greater obligation in curbing their "sisters'" excesses, since protestations like these

By permission of Michael E. Levin.

can always be dismissed as masculine insecurity. Yet acquiescence by men bending the knee to ingratiate themselves with "progressive" women is the more contemptible. A hen-pecked "Yes, dear" would have done.

It will be replied that willfully altering language, however unpleasant the process, will expunge from it sexist prejudices. Does not "minuteman" create a presumption against women taking up arms? To the large claim that English is anti-woman a general scholium must be entered in rebuttal. *Pace* the speculations of some sociolinguists, the use of a language does not commit the user to any special theses or view of the world. Anything can be affirmed, and denied, in a natural language. Take "shrew," cited by feminists as a case of linguistic sexism. That English does not commit us to the existence of shrews is shown by the fact that the existence of shrews may be denied in English: "There are no shrews." This would be *self-contradictory* if English were indeed sexually biased. Perhaps the feminists are aiming simply to eliminate the words for expressing certain thoughts (e.g., that some women are shrill and strident). This is Newspeak, whose dangers are patent.

Granted, English idioms change with social patterns. WWII gave us "Rosie the riveter." But we cannot even predict these changes, let alone try to dictate them. They occur at the same unconscious level as speech itself. Certainly it is hard to imagine how the English scheme of pronominal reference, centered on "he," could alter. It fits the natural iambic rhythm of English as the feminine "person" does not. "He or she who hesitates is lost" and "People are the measure of all things" fall flat.

I am not denying that language tells us something about ourselves. It is interesting to ponder the masculine and feminine nouns of languages which, unlike English, do have gender. Even more interesting are the inflected languages. In classical Greek the neuter coincides with the masculine roughly four times as much as it does with the feminine—and where it coincides with the feminine it coincides with the masculine as well. Were our ancestors telling us something?

Consider, then, the title: "Ms." Many people resist replacing the "Miss/Mrs." distinction by "Ms." but can only come up with a distasteful echo of caricatured Negro dialect as a reason. What actually is the function of the "Miss/Mrs." distinction? I suspect it is this. Evolution has selected bisexual intercourse as that reproductive method which maximizes genetic variety compatibly with fecundity. Under such a system one sex must be the aggressor, the other the accepter. If neither aggressed nothing would happen. If both did either nothing *but* mating would happen, or, more probably, the similarity of the mating behavior of the sexes would deprive members of one sex of grounds for pursuing the opposite sex rather than their own, and homosexuality would wipe the species out. In the human species Man is the aggressor and Woman the accepter. As man is the aggressor he has to know, when encountering a new female, if she is eligible for his overtures. A woman need know nothing similar of a new man, since she is not responsible for initiation. The Miss/Mrs. device signals the male immediately as to the potentials for his future relations with this new female. The possibility of sexual awareness always exists between man and woman, and Miss/Mrs. is one of the many ways of accommodating this. (To deplore this fact and call men beasts—or pigs, in the new argot—is to deplore human sexuality itself. This fact, incidentally, also creates unique complications for across-the-board on-the-job sexual integration.) Miss/Mrs. has come about through its evolutionary value and consilience with human nature.

I imagine the feminist reply would be to deny outright this essential difference between men and women, chalk it up to "society" (a useless hypothesis for so ubiquitous a phenomenon) and ask why women should not have the sexual prerogatives of men. I am reluctant even to argue for my own claim since to do so would imply that it is recondite or in some way less than completely self-evident. I can only appeal to each person's experience of trying to do things over the long haul in any other than what Bill Cosby once called "the regular way." But I must confess a certain desire to see the new feminist make the indicated reply, for it tips her real hand: not the desire to bring language into line with "equal treatment" but the desire to upset the whole sexual applecart. And they are succeeding. They have come near to making us self-conscious about the language of sexuality, and with that may come such self-consciousness about sex itself as to destroy spontaneity. We must begin to resist these encroachments.

ROBIN LAKOFF

Language and Woman's Place

Robin Lakoff presents examples of common English usage to illustrate two major claims: (1) that women are taught to speak differently from men, and (2) that the rules of our language cause all of us to describe men and women differently.

*A girl is taught to use less forceful words ("oh dear" instead of "damn") and to phrase questions, commands, and even statements in a mild and unassertive way ("It's too expensive, isn't it?" instead of "It's too expensive"). When she speaks this way in later life, it conveys the impression that her opinions are unimportant or not well founded and that she is generally less sure of herself than a man would be. There are also many words, used almost exclusively by women, which tend to make the subject or the speaker seem trivial or unserious (*divine, cute*).*

Lakoff further notes the ways we talk about women. The use of lady *and* girl *in place of* woman, *where* gent *or* boy *would be inappropriate, again makes women seem fragile, trivial, or immature. That* girl *and* lady *are euphemisms suggests that* woman *has sexual connotations which need to be covered by euphemism.*

Finally, Lakoff argues that these linguistic practices affect—and reflect—the way men view women and women view themselves. However, rather than calling for wiping out all the sexual imbalances in English, such as the generic he, *Lakoff suggests focusing on those words which do clearly demean one sex and which can be changed. Pronouns are probably here to stay, so Lakoff does not use alternative pronouns such as* tey, *adopted by Alison Jaggar earlier in this volume.*

Further Reading

ROBERT BAKER, " 'Pricks' and 'Chicks': A Plea for 'Persons,' " in *Philosophy and Sex,* R. Baker and F. Elliston, eds. (Buffalo, N.Y.: Prometheus Books, 1975), pp. 45–64.

VIRGINIA VALIAN, "Linguistics and Feminism," in *Feminism and Philosophy,* M. Braggin, F. Elliston, and J. English, eds. (Totowa, N.J.: Littlefield, Adams, 1977).

Women experience linguistic discrimination in two ways: in the way they are taught to use language, and in the way general language use treats them. Both tend, as we shall see, to relegate women to certain subservient functions: that of sex object, or servant; and therefore certain lexical items mean one thing applied to men, another to women, a difference that cannot be predicted except with reference to the different roles the sexes play in society.

· · ·

If a little girl "talks rough" like a boy, she will normally be ostracized, scolded, or made fun of. In this way society, in the form of a child's parents and friends, keeps her in line, in her place. This socializing process is, in most of its aspects, harmless and often necessary, but in this particular instance—the teaching of special linguistic uses to little girls—it raises serious problems, though the teachers may well be unaware of this. If the little girl learns her lesson well, she is not rewarded with unquestioned acceptance on the part of society; rather, the acquisition of this special style of speech will later be an excuse others use to keep her in a demeaning position, to refuse to take her seriously as a human being. Because of the way she speaks, the little girl—now grown to womanhood—will be accused of being unable to speak precisely or to express herself forcefully.

· · ·

TALKING LIKE A LADY

"Women's language" shows up in all levels of the grammar of English. We find differences in the choice and frequency of lexical items; in the situations in which certain syntactic rules are performed; in intonational and other supersegmental patterns. As an example of lexical differences, imagine a man and a woman both looking at the same wall, painted a pinkish shade of purple. The woman may say [1]:

[1] The wall is mauve,

with no one consequently forming any special impression of her as a result of the words alone; but if the man should say [1], one might well conclude he was imitating a woman sarcastically or was a homosexual or an interior decorator.

From Robin Lakoff, *Language and Woman's Place* (New York: Harper & Row, 1975), pp. 4–6, 8–12, 14, 16–17, 19–20, 22–26, 28, 31–32, 34–37, 40–41, 43–45. Copyright © 1975 by Robin Lakoff. Reprinted by permission of the publisher.

· · ·

Aside from specific lexical items like color names, we find differences between the speech of women and that of men in the use of particles that grammarians often describe as "meaningless." . . .

. . . Consider:

> [2] (a) Oh dear, you've put the peanut butter in the refrigerator again.
> (b) Shit, you've put the peanut butter in the refrigerator again.

It is safe to predict that people would classify the first sentence as part of "women's language," the second as "men's language." It is true that many self-respecting women are becoming able to use sentences like [2] (b) publicly without flinching, but this is a relatively recent development, and while perhaps the majority of Middle America might condone the use of (b) for men, they would still disapprove of its use by women. . . . The difference between using "shit" (or "damn," or one of many others) as opposed to "oh dear," or "goodness," or "oh fudge" lies in how forcefully one says how one feels. . . . Hence in a really serious situation, the use of "trivializing" (that is, "women's") particles constitutes a joke, or at any rate, is highly inappropriate.

> [3] (a) *Oh fudge, my hair is on fire.[1]
> (b) *Dear me, did he kidnap the baby?

· · ·

. . . Allowing men stronger means of expression than are open to women further reinforces men's position of strength in the real world: for surely we listen with more attention the more strongly and forcefully someone expresses opinions, and a speaker unable—for whatever reason—to be forceful in stating his views is much less likely to be taken seriously.

· · ·

Similar sorts of disparities exist elsewhere in the vocabulary. There is, for instance, a group of adjectives which have, besides their specific and literal meanings, another use, that of indicating the speaker's approbation or admiration for something. Some of these adjectives are neutral as to sex of speaker: either men or women may use them. But another set seems, in its figurative use, to be largely confined to women's speech. Representative lists of both types are below:

[1]In conformity with current linguistic practice, throughout this work an asterisk (*) will be used to mark a sentence that is inappropriate in some sense, either because it is syntactically deviant or used in the wrong social context.

Neutral	Women Only
great	adorable
terrific	charming
cool	sweet
neat	lovely
	divine

. . . Where a woman has a choice between the neutral words and the women's words, as a man has not, she may be suggesting very different things about her own personality and her view of the subject matter by her choice of words of the first set or words of the second.

[4] *(a)* What a terrific idea!
   (b) What a divine idea!

It seems to me that *(a)* might be used under any appropriate conditions by a female speaker. But *(b)* is more restricted. Probably it is used appropriately (even by the sort of speaker for whom it was normal) only in case the speaker feels the idea referred to to be essentially frivolous, trivial, or unimportant to the world at large—only an amusement for the speaker herself. Consider, then, a woman advertising executive at an advertising conference. However feminine an advertising executive she is, she is much more likely to express her approval with [4] *(a)* than with *(b)*, which might cause raised eyebrows, and the reaction: "That's what we get for putting a woman in charge of this company."

. . .

When we leave the lexicon and venture into syntax, we find that syntactically too women's speech is peculiar. To my knowledge, there is no syntactic rule in English that only women may use. But there is at least one rule that a woman will use in more conversational situations than a man. . . . This is the rule of tag-question formation.

. . .

There are situations in which a tag is legitimate, in fact the only legitimate sentence form. So, for example, if I have seen something only indistinctly, and have reason to believe my addressee had a better view, I can say:

[5] I had my glasses off. He was out at third, wasn't he?

Sometimes we find a tag question used in cases in which the speaker knows as well as the addressee what the answer must be, and doesn't need confirmation. One such situation is when the speaker is making "small talk," trying to elicit conversation from the addressee:

[6] Sure is hot here, isn't it?

In discussing personal feelings or opinions, only the speaker normally has any way of knowing the correct answer. Strictly speaking, questioning one's own opinions is futile. Sentences like [7] are usually ridiculous.

[7] *I have a headache, don't I?

But similar cases do, apparently, exist, in which it is the speaker's opinions, rather than perceptions, for which corroboration is sought, as in [8]:

[8] The way prices are rising is horrendous, isn't it?

While there are of course other possible interpretations of a sentence like this, one possibility is that the speaker has a particular answer in mind —"yes" or "no"—but is reluctant to state it baldly. It is my impression, though I do not have precise statistical evidence, that this sort of tag question is much more apt to be used by women than by men. If this is indeed true, why is it true?

These sentence types provide a means whereby a speaker can avoid committing himself, and thereby avoid coming into conflict with the addressee. The problem is that, by so doing, a speaker may also give the impression of not being really sure of himself, of looking to the addressee for confirmation, even of having no views of his own. This last criticism is, of course, one often leveled at women. One wonders how much of it reflects a use of language that has been imposed on women from their earliest years.

· · ·

TALKING ABOUT WOMEN

We have thus far confined ourselves to one facet of the problem of women and the English language: the way in which women prejudice the case against themselves by their use of language. But it is at least as true that others—as well as women themselves—make matters so by the way in which they refer to women. Often a word that may be used of both men and women (and perhaps of things as well), when applied to women, assumes a special meaning that, by implication rather than outright assertion, is derogatory to women as a group.

When a word acquires a bad connotation by association with something unpleasant or embarrassing, people may search for substitutes that do not have the uncomfortable effect—that is, euphemisms. Since attitudes toward the original referent are not altered by a change of name, the new name itself takes on the adverse connotations, and a new euphemism must be found. It is no doubt possible to pick out areas of particular psychological strain or discomfort—areas where problems exist in a culture—by pinpointing items around which a great many euphemisms are clustered. An obvious example concerns the various words for that household convenience into which human wastes are eliminated: toilet, bathroom, rest room, comfort station, lavatory, water closet, loo, and all the others.

In the case of women, it may be encouraging to find no richness of euphemism; but it is discouraging to note that at least one euphemism for "woman" does exist and is very much alive. The word, of course, is "lady," which seems to be replacing "woman" in a great many contexts. . . .

It might also be claimed that *lady* is no euphemism because it has exactly the same connotations as woman, is usable under the same semantic and contextual conditions. But a cursory inspection will show that this is not always the case. The decision to use one term rather than the other may considerably alter the sense of a sentence. The following are examples:

[9] *(a)* A (woman) that I know makes amazing things out of
     (lady)
    shoelaces and old boxes.
(b) A (woman) I know works at Woolworth's.
    (lady)
(c) A (woman) I know is a dean at Berkeley.
    (lady)

(These facts are true for some speakers of English. For others, *lady* has taken over the function of *woman* to such an extent that *lady* can be used in all these sentences.)

In my speech, the use of *lady* in [9] *(c)* imparts a frivolous or nonserious tone to the sentence: the matter under discussion is one of not too great moment. In this dialect, then, *lady* seems to be the more colloquial word: it is less apt to be used in writing, or in discussing serious matters. Similarly in [9] *(a)*, using *lady* would suggest that the speaker considered the "amazing things" not to be serious art, but merely a hobby or an aberration. If *woman* is used, she might be a serious (pop art) sculptor.

Related to this is the use of *lady* in job terminology. For at least some speakers, the more demeaning the job, the more the person holding it (if female, of course) is likely to be described as a *lady*. Thus, *cleaning lady* is at least as common as *cleaning woman, saleslady* as *saleswoman.* But one says, normally, *woman doctor.* To say *lady doctor* is to be very condescending: it constitutes an insult. For men, there is no such dichotomy. *Garbageman* or *salesman* is the only possibility, never **garbage gentleman.* And of course, since in the professions the male is unmarked, we never have **man (male) doctor.*

· · ·

Another realm of usage in which *lady* contrasts with *woman* is in titles of organizations. It seems that organizations of women who have a serious purpose (not merely that of spending time with one another) cannot use the word *lady* in their titles, but less serious ones may. Compare the *Ladies' Auxiliary* of a men's group, or the *Thursday Evening Ladies Browning and Garden Society* with **Ladies' Lib* or **Ladies Strike for Peace.*

What is curious about this split is that *lady* is, as noted, in origin a euphemism for *woman.* What kind of euphemism is it that subtly denigrates the people to whom it refers, suggests that they are not to be taken seriously, are laughing stocks? A euphemism, after all, is supposed to put a better face on something people find uncomfortable.

· · ·

This brings us to the consideration of another common substitute for *woman,* namely *girl.* One seldom hears a man past the age of adolescence referred to as a boy, save in expressions like "going out with the boys," which are meant to suggest an air of adolescent frivolity and irresponsibility. But women of all ages are "girls": one can have a man, not a boy, Friday, but a girl, never a woman or even a lady, Friday; women have girl friends, but men do not—in a nonsexual sense—have boyfriends. It may be that this use of *girl* is euphemistic in the sense in which *lady* is a euphemism: in stressing the idea of immaturity, it removes the sexual connotations lurking in *woman.* Instead of the ennobling present in *lady,* *girl* is (presumably) flattering to women because of its stress on youth. But here again there are pitfalls: in recalling youth, frivolity, and immaturity, *girl* brings to mind irresponsibility: you don't send a girl to do a woman's errand (or even, for that matter, a boy's errand).

· · ·

Suppose we take a pair of words which, in terms of the possible relationships in an earlier society, were simple male-female equivalents, analogous to bull: cow. Suppose we find that, for independent reasons, society has changed in such a way that the primary meanings now are irrelevant. . . . One good example of such a divergence through time is found in the pair *master* and *mistress.* Once used with reference to one person's power over another, these words became unusable in their original sense as the master-servant relationship became nonexistent. But the words are still common as used in sentences [11] and [12]:

[11] *(a)* He is a master of the intricacies of academic politics.
     (b) *She is a mistress . . .
[12] *(a)* *Harry declined to be my master, and so returned to his wife.
     (b) Rhonda declined to be my mistress, and so returned to her husband.

. . .

The sexual definition of women, however, is but one facet of a much larger problem. In every aspect of life, a woman is identified in terms of the men she relates to. The opposite is not usually true of men: they act in the world as autonomous individuals, but women are only "John's wife," or "Harry's girl friend." Thus, meeting a woman at a party, a quite normal opening conversational gambit might be: "What does your husband do?" One very seldom hears, in a similar situation, a question addressed to a man: "What does your wife do?" The question would, to a majority of men, seem tautological: "She's my wife—that's what she does." This is true even in cases in which a woman is being discussed in a context utterly unrelated to her relationships with men, when she has attained sufficient stature to be considered for high public office. In fact, in a recent discussion of possible Supreme Court nominees, one woman was mentioned prominently. In discussing her general qualifications for the office, and her background, the *New York Times* saw fit to remark on her "bathing-beauty figure." Note that this is not only a judgment on a physical attribute totally removed from her qualifications for the Supreme Court, but that it is couched in terms of how a man would react to her figure. Some days later, President Nixon announced the nominations to his Price Board, among them one woman. In the thumbnail sketches the *Times* gave of each nominee, it was mentioned that the woman's husband was a professor of English. In the case of none of the other nominees was the existence of a spouse even hinted at, and much less was there any clue about the spouse's occupation. So here, although the existence of a husband was as irrelevant for this woman appointee as the existence of a wife was for any of the male appointees, the husband was mentioned, since a woman cannot be placed in her position in society by the readers of the *Times* unless they know her marital status. The same is not at all true of men. Similarly in the 1971 mayoral campaign in San Francisco, the sole woman candidate was repeatedly referred to as *Mrs. Feinstein,* never *Feinstein,* when her opponents were regularly referred to by first and last names or last names alone: *Joseph Alioto,* or *Alioto,* not *Mr. Alioto.* Again, the woman had to be identified by her relationship to a man, although this should bear no relevance to her qualifications for public office.

. . .

Now it becomes clearer why there is a lack of parallelism in men's and women's titles. To refer to a man as *Mr.* does not identify his marital status; but there is no such ambiguous term for women: one must decide on *Mrs.* or *Miss.* To remedy this imbalance, a bill was proposed in the United States Congress by Bella Abzug and others that would legislate a change in women's titles: *Miss* and *Mrs.* would both be abolished in favor of *Ms.* Rather less seriously, the converse has been proposed by Russell Baker, that two terms should be created for men, *Mrm.* and *Srs.*, depending upon marital status. . . . Why do we feel that Baker's suggestion (even if it did not come from Baker) is somehow not to be taken as seriously as Abzug's? . . .

. . . A title is devised and used for a purpose: to give a clue to participants in social interaction how the other person is to be regarded, how he is to be addressed. In an avowedly class-conscious society, social ranking is a significant determining factor: once you know that your addressee is to be addressed as "lord," or "mister," or "churl," you know where he stands with respect to you; the title establishes his identity in terms of his relationship with the larger social group. For this reason, the recent suggestion that both *Mr.* and *Mrs./Miss* be abolished in favor of *Person* is unlikely to be successful: *Person* tells you only what you already know, and does not aid in establishing ranking or relationship between two people. Even in a supposedly classless society, the use of *Mr.* (as opposed to simple last name or first name) connotes a great deal about the relationship of the two participants in the discourse with respect to each other. To introduce yourself, "I'm Mr. Jones" puts the relationship you are seeking to establish on quite a different basis than saying, "I'm Jones," or "I'm John," and each is usable under quite different contextual conditions, socially speaking. As long as social distinctions, overt or covert, continue to exist, we will be unable to rid our language of titles that make reference to them.

. . .

CONCLUSION

Linguistic imbalances are worthy of study because they bring into sharper focus real-world imbalances and inequities. They are clues that some external situation needs changing, rather than items that one *should* seek to change directly. A competent doctor tries to eliminate the germs that cause measles, rather than trying to bleach the red out with peroxide. I emphasize this point because it seems to be currently fashionable to try, first, to attack the disease by attempting to obliterate the external symptoms; and, second, to attack *every* instance of linguistic sexual inequity, rather than selecting those that reflect a real disparity in social treatment, not mere grammatical nonparallelism. We should be attempting to single out those linguistic uses that, by implication and innuendo, demean the members of one group or another, and should be seeking to make speakers of English aware of the psychological damage such forms do. The problem, of course, lies in deciding which forms are really damaging to the ego, and then in determining what to put in their stead.

A good example which troubles me a lot at present, is that of pronominal neutralization. In English, as indeed in the great majority of the world's languages, when reference is made individually to members of a sexually mixed group, the normal solution is to resolve the indecision as to pronoun choice in favor of the masculine: the masculine, then, is "unmarked" or "neutral," and therefore will be found referring to men and women both in sentences like the following:

[13] *(a)* Everyone take his seat.
     (b) If a person wants to ingratiate himself with Harry, he
                                 *herself   *she
     should cook him moo-shu pork.

                     . . .

That is, although semantically both men and women are included in the groups referred to by the pronouns in these sentences, only *he* and related masculine forms are commonly possible. An analogous situation occurs in many languages with the words for *human being:* in English, we find *man* and *mankind,* which of course refer to women members of the species as well. This of course permits us innumerable jokes involving "man-eating sharks," and the widespread existence of these jokes perhaps points up the problem that these forms create for a woman who speaks a language like English.

I feel that the emphasis upon this point, to the exclusion of most other linguistic points, by writers within the women's movement is misguided. While this lexical and grammatical neutralization is related to the fact that men have been the writers and the doers, I don't think it by itself specifies a particular and demeaning role for women, as the special uses of *mistress* or *professional,* to give a few examples, do. It is not insidious in the same way: it does not indicate to little girls how they are expected to behave. Even if it did, surely other aspects of linguistic imbalance should receive equal attention. But more seriously, I think one should force oneself to be realistic: certain aspects of language are available to the native speakers' conscious analysis, and others are too common, too thoroughly mixed throughout the language, for the speaker to be aware each time he uses them. It is realistic to hope to change only those linguistic uses of which speakers themselves can be made aware, as they use them. One chooses, in speaking or writing, more or less consciously and purposefully among nouns, adjectives, and verbs; one does not choose among pronouns in the same way. My feeling is that this area of pronominal neutralization is both less in need of changing and less open to change than many of the other disparities that have been discussed earlier, and we should perhaps concentrate our efforts where they will be most fruitful.

But many nonlinguists disagree. I have read and heard dissenting views from too many anguished women to suppose that this use of *he* is really a triviality. The claim is that the use of the neutral *he* with such frequency makes women feel shut out, not a part of what is being described, an inferior species, or a nonexistent one. Perhaps linguistic training has dulled my perception, and this really is a troublesome question. If so, I don't know what to advise, since I feel in any case that an attempt to change pronominal usage will be futile. My recommendation then would be based purely on pragmatic considerations: attempt to change only what can be changed, since this is hard enough.

ROSE DE WOLF

The Battle for Coed Teams

Rose DeWolf describes an actual controversy over equality in Pennsylvania: should high schools be permitted to maintain sex-segregated teams? Each side claims it has found the "equal" arrangement.

Because few girls can compete successfully on the boys' teams, one side argues that the "equal" arrangement is to maintain separate teams but with equal coaching, equal funding, and equal facilities. The other side cites the Supreme Court statement that "separate is inherently unequal." That statement, in
Brown *v.* Board of Education, *was made in regard to racial segregation of schools. It can be argued, however, that sex is relevant to sports (because of size, strength, etc.) in a way that race is not relevant to education. For example, featherweight boxers do not object to being offered separate weight classes in which to compete; nor do Little Leaguers feel it unjust that adults are prohibited from playing on their teams.*

An elusive element here is the question of fame, encouragement, and public attention. If separate teams are used, and if the boys' basketball team can beat the girls' team, the public may prefer to see and read about the boys. Again the arrangement is unequal in this dimension. DeWolf looks forward to the day when a new emphasis on participation and enjoyment at all skill levels will replace the stress on competition, winning, and fame.

Further Reading

ANN CRITTENDEN SCOTT, "Closing the Muscle Gap," *Ms.,* 3 (September 1974), 49–55, 89.

ELLEN WEBER, "Boys and Girls Together: The Coed Team Controversy," *womenSports,* 1 (September 1974), 53–55.

DOROTHY HARRIS, *D.G.W.S. Research Reports: Women in Sports,* vol. 11 (Washington, D.C.: American Association for Health, Physical Education and Recreation, 1973).

PROJECT ON THE STATUS AND EDUCATION OF WOMEN, "What Constitutes Equality for Women in Sport?" (Washington, D.C.: Association of American Colleges, 1974).

RICHARD ALAN RUBIN, "Sex Discrimination in Interscholastic High School Athletics," *Syracuse Law Review*, 25 (1974), 535–74.

Sometime in the future (and maybe not too far off, either) there will no longer be "boys' teams" and "girls' teams" down at the local high school. There will just be teams, period. School sports are going unisex. That seems to be the inevitable outcome of court decisions which have been handed down in the past few years and seem likely to be handed down in the next few. Take these examples:

In Nebraska, a girl named Debbie Reed wanted to play golf for her high school but was rejected—despite her powerful swing. It seems her school had only one golf squad and that was for boys. Debbie charged discrimination, sued for the right to join the team and in 1972, won.

In Minnesota, a court agreed to let Peggy Brenden join a boys' tennis team. The judge felt that Peggy, who was ranked the number one eighteen-year-old player by the Northwestern Lawn Tennis Association, was clearly too good for her school's girls' team, which had only informal coaching, sporadic practice, and no interscholastic competition.

And, just this year, Heidi Beth Kaplan won for girls the right to swim on boys' teams in Philadelphia. Heidi, one of the outstanding swimmers at University City High School, hadn't been able to compete because there was no girls' team and girls were not allowed on the boys' team. Heidi complained to her sister, Sharon Wallis, who happened to be a feminist *and* a lawyer. Ms. Wallis filed a suit and before it ever reached the court, the school board relented and said girls could join the boys' swimming teams. When reporters asked the coach at rival Bartram High School how he felt now that his team would have to compete with Heidi, he said, "I think she'll probably kill us." And he added: "There was a girl here two years ago who wanted to swim but I was told I definitely could not use her. She could beat anybody at any stroke at any distance. Unfortunately, her sister was not a lawyer."

Additionally, several states have taken action to integrate their schools' teams. In New York, after a sixteen-month study showing that neither girls nor boys suffered adverse effects from coed competition, the State Board of Regents decided to allow integrated sports. Unfortunately, it exempted almost as many—baseball, basketball, field hockey, football, ice

Reprinted in full by permission from *womenSports*, 1 (July 1974), 61–63.

hockey, lacrosse, soccer, softball, handball, power volleyball, and wrestling —as it included. So far the state with the most progressive legislation is probably Michigan, which passed a law allowing coed competition in all but body contact sports. Current Michigan policy is to have separate programs for boys and girls but to let a girl, who elects to do so, participate in the boys' program—and vice versa.

The direction toward unisex is clear, but so far victories for integration have only been partial. Debbie Reed and Peggy Brenden won only the right for themselves as individuals to play on boys' teams.

Other girls who want to win on the playing fields will have to win in the courts as they did. Heidi Beth Kaplan's complaint achieved integration for all Philadelphia girls but only in one sport. New York State has said that there *may* be coed teams but not that there must be. And Michigan is maintaining separate sports leagues although allowing some interchange between the two.

But now in Pennsylvania, an all-out, total attack on sex-segregated sport has been launched. Last November the state attorney general filed suit in the Commonwealth Court to force the Pennsylvania Interscholastic Athletic Association (the body that controls school sports in Pennsylvania) to integrate all sports except wrestling and football. If Pennsylvania wins its suit—a decision may well be ruled just as you are reading this—what is now a slow trend toward unisex may turn into a rout. Two things make the Pennsylvania case different from those that have come before.

1. It is the first challenge to sex-segregated sports brought by an agency of a state rather than by an individual athlete.

2. It asks for more than the mere right of an individual girl athlete who wishes to compete with boys to do so. It asks the court to *order* the integration of all teams except football and wrestling and would require affirmative action to bring female athletes onto presently all-male teams.

How does it come about that this precedent-setting challenge is being made in Pennsylvania rather than any other state? The suit owes its existence to a fortunate collaboration between two state officials: a forward-looking secretary of education named John Pittenger and a feminist deputy attorney general named Kathleen Herzog Larkin. It all began when an irate father called Pittenger last year to ask him to somehow force the PIAA to reinstate riflery as a recognized sport. It seems the man's daughter had been on her school's coed rifle team when riflery—which had been a PIAA-approved sport for thirty years—was suddenly dropped. The widespread suspicion, though the PIAA denied it, was that riflery had been dropped to maintain a PIAA rule adopted in 1970 prohibiting girls from playing

with, or even practicing with, boys. Presumably, such a rule was unnecessary before 1970 since unwritten rules sufficed. It seems likely that, as the
movement for equal rights for women gained momentum in every area of
life, the PIAA saw the "writing on the wall" and decided to put some
writing on its books.

But the riflery complaint wasn't the only one Pittenger got. Women
complained that the PIAA, a quasi-public body supported by dues paid by
each school district (in other words, public funds), had an all-male board
of control. Women coaches complained that they didn't get paid the same
as men when officiating for PIAA events. Parents complained that PIAA
rules make it clear that girls are to be considered not just separate but
unequal. The maximum number of games a boys' basketball team can play
is twenty-two. But the maximum number a girls' team can play is sixteen.

And the PIAA code reads: "Schools have a responsibility to encourage
ladylike qualities in girls participating in sports. Although athletic attire
must permit freedom of movement, a competitor must wear clothing
which is clean and so designed and worn as not to be objectionable or
sensational. The clothing must be made of material which is not transparent, even when wet."

Irate girls called that patronizing, pointing out that there is no similar
language in the code directed at boys. Are boys not to have "gentlemanly
qualities"? Is it okay for a boy to wear a dirty, transparent bikini?

The complaints were not all individual ones. Some came in the form of
documented reports from study groups. The Inter-School Council of
Lower Merion Township, for example, wrote up a report on sexism in
athletics and mailed it to Pittenger. Charlotte Thurschwell, who was co-
chairman of the project, recalls it all got started because one mother complained that her daughter had to bring her team uniform home to be
laundered while boys' uniforms were laundered by the school. She called
that discrimination against the mothers of girls as opposed to the mothers
of boys since it ends up being the mother who washes the uniforms. The
Lower Merion report thumped not only discrimination in laundry services,
but discrimination in use of cheerleaders (the cheerleaders—all girls—
cheered only for teams that were all boys) and discrimination in budget
(boys' sports got the lion's share).

All these complaints found a responsive listener in John Pittenger. It
isn't that he considers himself a crusader for women's rights—he concedes
he'd never given the matter much thought—but he believes in doing
what's "right and fair." So he took the complaints to the attorney general's
office for review because any legal action would have had to be handled
by the Pennsylvania Department of Justice. There the matter fell into the
sympathetic hands of Deputy Attorney General Kay Larkin. She and the
rest of her department felt the PIAA should be sued—but not just to

reinstitute the riflery team or to change a few rules—but to totally integrate sports. And so the suit was filed that way. Only football and wrestling were left out, not on legalistic grounds, but just because the opposition would be tough enough without encouraging emotional arguments about "orgies" on the mat or fatal injuries on the fifty-yard line.

The uproar was, of course, immediate. Charles McCullough, deputy director of the PIAA, voiced the most prevalent fear about the suit when he said that girls' sports would be hurt more than helped if the sex-segregation rule were declared unconstitutional. "If girls are permitted on the same teams as boys," McCullough said, "then very few girls will be on any team at all. The average girl is physically weaker than the average boy and could not win a place on the team if try-outs were open to everyone. The rule against boys and girls competing together forces schools to fund two separate teams and that way more girls actually get more opportunity to play."

Women coaches in Pennsylvania, by and large, agreed with that point of view. "What we want," said Mrs. Hilda Thompson, president of the Pennsylvania Association for Health, Physical Education and Recreation and a teacher-coach for the York City School District, "is equal funding for women's teams and equal access to school facilities."

"Only a policy of separate but equal will keep girls' sports alive," commented Barbara Rankin, a hockey coach in Berks County schools. "Once teams are allowed to be mixed, the girls will be pushed out."

McCullough contended that the law suit was unnecessary because "nobody has done more for girls' sports in Pennsylvania than we have." What has been done is that since 1968, the number of teams for girls in the state of Pennsylvania has increased from 500 to over 2,500. In 1968, there were no championship tournaments for girls. In 1974, there are ten—just as there are ten for boys. And in 1968, there were practically no women sports officials outside the major cities. Now there are more than 2,000 women officials registered by the PIAA.

But that's still not equality. In Pennsylvania, as in most other states, boys' programs are favored over girls', whether it comes to funds, facilities, coaching services, or even cheerleading. As Pittenger puts it, "If you see an athletic program budget in which the boys get $50,000 and the girls get $2,000 you sure know something's wrong."

The real issue—and there are respected women's rights advocates on both sides of the argument—is what constitutes "equality." Some, like Hilda Thompson and Barbara Rankin, argue that girls will only be equal if they have programs that are separate from but as richly funded as boys' programs. Others, like Kay Larkin, say that separate-but-equal just isn't equal. "I know there are practical problems," she said. "And I don't have any illusions that even if we win the suit, all teams will immediately be sexually integrated just like that. The Supreme Court decided that schools should be racially integrated back in 1954 and it hasn't totally come about yet." But she added, "That decision of 1954 said that separate was inherently unequal. And it is. There are intangible benefits to be gained from playing on a winning team—there is acclaim, newspaper publicity, honors, awards, trips, scholarships and the like. If the possibility of playing on a winning team is determined by sex—rather than by ability—that's discriminatory."

But how do you get around the fact that most girls are poorer athletes than most boys?

"The courts have already ruled," Larkin said, "that every male high school student is not stronger than every female high school student. Therefore, athletes should be grouped by ability. Everyone knows it is no fun to play with someone who is either much better or much worse than you. If you always win or always lose, you aren't motivated to improve. If girls are never given the opportunity to play against strong competition, if girls are never given the access to the same quality of coaching as boys, then you are saying they are never going to be given an opportunity to be equal. That isn't the kind of policy a Department of Education should have."

What is true for female students is also true for female coaches, she added. If they are never to get the opportunity to coach the best, their opportunities, too, are forever limited.

Oh, c'mon. Girls are not equal. They are shorter, lighter. They are built differently. Their hips are wider. Their muscles are different, they have a smaller lung capacity.

Testimony to that effect has been offered in every case tried so far, Larkin says. But the argument used to counter it is this: Physical characteristics are not the only ones necessary for success in athletics. Other factors, not unique to either sex, can compensate for lack of speed and strength. Like mind-body coordination, mental determination, sensory perception, courage, intelligence, willingness to practice, and experience. A large oxygen consumption rate is not necessary for golf. But concentration and coordination [are].

Well, what about the argument that if schools are forced to integrate, they'll have just one team which most girls won't make? What about the argument that there won't be as many teams for girls and that there will be less opportunity for girls, instead of more?

Larkin admits that it may be true at first that only one outstanding girl athlete will make the varsity squad. But eventually, other girls will be emboldened to try, she said.

"For years there was a boy-only punt and kick competition in State College, Pa. Last year a girl entered it—and came in second. This year fifteen girls entered. And the girl who'd come in second last year came in first."

And the Pennsylvania suit doesn't just ask that girls be allowed to try out for boys' varsity teams. It requests the development of a plan for integrating sports that will maintain the present level of participation for women. Says Pittenger: "We have no intention of destroying girls' sports. If we found a school district was using the idea of coed sports in order to avoid its responsibility to provide a total equal sports program for girls, we'd have to take some affirmative action to solve that."

For Pittenger, the lawsuit is only part of a whole program to change sports in Pennsylvania. He contends that the present "American Way of Sport" discriminates not only against girls, but also against most boys. The system, he says, is designed for the talented as opposed to the just-interested. (The varsity team gets all the emphasis.) It is designed for the few as opposed to the many. (The football team will have six coaches but there is no volleyball squad.) It is designed to emphasize sports that benefit the school (those that bring in gate receipts) rather than sports that benefit the students (those that can be played for a lifetime). And so he has asked the State Board of Education to adopt new regulations on school athletics.

His proposed regulations, which would have the force of law, would have athletic programs starting in grade school as part of an over-all program for growth. They would be as much designed for kids who are over-weight or poorly coordinated as for those who run the fastest and jump the highest. They would be equally for boys and girls. There would be more overlap than presently exists between athletic programs in the schools and in the community. Adults would be invited into the school to use the gymnasium; kids would be taken to the local bowling alley to learn to bowl. Participation in a church-sponsored softball league or Boy Scout camping program would qualify for physical education credit.

Schools would emphasize sports that last a lifetime—like bowling, ping pong, volleyball, swimming, canoeing, tennis, or golf—rather than sports like basketball or football that you can't play after forty without risking a heart attack.

Pittenger's aides claim that when the realization gets around that these new regulations could mean a smaller budget for the football team, revolutions will be organized in school basements. "Could be," one staffer cracked, "that all of western Pennsylvania will secede and annex itself to Ohio."

But Pittenger intends to stand firm. "If sports have virtues that have been claimed for them by coaches and others—and I think they do," he says, "then those advantages ought to be available to everybody—male or female, talented or clumsy, young or old. And the disadvantages, too, I suppose. Just as boys are injured in competitions, I suppose girls will be, too. I am concerned that we don't turn girls into win-at-all-costs-put-a-knee-in-the-groin-and-keep-going types, but I don't favor turning boys out that way either."

One thing is clear: the way the wind is blowing, change is sure to come, one way or the other. And when it does, there will be a lot of gyrating in the gymnasiums, a lot of fuming on the playing fields, before all the issues that have been raised are settled. Pittenger would like to see them settled in favor of more equality of opportunity for all.

"I don't think I'm fighting this all alone," he says. There are a great many parents whose youngsters are not football heroes who want to see their kids benefit more from a school sports program.

And there are a lot of girls who don't want to return to the "old way."

Ginger Rossnagel, of Cherry Hill (N.J.) High School, was discussing with a reporter her feelings about competing with boys in cross-country. "It makes me a better runner," she said. "Everytime I get exhausted and close to quitting . . . I ask myself if I'd rather be on the cheerleading team . . . and I keep going."

MADELON BEDELL

Supermom!

This article is indirectly about self-respect. Madelon Bedell describes the conflict she experienced in a world which demands two different kinds of success from women. On the one hand, a successful person has a promising career and is not "just" a housewife. Bedell's friends with no career felt inferior for that reason. On the other, a successful woman cooks exquisitely and has a clean house, a contented husband, and pampered children. As a woman with a career, she felt inferior and guilty for not putting full time into this job.

The result? A "Super Mom" who attempts to carry out a full-time career and feels she must justify this by working twice as hard as a full-time homemaker. Bedell describes her difficulty in relating to other women, both those with "outside" careers and those without. She concludes that the "Super Mom" becomes a nervous wreck and an obnoxious person.

The problem, of course, arises from the double-bind society has set. Bedell felt she would fail to be either a successful person or a successful woman. When she began to reject these incompatible demands, reasoning that she had a right to be successful and happy without being either obnoxious or a nervous wreck, she gained in self-respect.

Further Reading

JESSIE BERNARD, "The Paradox of the Happy Marriage," in *Woman in Sexist Society*, Vivian Gornick and Barbara Moran, eds. (New York: Basic Books, 1971), pp. 145–62.

PAULINE BART, "Depression in Middle-Aged Women," in *Woman in Sexist Society*, Vivian Gornick and Barbara Moran, eds. (New York: Basic Books, 1971), pp. 163–86.

JOHN KENNETH GALBRAITH, "The Economics of the American Housewife," *Atlantic Monthly*, 232 (August 1973), 78–83.

ANN OAKLEY, *The Sociology of Housework* (New York: Pantheon Books, 1974).

Although I have been one for twenty years, it was only six months ago that I realized that I was a Super Mom. The revelation occurred in a flash, one Saturday afternoon, as I was preparing dinner for ten. It was one of my usual masterpieces, a glorified lamb stew, called *navarin printanier.* If you follow the three-and-one-half-page Julia Child recipe carefully, without cheating, it takes most of the day to fix. I never cheat.

So it happened at about 5 P.M.—after I had successfully caramelized the sauce, poured it through a strainer, separated each stubborn bone from each hot, glutinous piece of lamb, returned the whole dish to the clean casserole, and was beginning to add my peeled carrots, turnips, and potatoes (sculptured into one-and-one-half-inch ovals)—that the guest of honor, my brother, walked into the kitchen. As I started to put in the final *bouquet de légumes,* he essayed a sip of the sauce and gave forth a sigh of delight. "Oh, Madelon," he said, "what a heavenly dish. Just look at everything you do—your house, your children. You're really a Super Woman, do you know that?" I beamed.

My ten-year-old son, who had just spied his favorite dessert, *mousse au chocolat,* in the refrigerator, turned around. "She's not a Super Woman," he said. "She's a Super Mom, that's what." I radiated.

After the guests had gone, I told my husband to go to bed—I knew he'd had a hard day. It was about 3 A.M. as I was cleaning up the last dish and putting the last chair in place and thinking about breakfast the next morning (sour cream omelet or waffles, ham or bacon?) that I said to myself, "Yes, it's true, I *am* a Super Mom." Are there other Super Moms, I wondered, as I went upstairs, stretched out in bed, and rubbed my aching legs, or am I unique?

Not at all, I realized. The world is full of women like me. All of us who are married and have children and also have full-time jobs are—or are expected to be—Super Moms. We're quite different from our male counterparts, fathers who also have jobs. The difference is that they just have one job, the one that pays. We have two, and the one that doesn't pay is the more important. At various times in my working life, I have been a researcher, a reporter, a writer, and a publicist, but in my mind, I was first and foremost a Mom. A Mom with a job. A do-it-all woman. That's me. Super. How did I get that way?

Let me go back in time to the 1950s when I took the first step on the long march to Super Momism, with the birth of my first child. Everybody knows about the fifties. This was the era of the silent generation and the Feminine Mystique. World War II was over. Women who had held jobs in factories and offices all over the country and had been hailed as the Girl Behind the Man Behind the Gun, were told to go back home and start being the Mom Behind the Pop Behind the Desk.

There were only a few of us who did not succumb. For one reason or another (in my case, a blind conviction that staying at home all day was like being in prison, however gilded the bars), we were determined to keep our jobs and have a family as well. That made us instant pariahs, outcasts from society. All sorts of authorities told us in no uncertain words that in leaving home (you were presumed to have "left home" permanently even if it was only between the hours of nine and five every day), we were behaving in an Unnatural Way. Sigmund Freud and Dwight Eisenhower told us that, and I am sorry to say we believed them.

One ray of hope was offered to us. The host of kindly advisers who assaulted us daily in person or via every known communications medium —psychiatrists, psychologists, social workers, teachers, pediatricians, obstetricians, and marriage counselors—did go so far as to say that if we felt we "really *had* to work outside the home," it just might be all right, provided we did not neglect children, husband, and home. It took cleverness and organization, and unceasing effort, but if we persevered, we could do it. They threw us a crumb of hope, the stock phrase of the times offered to the working mother, "It's not the quantity of time you spend with your children, it's the quality."

Oh, how I snatched at that crumb and tried to turn it into a cake, the one that I might eat and have, too. In search of that quality, I read all about nutrition, child psychology, and homemaking, as well as books and columns of advice to working mothers. I discussed my "problem" with teachers, doctors, and other anxious mothers who had jobs. Out of it all I began to formulate my composite picture of the ideal Super Mom, the one I was trying to be.

(1) *Occupation.* Super Moms can be found in nearly every type of job, white or blue collar. I recently met one Super Mom who was a taxicab driver. Our number is greatest, however, among the professional classes— writer, editor, designer, doctor, scientist—because these jobs can usually be tailored to meet the need of the Super Mom for combining demands of work and home. (Or should I say, work and more work?)

The professional working mother can usually fix things ("plan her schedule" is the usual term) so that she can leave the office for interviews with children's teachers or visits to the doctors, take her children to or from school, do family errands, stay home when the children are sick (she simply calls up and says *she's* sick), and otherwise assuage her guilt. The latter phrase is important. No one can be a Super Mom unless she feels guilty.

(2) *Pregnancy and Childbirth.* The earliest—and still the most fervent—

advocate of natural childbirth, breast-feeding, and large families was the Super Mom. Super Moms soar through pregnancies. They are never afraid. They are never tired. They work until the day (sometimes until the very hour) of delivery and go back to their jobs no later than one month after returning from the hospital. Back to work, they continue to breast-feed, at least partially, rising at 5:30 A.M. for the first feeding and rushing home at the end of the day, so as to be there for both nighttime feedings.

(3) *Male Attitudes Toward Super Moms.* All male chauvinists like and approve of Super Moms. With shrewd practicality they recognize that a Super Mom gives a man his money's worth and asks no sacrifice of male privilege. "You mean you take care of the kids and manage the house and bring home an income, too? Gr-oovy!"

(4) *Homemaking.* This is where Super Mom shines. Her house is never in disorder, always competently organized. She knows how to sew as well as clean, cook, do the laundry, and iron, even if she doesn't do these things on a daily basis. Sometimes she even makes her children's clothes, just to show she can. If she both designs *and* makes them, well, can anyone, even Sigmund Freud or Dwight Eisenhower, ask for more?

(5) *Husbands.* A crucial area, delicate to handle, subtle, infinitely complex, full of booby traps. First of all, there is the problem of the initial selection of a husband. No weakling, no passive partner will do. Even intellectuals are suspect. Unless the egghead husband is a *somebody,* his cerebral attributes may reflect on Super Mom's womanhood, which is at all times under societal surveillance. Her ideal mate is the rangy athletic type whose overt "masculinity" protects her against accusations of emasculating her man. He likes to sail, ski, and go camping—and take the kids with him. Mom goes along too, of course, participates in the activities, makes the sandwiches, takes care of the younger children, and when Pop is tired after his long day's outing, drives home.

Inside the household, husbands are given special treatment. It is clearly understood that even though both are wage earners, at home Mom is still Mom and Pop is still Pop. The care and feeding of the children is Mom's job and so is the care and feeding of Pop. Thus, Super Mom hurries home from work to bathe the children, feed them, read to them, help them with their homework, and put them to bed. This is the children's hour and it is sacred. If Mom fails to observe it, or lets Pop take over, the children will be traumatized for life, or at the very least, Mom will feel that she failed as a "real woman, fulfilling her natural role."

She must also be careful, however, not to traumatize Pop or let him think she is neglecting him for the children. She is also home from work ahead of *him,* ready to greet him, cheerful and smiling, chilled martini in one hand, a platter of hot hors d'ouevres in the other, just as if she hadn't been gone all day. This is Pop's hour and it is sacred. The fact that it occurs at precisely the same time as the equally sacred children's hour is not important. Super Mom will figure out a way to "plan her schedule" so that the two previous interludes can be accomplished at the same time.

At all times, Mom is always careful to preserve Pop's male prerogatives. She makes sure that he has his free time on Saturday afternoons while she takes the children to the zoo, park, or museum. She is grateful when he helps out with household chores but never lets him help too much. She sees to it that he does the ordering at restaurants and the talking at social gatherings. She even lets *him* talk about *her* work. In this manner, the essential values of society are preserved, even though Mom does work. Crucial!

That's it, the profile of Super Mom: worker, homemaker, wife, and mother . . . oh yes, there is an additional point:

(6) *The Super Mom is a nervous wreck.*

And another which may have already occurred to you:

(7) *The Super Mom is an obnoxious person.*

Fortunately, or unfortunately, during my twenty-year stint as a Super Mom, I never clearly grasped those last two points, although Number 6 did occasionally suggest itself to me, and in my subversive unconscious, so did Number 7. Most of the time, however, I was too busy striving, ever striving to meet the five major demands.

It was rough going, you may be sure of that. It's not easy to be something you are not. More: something you don't really want to be. It requires the maintenance of a perpetual state of alertness. Alarm bells go off every hour on the hour. Enemies are everywhere, waiting to pounce on you at the slightest slip.

Over the years I grew to recognize those enemies and to be able to identify them before they even got started about their vicious business. First and foremost among them were Other Women. Most of them were wives and mothers like myself, but unlike me, they had given up their outside jobs to devote full time to their Real Jobs. My attitude toward them was ambiguous. I felt *guilty;* they worked harder, couldn't leave the house every day as I did, didn't have household help. I was also *envious;* they never had to deal with problems of job performance, job security, and job competition the way I did. In truth I also felt *superior.* I did two jobs and made money on my own, while they did only one and were financially dependent on their husbands. Finally and perhaps most of all, I felt *inferior.* You know why? They were Real Women and I was not.

I was never quite sure what they thought of me and my double life, because we never discussed it. Nevertheless, I did get occasional vibes that indicated their feelings were a kind of mirror image of my own. I sensed that, toward me, they felt *guilty* because I earned income and helped support the family and they didn't; *envious* because I wasn't bound to the house and kids the way they were; *inferior* because I did "real work" and they didn't; and, of course, *superior* because—you know why—they were Real Women and I was not.

The Other Other Women, mothers with jobs like myself, should have been a consolation, but they weren't. For one thing there were too few of them. But, mainly, it was because they seemed to have no difficulty handling the double life of the Super Mom as I did. When we got together, most of the talk was about How Good We Were and How We Did It. I felt like a charlatan because I knew I wasn't very good and didn't do very well. Beside these magnificent achievers, I weighed myself and was found wanting. It never occurred to me that they might be feeling the same about me.

My last enemy was the most powerful of all, and also a woman: myself. Not the Super Me, but the Secret Me, the one I tried to keep hidden from everyone else. She was about as Unreal a Woman as you could ever want to see: lazy, absent minded, impatient, loud-voiced, argumentative and ambitious. She didn't care in the slightest about such things as whether her children occasionally went to school with socks that didn't match. She did not like to sail, hike, or go camping. She was prone to latenight reading and early morning snoozing, liked to take solitary walks, and sometimes preferred her own company to that of all other people, including her husband. She was stubborn, persistent, and indomitable. For years, I conducted a daily battle with her and I never knew which of us was really winning.

Until the evening of the lamb stew dinner, the event that I think of as my *crise de navarin.* That night I lay in bed, arguing, as always with myself, my enemy. As I recall, the conversation went something like this:

"I don't feel like making breakfast tomorrow." (That was she, the enemy; she always started things.)

"That's too bad. You'll just do it, that's all."

"Why?"

"Why? What do you mean, why? Because the family has to have a special Sunday breakfast, that's why."

"Why?"

I was speechless. Suppose I stopped fighting her and started listening to her? Suppose I stopped playing a role and started being myself? Suppose, suppose. . . . It was all too tiring to think about. I rolled over and went to sleep and didn't wake up until noon the next day, by which time my husband and children had made their own breakfasts. None of them seemed traumatized. My consciousness was raised. I was ready to abdicate my throne. But it wasn't that easy. If I had struggled with a battalion of enemies during the years of the making of a Super Mom, they were nothing compared to the forces I had to contend with in trying to unmake her. Regiments.

At first I tried grandiose schemes of the type I had read about: a marriage contract with twenty-five separate clauses outlining the division of household and family duties between husband and wife; an indoctrination program in which the family was required to read *Sexual Politics, The Dialectic of Sex, Sisterhood Is Powerful,* and *The Origin of the Family, Private Property and the State;* a family commune with all responsibilities shared according to age and occupation. None of them worked. No one would read the books. My husband laughed at the marriage contract. My three children (ages eighteen, fifteen, and ten) made it clear that they preferred the autocracy of a nuclear family to the democratic family commune. No matter what I tried, it always ended up the same way, with my giving up and doing everything myself. After two months of experimentation I was back where I started, still making my scrumptious, nutritious breakfasts, still rushing home to make dinner, closer than ever to Stage Number 6 of Super Momism.

Those communes and contracts and indoctrinations changed the structure but not the personnel. Who was in charge of the whole business? Who was the Chairperson of the Commune? Who was the Educational Director of the Indoctrination Program? Who felt superior organizing the whole thing? Who felt guilty when it didn't work? Who expiated her guilt by taking charge again and running the household? You know who. And so did I. Before I could start changing my family, I had to change myself.

It was all clear. In order to change myself, I had first to change certain fixed behavior patterns. No point, at this stage, in trying to do new things. The trick was to stop doing the old ones. Stop reacting to familiar stimuli in the familiar way. Proceed cautiously. Begin in little ways. Let me illustrate.

It is after dinner. My husband raises his head from the newspaper and says: "Is there coffee?"

I raise my head from my novel and say: "I don't know. Is there?" Shattering.

Or another. My youngest son comes home from school and says: "Did you bake the cake for the sale tomorrow?"

"No, son, I didn't. Here's a dollar. Run out to the store and buy one, will you?" Mind-blowing!

From here on, I broadened out into more dangerous areas of experimentation. I began talking to other women about the way I felt instead of the way I was supposed to feel. One time when the question of costumes for the school play came up, I took a deep breath and stated that I Could Not Sew. To my amazement, several women said they couldn't, either. We ended up forming a delegation to request the school to simplify the costumes. I stopped rushing downstairs at dawn to get my teen-age daughter's breakfast in time for the first session at high school. Instead, I let her make her own. She was delighted and didn't love me one little bit less for it. Maybe more. I told my oldest son that nobody was going to pick up around his room for him any more. I felt pretty guilty every time I walked by his open door with all those mounds of dirty clothes, open bureau drawers, and half-drunk Coke bottles. I solved the problem by the simple process of shutting the door. So far, he has not contracted any disease from the accumulated mess.

When my youngest son called my office and complained that he was all alone with nothing to do, I stifled the sharp stab of guilt. The point was not that I was neglecting him by not being at home but that he had not developed the capacity to amuse himself. I refrained, therefore, from issuing my usual Ten Frantic Suggestions for Constructive Activity. Instead, I made one suggestion, said I was busy, and hung up. When I arrived home, nervous and trembling, he was outside playing ball, and there was no policeman at the doorstep, waiting to arrest me for child neglect. Little by little, so far as the kids were concerned, we began easing into our own version of the family commune.

The holdout was my husband. He had never objected to some of the more superficial aspects of my newfound consciousness, such as going to women's meetings or taking time to pursue my own interests. He was relieved when I did things like calling waiters myself instead of insisting that he play the prescribed male role in such situations. All that stuff was pretty silly, he agreed. After all, he had always been a male feminist, hadn't he?

What he did *not* like was what nobody likes: doing the dirty work. He never refused outright to do any of it; he was much too clever for that. He agreed that it was not fair for wives to assume the entire burden of home and child care, certainly not! But, he asked, wasn't I exaggerating the weight of the burden?

To prove his point, he cooked dinner seven nights in a row, producing a series of exquisite meals, all the while humming as he worked, proclaiming how *easy* it was, how positively joyful a task. Too bad, he said on Sunday night as we were all enjoying the last delicious bite of his homemade *tarte framboise,* that he had to leave the next day for Texas on a business trip. He arrived back five days later at 10 P.M. Even then, he offered to make his own dinner, saying he had never asked anybody to make dinner for him, ever, and he would do it immediately, as soon as he lay down for just a few moments' rest after traveling halfway across the country and back.

Another masterful strategy he worked out utilized exactly the opposite technique. He offered to take over the weekly laundry chore and then proceeded to make such a fuss over it that everybody was miserable. He woke everyone at 7 A.M. on Saturday to strip their beds of sheets, so that he could get on with his job. He put all the dirty socks to soak in the bathtub for twenty-four hours, thus preventing anyone from taking a bath during that period. Sometimes, unable to do the task on Saturday due to pressing business demands, he left it until Sunday. It was pretty hard to take, watching him get up early on his one day of rest, wearily getting out his bleach, detergent, and softener.

But I held firm, waiting for the tide to turn. This waiting period is the most difficult stage in the unmaking of a Super Mom. At times, divorce seemed imminent, and I was overwhelmed by feelings of guilt and fear. Did I really want to be an independent woman if this was the price I had to pay? More than once I decided to forget the whole idea. At these points, I would take a hitherto forbidden solitary walk and come back with renewed determination.

Eventually, as battle fatigue began to weary both contenders, a truce was declared and we came to an agreement. It isn't exactly a contract. It has no ironclad clauses. It is subject to continual revision; it occasionally breaks down completely and must be painfully reassembled. On the whole, it goes something like this. We'll both do what we can and both support each other in getting the kids to do what they can. Nobody will try to be perfect. We will agree on three things. Your work is important and so is mine. Care of the children and home is also important—to both of us. None of these things is as important to either of us as each of us is to ourselves. Not bad for a twenty-year-old marriage begun in the fifties.

And so it is, in the quiet of the early evening, as the children and their father prepare dinner, that I am able to be alone in my study, at peace before my typewriter, writing these confessions—and luxuriating in my newfound freedom to be less than perfect and therefore much more human.

BIBLIOGRAPHY

General Feminist Anthologies

BETTY ROSZAK and THEODORE ROSZAK, *Masculine/Feminine* (New York: Harper & Row, 1969).

CYNTHIA FUCHS EPSTEIN and WILLIAM J. GOODE, eds., *The Other Half: Roads to Women's Equality* (Englewood Cliffs, N.J.: Prentice-Hall, 1971).

ROBIN MORGAN, *Sisterhood Is Powerful* (New York: Random House, 1970).

VIVIAN GORNICK and BARBARA MORAN, eds., *Woman in Sexist Society* (New York: Basic Books, 1971).

Political Theories and Radical Feminism

KATE MILLETT, *Sexual Politics* (Garden City, N.Y.: Doubleday, 1970).

BETTY FRIEDAN, *The Feminine Mystique* (New York: Dell, 1963).

SHULAMITH FIRESTONE, *The Dialectic of Sex* (New York: William Morrow, 1970).

JULIET MITCHELL, *Woman's Estate* (New York: Vintage Books, 1971).

Introductory Ethics

WILLIAM K. FRANKENA, *Ethics*, 2nd ed. (Englewood Cliffs, N.J.: Prentice-Hall, 1973).

BERNARD WILLIAMS, *Morality* (New York: Harper & Row, 1972).

ALASDAIR MACINTYRE, *A Short History of Ethics* (New York: Macmillan, 1966).

RICHARD BRANDT, *Ethical Theory* (Englewood Cliffs, N.J.: Prentice-Hall, 1959).

Social and Political Philosophy

JOEL FEINBERG, *Social Philosophy* (Englewood Cliffs, N.J.: Prentice-Hall, 1973).

HUGO BEDAU, ed., *Justice and Equality* (Englewood Cliffs, N.J.: Prentice-Hall, 1971).

ALAN GEWIRTH, ed., *Political Philosophy* (New York: Macmillan, 1965).

Psychological Differences and Sex Roles

ELEANOR MACCOBY and CAROL JACKLIN, eds., *The Psychology of Sex Differences* (Stanford, Ca.: Stanford University Press, 1974).

M. KAY MARTIN and BARBARA VOORHIES, *The Female of the Species* (New York: Columbia University Press, 1975).

JUDITH BARDWICK, *Psychology of Women* (New York: Harper & Row, 1971).

MARGARET MEAD, *Male and Female* (New York: William Morrow, 1949).

Sexuality

BOSTON WOMEN'S HEALTH BOOK COLLECTIVE, *Our Bodies, Ourselves,* 2nd ed. (New York: Simon & Schuster, 1976).

ROBERT BAKER and FREDERICK ELLISTON, eds., *Philosophy and Sex* (Buffalo, N.Y.: Prometheus Books, 1975).

JOEL FEINBERG, ed., *The Problem of Abortion* (Belmont, Ca.: Wadsworth, 1973).

Education

JUDITH STACEY, SUSAN BÉREAUD, and JOAN DANIELS, eds., *And Jill Came Tumbling After: Sexism in American Education* (New York: Dell, 1974).

BARBARA GRIZZUTI HARRISON, *Unlearning the Lie* (New York: Random House, 1973).

NANCY FRAZIER and MYRA SADKER, *Sexism in School and Society* (New York: Harper & Row, 1973).

Report on Sex Bias in the Public Schools (New York: National Organization of Women, 1973). Available from Educational Resources Information Center, #ED-090-131.

Historical Selections

ALICE S. ROSSI, ed., *The Feminist Papers* (New York: Columbia University Press, 1973).

MIRIAM SCHNEIR, ed., *Feminism: The Historical Writings* (New York: Random House, 1972).

ELEANOR FLEXNER, *Century of Struggle* (Cambridge, Mass.: Harvard University Press, 1959).

Men's Liberation

JACK NICHOLS, *Men's Liberation: A New Definition of Masculinity* (New York: Penguin Books, 1975).

WARREN FARRELL, *The Liberated Man* (New York: Random House, 1974).

JOSEPH H. PLECK and JACK SAWYER, eds., *Men and Masculinity* (Englewood Cliffs, N.J.: Prentice-Hall, 1974).

KARL BEDNARIK, *The Male in Crisis* (New York: Alfred A. Knopf, 1970).